The Act of Thinking

The Act of Thinking

Derek Melser

A Bradford Book
The MIT Press
Cambridge, Massachusetts
London, England

Set in Stone sans and Stone serif by The MIT Press. Printed and bound in the United States of America.

Library of Congress Cataloging-in-Publication Data

Melser, Derek.
The act of thinking / Derek Melser.
p. cm.
"A Bradford book."
Includes bibliographical references and index.
ISBN 0-262-13446-2 (alk. paper)
1. Thought and thinking. 2. Act (Philosophy). I. Title.
B105.T56M45 2004
128'.3—dc22   2004044979

10 9 8 7 6 5 4 3 2 1

to Helen

Contents

Foreword

Aims

The main aim of this book is to present a new theory about the nature of thinking. I mean *thinking* in a broad sense that includes most of the various "mental phenomena." The theory equates thinking with the covert "token performance" or "tokening" of actions of one kind or another. The covert tokening of actions is identified as itself a species of action. As well as being intended as a contribution to the philosophy of mind, the book aims to contribute to a larger project that I mention only in this foreword and at the end of the book. The larger project is to establish actions as a legitimate philosophical given. The claim here is that the concept of "something one does" is self-sufficient and sui generis. Our knowledge of actions need not be, nor can it be, justified or explained by knowledge of any other kind. Actions are philosophical hard currency in themselves.

The conventional assumption is that the concept of an action includes and presupposes concepts of mental phenomena—beliefs, desires, decisions, intentions, volitions, etc.—and that these latter are concepts of a fundamentally non-actional kind. If the theory in this book is right, the conventional assumption is mistaken and mental concepts are really actional concepts. If this is so, then, in specifying the thinking that leads to and/or accompanies actions, one is not specifying the action plus some other kind of phenomenon, rather, one is specifying a more complex kind of action, or specifying an action plus some ancillary actions. In this case, the claim that actions are a basic philosophical "given" would no longer be vulnerable to the fact that actions often, or always, involve thinking.

In order to perform any action, the agent must (among other things) perceive things in the world that are relevant to that action—that is, the action's patient, venue, instrument, product, goal state, etc. It is assumed that perception is an impersonal natural process—something that happens to a person, more than an action the person performs. Thus, the agent's perceivings of relevant things would introduce another necessary but non-actional element into actions, also jeopardizing actions' ontological independence. However, if it can be shown that perceiving is not a natural (say, physiological) process but a form of personal action, then the "actions as given" thesis would be defensible here too. My attempt in chapter 6 to show that perceiving is an action may be too brief to convince. Even so, I thought it worth indicating how this might be argued. Actions do have an essential perceptual component, but in my view this perceptual component is itself actional and not an impersonal process. Thus, the actional status of actions is not compromised by their perceptual component.

It is widely assumed that actions must, like everything else in the world, be in-principle specifiable in objective, scientific terms. It is assumed that scientific descriptions of actions would primarily concern macro- and micro-physiological events but would also encompass complex causal interaction between external objects and these physiological events. The physiological events believed to underpin actions are thought to include perceptual and mental (brain) events as well as muscular ones. In opposing this assumption, proponents of the "actions as given" view could agree that, if actions are real things in the world, they must be scientifically describable. However, while continuing to assert the reality of actions, they could claim that actions are not "things in the world" in the required sense. And they could claim that actions are not explicable in physiological terms. I argue both of these claims, albeit briefly, in chapter 11.

The question of the possibility of scientific analysis of people's actions is as large and controversy-fraught as the questions about the nature and relation to action of thinking (or "mental phenomena") and perception. To establish that actions are sui generis would require addressing all three questions at length. In this book, I devote a chapter each to the questions relating to perception and scientific explanation of actions. My main aim is to tackle the question about thinking and its relationship with action.

Excuses and Apologies

At some points in this book I make large claims, sometimes in relation to issues around which there is ongoing controversy in the philosophical literature. This is due partly to my mooting what is, for better or worse, a large theory—a theory of thinking that has applications not only in the philosophy of mind but also in several other philosophical areas. I have chosen to paint with a broad brush rather than concentrate on details. I am aware that many philosophers would disagree with much or all of the theory of thinking I advance. However, it would be impossible in one book to properly integrate my theory into the vast contemporary literature, or even to argue the theory closely enough to persuade a skeptical lay reader. Yet if I had hedged all my claims with enough caveats to make them acceptable, you would be reading a boring and much longer book. Undue deference to skepticism is anyway premature, since I am introducing a theory and not defending one.

I also wanted to keep the book fairly short. The present book is an abbreviation, by about a third, of a doctoral dissertation that is itself a considerable reduction of the germane material I accumulated during my doctoral research. The result of my desire for comprehensiveness and brevity is a style that might sometimes seem peremptory. I have tried to avoid giving this impression; if I have not succeeded, I apologize. Anyway, if what this book adumbrates is the large new area for philosophical research and discussion I believe it is, then it might not be too long before detailed maps of the area are made by others and the preliminary sketchwork this book offers can be set aside.

Acknowledgements

The preparation of the Ph.D. thesis on which this book is based was assisted by a Massey University Doctoral Scholarship. I thank the Philosophy Department staff, the Doctoral Research Committee, and the University for so generously demonstrating their confidence in me.

I thank above all my chief Ph.D. supervisor, Dr. Tom Bestor, for his major contribution to my project. I could not have formulated many of the ideas in this book without Tom's help nor, in the case of the central idea, without his insistence. Tom's generosity with his time and his patience, percipience, and companionship made my preparation of the thesis a pleasure as well as an adventure. Tom also greatly improved my head-butting abilities.

I thank my second and third supervisors as well—Dr. Roy Perrett, for useful suggestions as to reading and for tactical advice, and Prof. Peter Schouls for his staunch support at both official and personal levels. I am much indebted to Drs. Alex Frame, John Horrocks, Jenny Mackenzie, Peter Melser, and John Patterson, and to Prof. Andy Lock, for valuable discussions on a variety of topics, including Mount Helvellyn. I would also like to register my gratitude to the late Dr. Harry Orsman for advice about the etymology of *mind*. I thank Melanie Staines M.A. for suggesting to my son Anton that, for the sake of simplicity, writers should use their own gender for the generic third person. I have adopted Ms. Staines's suggestion in this book.

I am deeply grateful to Sir Stuart Hampshire for writing to me about my Ph.D. project and for his generous opinion of its central thesis. Finally, I would like to thank my wife and my two sons for their patience, optimism, and cheerful skepticism in regard to the book project. This added considerably to my motivation to complete the book.

Introduction: Is Thinking a Natural Process, or Is It an Action?

By *thinking* we usually mean such activities as calculating, cogitating, pondering, musing, reflecting, meditating, and ruminating. But we might also mean any of a broader range of actions or activities (or dispositions, states, processes, or whatever). I mean remembering, intending, imagining, conceiving, believing, desiring, hoping, feeling emotion, empathizing, following what someone is saying, minding, being conscious of something, and so on. This is admittedly a mixed bag. It might seem that feeling, in particular, should be separated out. Certainly thinking and feeling can be contrasted, but in the context of this book it is what they have in common that is interesting. Anyway, I would like to include all the above as "thinking." The general term most philosophers would use is *mental phenomena*, but, for various reasons, I want to try to do without it. We can use *thinking* instead.

The notion of thinking helps us to explain people's behavior. We appeal to thinking to explain actions, qualities of action, abilities and dispositions to act, and even certain kinds of bodily agitation. Consider the distinctive posture of Rodin's Penseur, an attentive and methodical performance, any goal-directed activity, explaining to someone what one is doing, producing a list of relevant facts, finding the solution to a problem of woodworking or arithmetic, having a disposition to racist remarks or effusive greetings, and trembling or blushing at what someone is saying. We explain these different behaviors and aspects of behavior, and many others, by positing different kinds of thinking going on behind the scenes. The thinking determines the nature of the behavior, then motivates and guides its performance, from within.

What kind of thing is thinking? Is it a "mental" process? Is it a physiological process in the brain? Is it both? Or is it something different again—an action or activity the person performs?

Cognitive Science

According to the currently dominant theory as to the nature of thinking, thinking is the brain's computer-like processing of "mental representations." The brain acquires information about reality via the sense organs and encodes it into neural form as mental representations. The brain stores each representation and computes from it—and from other current and previously stored representations—a program of neuron firings that will produce a behavioral response appropriate to the current situation. This representational and computational understanding of the mind/brain is the basis of "cognitive science," the approach to psychology and philosophy of mind that took over from behaviorism in the mid 1970s.[1]

Cognitive scientists believe their theory is a more sophisticated and scientific version of the "folk" theory that ordinary people believe in. According to folk theory, thinking is a "mental" process carried out in and/or by "the mind." And the mind is assumed to be some kind of non-physical agent inside people's heads. Cognitive science agrees that thinking goes on inside the head. For the cognitive scientist, however, thinking is information processing done by or in the brain. Mind is redefined as a brain function.

The question to what extent the concepts of folk theory can be retained in scientific explanations of behavior is still a cause of philosophical debate. Nearly all cognitive scientists accept that the entities postulated by folk theory—mental phenomena such as beliefs, desires, intentions, and fears, and minds themselves—have some reality. They agree that folk theory of mind has not only practical utility but also some theoretical justification. Furthermore, cognitive scientists assume that the entities postulated by folk theory are real enough to be studied scientifically. This is implicit in the scientific-sounding terms cognitive scientists employ when referring to these entities: *mental phenomena* (or *processes, events, entities, states, representations*), *cognitive processes, conscious processes, conscious states, intentional states, propositional attitudes,* and so on.

Bald identification of the various mental phenomena with brain processes is the exception in current theory. However, mental phenomena are universally believed to be in some way intimately related to brain processes and brain areas. Various theories—with names like "identity theory," "functionalism," "anomalous monism," and "connectionism"— opt for one intimate relationship or another.

As well as developing formal theories about the relations between mental phenomena and brain processes, cognitivist philosophers often make do with metaphors. Brain researchers often use the same expressions. Consciousness and other mental phenomena are said to be "dependent on," "supervenient on," "underpinned by," "caused by," "correlated with," or "the product of" neurophysiological processes. Or the latter are held to "support," "be the mechanism for," "be responsible for," "give rise to," "determine," or "underlie" mental phenomena. Such language clearly implies that, even if mental phenomena are not strictly identical with brain processes, brain processes are still where the action is as far as mental phenomena are concerned. The following is a typical statement of the task of cognitive science:

We believe that at the moment the best approach to the problem of explaining consciousness is to concentrate on finding what is known as the neural correlates of consciousness—the processes in the brain that are most directly responsible for consciousness. By locating the neurons in the cerebral cortex that correlate best with consciousness, and figuring out how they link to neurons elsewhere in the brain, we may come across key insights into . . . the hard problem: a full accounting of the manner in which subjective experience arises from these cerebral processes.[2]

Here, despite the modest hopes of progress, it is unquestioned that brain processes constitute the underlying reality and that the task of explaining mental phenomena is just the task of finding the relevant brain processes and seeing how they work.

The important thing for the purposes of this book is that both the layperson and the cognitive scientist, by assuming that thinking is a process that goes on inside people's heads, are excluding in advance the possibility I want to consider: that thinking may be a kind of action, something the person actively does. In both popular and scientific views, thinking is seen as an impersonal internal process rather than an action the person performs for himself. In the folk view, thinking is a mental process; in the scientific view, it is a neurophysiological one. But the same "impersonality" applies. In neither view is the person doing the thinking. Rather, as with natural processes such as gestation, blood circulation, and digestion, a dedicated organ or mechanism carries out (or hosts, or is responsible for) the process. The main difference between the popular and scientific theories is the nature of the organ or mechanism that is nominated for the job. In the one case it is the non-physical "mind"; in the other it is the physical brain.

The Possibility of an Actional Account of Thinking

In chapters 1 and 2, I review several theories of thinking I call "action-based." While all of the theorists I talk about in those chapters see thinking as having intimate logical and practical ties to action, none of them regards thinking as itself an action. Their accounts are "action-based" but not "actional" theories of thinking. For none of them is thinking something the person does. In Gilbert Ryle's *logical behaviorist*, *adverbial*, and *refraining* theories, thinking is a behaviorally vacuous "grammatical construct" or some such. For *methodological behaviorists*, it is a theoretical construct: a hypothetical intervening variable between stimulus and response. *Physiological abbreviationists* believe thinking is an internal physiological process involving not just brain events but subtle physiological events throughout the body. For the various *internalized social activity* theorists, thinking is also an internal and hence impersonal process—it is social action that is so abbreviated as to be "internalized" in a person. But the emphasis in internalization theories is on the action's becoming non-physical rather than on its becoming subtle and physiological. In these theories, thinking remains, effectively, a mental process in the folk sense.

It seems that every theory of thinking—from the folk theory of mind (which has been around since before Plato) through the various behaviorist, abbreviationist, and social internalization theories of the early and mid twentieth century and the contemporary orthodoxies of cognitive science—either discards or ignores the possibility that thinking is something people do. What I suggest in this book is that, despite the weight of popular and expert opinion, the possibility of thinking's being an action of the person is a very real one. And by "action" I mean an ordinary, albeit unique, learned and voluntary action.

There are several initial grounds for believing that thinking must be an action. I will list some of these very shortly. However, first it is worth getting clear about the difference between impersonal (natural) processes and people's actions.

Natural Processes vs. Personal Actions

In everyday speech, the word *process* is often used to mean things other than natural processes. In one usage it means much the same as *procedure* and refers to an action or course of action with clear stages, often with more than one person contributing. Thus we might talk about a legal process or a manufacturing process, or being in the process of shaving, or something's being in the process of construction. For the purposes of my argument, these procedure-type processes can all go into the "action" bag.

In a closely related usage, we speak of a "process" when the contribution made by people's actions is about equal to, and intertwined with, one or more natural processes. This is true especially of technical processes. Industrial processes, such as steelmaking or electric power generation, involve natural processes that are everywhere controlled by people's actions. And there are mechanical and electronic processes that, once initiated, can proceed with little human intervention, but which nevertheless require people to design, make, and employ the mechanism (or other device or system) the functioning of which constitutes the process in question. The mechanism operates in conformity with natural laws of cause and effect, but putting it into operation is something people do. The respective actional and natural-process contributions to technical processes are often difficult to disentangle. Consider sorting out the actions from the natural processes in, say, drying one's hair with a hair dryer.

For present purposes, we can safely ignore these technical processes. Despite popular conceptions of the brain as a computer, and despite talk of neurophysiological "mechanisms" in the brain, no one believes that thinking is literally a technical process involving people using technology to manage natural processes. The question whether thinking is an action or a process is not complicated in the way the same question about hair-drying might be. If thinking is a process, then it is a purely impersonal and natural kind of process that goes on in the brain unaided by technical interventions from us. In the case of thinking there is no problem of disentangling natural processes from the functioning of mechanisms and from the actions we perform in operating those mechanisms. Thinking is either all action or all process. The question is: How does thinking take place? Do people do it, or is it a natural process occurring in the brain?

Despite the variety in the everyday uses of *process*, I will restrict my use of the word to natural processes, such as biological, physiological, and chemical processes. It is natural processes that I want to distinguish actions, especially thinking, from. I will assume that the distinction between natural processes and learned and voluntary doings of people is obvious. If it is not now, it should be by the end of the next section.

I also assume for now that the two categories are mutually exclusive—that a natural process cannot be an action, and vice versa. There is in fact a widely held philosophical assumption, which I call "action physicalism," according to which the distinction between an action and a natural process is only superficially valid. It is valid "at the everyday level" perhaps, but not "at a deeper scientific level." Action physicalists argue that people's actions are physical events and can therefore, in principle, be analyzed down to and explained in terms of physiological and other natural causal processes. If action physicalism is true, showing thinking to be an action is pointless. Thinking still could (or would) be a natural process, such as a brain process. I tackle action physicalism in the final chapter. Until then, I assume that the everyday distinction between natural processes and actions is valid, and valid all the way down.

Initial Indications That Thinking Is an Action

Thinking Is Usually Self-Aware

Actions are characteristically, even by definition, self-aware. That is, when performing an action we are generally aware of and can describe what it is we are doing. One indication that our concept of thinking is a basically actional concept is that this automatic self-awareness feature also applies to thinking. We generally know, and can say, both that we are thinking and what we are thinking. This cannot be said of the natural processes going on in our bodies. Such inner goings-on as digestion, circulation and oxidation of the blood, insulin secretion by the pancreas, and conception are not usually—and certainly not characteristically or by definition—subject to awareness by the host person. Some internal processes are sometimes accessible to awareness; however, few are characteristically so, and none necessarily. In the normal course of events, we are never aware of the neurophysiological goings-on in our own brains—and yet we usually are aware of our thinking.

Thinking Is Often Publicly Observable

Actions nearly always involve overt movements, so normally one can see people performing actions. On the other hand, internal bodily processes—

including brain processes—generally don't involve overt movements. One reason people might have for believing that thinking is an internal process rather than an action is that one often, and perhaps characteristically, cannot see it going on. This alleged characteristic unobservability of thinking could easily be equated to the characteristic unobservability of internal processes. From there, one could easily infer that thinking is an internal process too.

However, there are actions that one can perform without making observable movements. "Staying absolutely still" is one such action. Deliberately refraining from doing X may also involve "doing nothing." In these cases, the person is making no overt movement yet is performing an identifiable action. What is more, although it involves no movement, the action—staying motionless, say—is not unobservable at all; it can easily be observed.

Thinkers often deliberately stay still. They may freeze in a particular posture—grip their hair, say, or put on a particular intent expression, or hold up their index finger, or do a full Le Penseur. Such conspicuous, even ostentatious, immobility is plausibly an "overt behavior." It can also be a deliberate display of one's thinking, with an implied *Do not disturb*. At any rate, here is a perfectly good sense in which we very often, even usually, can see people thinking in just the way we can see them walking or knitting. And this too counts against thinking's being an intracranial process.

In fact, a considerable range of overt behaviors and mini-behaviors are associated with and reliably indicative of thinking. Apart from immobility, these include frowning, giggling, fist-clenching, and sotto voce muttering. Admittedly, there is an important distinction—which I will revisit later—between behaviors that are part of (or constitutive of) an action or activity and behaviors that are mere contingent by-products of an action or activity. There are certain movements with knitting needles that are constitutive of knitting, but the squinting and frowning that may also be associated with knitting are not parts of knitting; they are only by-products. In cases of a third kind, an action may occur in connection with knitting that is neither a part of it nor a by-product of it but rather is ancillary to it—as when you purl exaggeratedly so I can see it better.

On the "internal process" view, any overt behavior associated with thinking can only be either a by-product of it or ancillary to it. Nothing observable could count as constituting, or as part of, the actual thinking. It is true that many of the behaviors and micro-behaviors that go with thinking are merely involuntary by-products of it. Into this bag we should put blushing or blanching, sweating, trembling, becoming sexually aroused, having one's voice crack, and being "paralyzed." However, involuntary bodily agitations are not the only kind of behavior associated with thinking. There are other kinds of overt movement—such as muttering words, adopting specific facial expressions, making eye movements as if inspecting things, tensing specific muscles, feinting gestures (e.g., drawing in the air), and arguably the above-mentioned immobility. These movements are deliberate actions, and they do seem to help *constitute* the thinking performance.

Thus, although thinking often occurs in the absence of readily observable movement, it is still true that overt behaviors of certain kinds may some-times be integral to and constitutive of thinking. Thinking out loud is one kind of thinking, just as reading out loud is one kind of reading.

Is Thinking Voluntary, or Is It "Automatic"?

Actions are performed by people, whereas natural processes just happen. This means that actions, but not natural processes, are characteristically subject to the imperative. Other things being equal, one can get people to do things or stop doing things just by asking or telling them to. As King Canute found out, however, natural processes are not similarly subject to the imperative. The very idea is odd.

The fact that actions are normally performable on request is logically tied to the fact that they are normally voluntary. That is, a person P being asked to do X has, in principle, a choice. P may do X or refrain from doing X. It is the idea of natural processes' being voluntary—e.g., of the wind's choosing to dry someone's hair—that is odd, fanciful, or incomprehensible.

In any event, thinking is both subject to the imperative and voluntary. One can sensibly ask someone to think of or about something, or to remem-ber, imagine, heed, hope, or fear—and to at least try to believe, desire, or love. Although there is always a chance that one's request will fail, asking someone to do thinking of some kind is seldom if ever logically odd. It would always be logically odd if thinking were a natural process.

Actions normally require at least some effort. Another possible reason for believing that thinking must be a natural process and not an action is that it often seems to proceed without our trying. In familiar situations and when responding to everyday speech, our imagining, remembering, antici-pating, or inferring is mostly so habitual as to be quite effortless. The thinking seems to get done automatically, without our consciously doing it. We can even "tune out" and still follow what is happening or what is being said. However, the *automatically* is only metaphorical. Like all metaphors, apt or otherwise, it is false when taken literally. What is actually being talked about is the kind of facility that any very habitual action would acquire. It is not that one is not doing the thinking, let alone that a mechanism inside one's head is doing it; it is just that we are so good at doing this particular bit or kind of thinking, so practiced, that we can do it without attending to our doing of it, and perhaps even while doing and attending to something else. And, of course, not all thinking is effortless. One may have to pound one's forehead to remember the name of Claire's husband, or to multiply 3 by 14.

Thinking can happen out of the blue sometimes too, as if spontaneously. Realizations can suddenly dawn, pennies drop. Here also, thinking seems to be something that happens, rather than something one does. In these cases, however, the realization generally comes as a result of past thinking that was both effortful and aware. Discoveries are the culmination of work. Unless one has in the past been actively and persistently interested in some possibility, then finding that that possibility is an actuality will not be a "realization." Similarly, when a poet "hears" lines and has only to write them down, this is in fact the outcome of untold previous aware, or half-aware, apparently fruitless strivings.

In other cases, thinking can persist despite the best efforts of the thinker. One may be gripped by anxiety, suspicion, envy, jealousy, or a memory that one would fain be rid of. It keeps coming back. Some people hear voices in their heads, voices they cannot shut out. Faith, hope, or love may be similarly compulsive, as if the person is in thrall. Surely compulsive thinking, at least, cannot be an action of the person. However, I suggest that the situation is much the same with compulsive thinking as with compulsive doings of other kinds—addictions, for example. We might say figuratively that a person is "struggling in the grip of" something, or is a "helpless victim," but we would never go so far as to say that taking an extra drink is not something an alcoholic himself *does*. Although the person may find it in practice difficult or impossible to refrain from taking the drink, it is still something he is doing and not an impersonal process.

It is always possible in principle, if not in practice, that the victim of an addiction or an obsession might refrain from doing or thinking whatever it is. Although it might be surprising, it would never be incomprehensible, or logically odd, for an alcoholic to refrain once in a while, or for a schizophrenic to once in a while ignore and thus quell the voices. Yet if drinking or thinking were natural processes, it would be logically odd to speak of the person's "refraining" or "desisting," even once. In at least this sense, even the most terrifying compulsions, delusions, and obsessions are voluntary actions.

We Evaluate Thinking Morally

Another near-universal feature of people's actions, related to their voluntariness, is their moral relevance. We hold people responsible for their actions, and we evaluate those actions morally. In any society, everyone's actions are at all times subject in principle to moral evaluation. One's own welfare depends to a considerable extent on what others do, on what is acceptable and customary, and the question whether a given action is acceptable or not is everyone's business and always relevant. Furthermore, praise and condemnation are useful instruments in improving the behavior of others.

Natural processes lack the moral dimension entirely. Natural processes may be good or bad news for people, but they are never morally right or wrong. We may take practical steps to prevent or enhance natural processes, but these steps never include praise or blame. Yet we do evaluate people's thinking in the moral way. Although much of what most people think is morally neutral (as is much of what they overtly do), some thoughts are worthy, virtuous, kind, or thoughtful and others are unkind, disgusting, despicable, or otherwise bad. They are unthinkable, for moral reasons. It is not just that one may sin in thought as well as in deed. To sin in thought *is* to sin in deed. To contemplate a horrible possibility, especially while smiling, is already to do something bad. The thinking may be morally bad even if it is never voiced and has no effect on anyone else.

Why this is, I am not sure. Perhaps there are issues here of psychologically harming or demoralizing oneself. In any event, as I have said above, the same cannot be said of natural events and processes. By definition, they are never morally bad. No one would think of condemning a natural process or condemning a person on account of a natural process going on inside him. In this respect also, thinking looks to be much more like a personal action than like an impersonal process.

Thinking Is Something We Learn to Do

Unlike natural bodily processes, actions must be learned. In most cases this means that they must be taught. Most commonly, actions are taught by demonstration and imitation. Thus, typically, actions must be demonstrable. Wittgenstein suggests that being demonstrable is part of what it means to be an action: ". . . doing is something that one can give someone an *exhibition* of."[3]

The prevailing view, in both lay and professional circles, is that thinking—or consciousness—is not something we learn but is rather a natural, biologically evolved, genetically programmed-in ability, similar in this respect to digestion or breathing. Consciousness is a gift rather than something we earn by learning. This assumption seems to be borne out by several considerations. First, consciousness seems to be a precondition for any learning, rather than something that is itself learned. Second, no one can remember learning to think in the way one might conceivably remember learning to speak. Third, because thinking or consciousness is usually or characteristically unobservable, it is difficult to see how it could be learned. At least, it could not be taught by demonstration in the way most learned skills are.

In chapter 3, I claim that infants are at birth neither able to think nor conscious (except in their being able to imitate in a rudimentary way) and that they must learn how to think. And in a long argument put forth in chapters 3–7, I claim that infants learn, for the most part, by being taught—and taught in the way that is usual for actions, that is, by having the thinking trick demonstrated to them.

That thinking is in any way demonstrable might seem mysterious. What I argue is that the ability to think begins with the infant's acquisition of abilities to perform certain kinds of overt communicative action, such as speech and gestures. These are all taught by demonstration and practice in the normal way. Thinking is the "performing" of the relevant communicative actions in an especially rapid, subtle, and covert way. Although the fully covert version may not be demonstrable, the covertizing process is. The progressive abbreviation of originally overt communicative performances can be demonstrated. And I claim that many familiar mother-infant games and other interactions have just this purpose. Thus, I argue that, despite appearances, there is a plausible story according to which infants and children are taught, and taught largely by example, how to think. They are taught how to be conscious of things.

There are other reasons for believing thinking to be a learned skill. The concepts of natural ability, practice, skill, quality of performance, degree of care in performance, and level of effort all apply naturally to actions and reflect the learnability of actions. And none of them is logically applicable to natural processes. We cannot speak of natural ability, of practice's improving skill, of care and quality of performance, or of effort in connection with natural bodily processes such as digestion or blood circulation.

Again, though, these skill concepts readily apply to thinking. Thinking is a performance; it is something one may do well or badly. One may think something out half-heartedly, perfunctorily, carelessly, or one may think it out enthusiastically, thoroughly, carefully, systematically. Some people have a talent for thinking and are better at it than others. Some thinking is slow, routine, and dull; other thinking is clever, quick, creative, and adventurous.

As we will see in chapters 1 and 2, Ryle is generally adamant that thinking is neither an intracranial process nor an action of the person. According to Ryle, thinking is closely tied to actions but is not a "proprietary activity" in its own right. However, in the following passage Ryle insists that thinking has at least the distinctively actional quality of skill and teachability I am talking about. And he equally insists that natural processes lack that quality:

. . . thinking is an art, like cricket, and not just a natural process, like digesting. Or, to put it less bluntly, the word *thinking* covers a wide variety of things, some, but not all of which embody, in differing degrees and respects, such things as drills, acquired knacks, techniques and flairs. It is just in so far as they do embody such things that we can describe someone's thinking as careless or careful, strenuous or lazy, rigorous or loose, efficient or inefficient, wooden or elastic, successful or unsuccessful. Epithets like these belong to the vocabularies of coaches and umpires, and are inapplicable to such natural processes as digesting. We cannot be clever or stupid at digesting. . . .[4]

The Argument of This Book

My aim in this book is to present a coherent account of thinking as a learned action. The mid-twentieth-century action-based theories of thinking come reasonably close to doing this, but, as I said, none of them goes the whole hog and identifies thinking as an action. For several reasons, however, these theories are worth looking at, and I devote chapters 1 and 2 to reviewing them.

The above brief arguments as to the actional nature of thinking could be extended and buttressed. On the other hand, no argument that thinking is an action we perform, however cogent, could be as compelling as a plausible account of just what kind of action it is. That is what I attempt in chapters 3–7.

I claim that there are two key ingredients in the act of thinking, both themselves actional. The first is our ability to do things in concert. The second is our ability to—jointly with others or alone—perform concerted activity in merely token form. I identify the concerting of activity as the matrix out of which solo action, cooperation, language use, solo perceiving, and thinking develop. And I say that the main instrument of development, the means by which all these other abilities derive from concerting, is our ability to "token" actions. Tokening is a learned skill whereby parts and aspects of concerted activity are merely incepted by participants, rather than being fully performed. As the child masters more sophisticated and covert ways of tokening actions, he eventually becomes able to, in this special token way, "rehearse" concerted activity while alone. And the rehearsing may be done without any overt movement. Basically, this is thinking.

If the initial hypothesis that thinking is an action and not a natural process is correct, and if my description in chapters 3–7 of what kind of action it is isn't too far astray, then both popular and expert opinion according to which thinking is an impersonal process that goes on inside people's heads must be gravely mistaken. This would require explanation. An "error theory" would be required, to show how so many could have got it so wrong for so long. In chapters 8 and 9, I offer an error theory. The gist of it is that the assumption common to both popular and scientific theories— that thinking goes on in people's heads—stems from most people's naively literal understanding of certain metaphors in the colloquial vocabulary for talking about thinking.

The colloquial vocabulary for talking about thinking is, I argue, basically figurative. The stock expressions in it are nearly all metaphors, and most of the central nouns—including *mind*—are derived by nominalization from the corresponding verbs. I suggest that the content of the metaphors, the especially seductive power of metaphors used in conjunction with nominalized verbs, and the propaganda-like repetitiveness of these idioms in everyday speech combine to foster the illusion that there is a mysterious agent and/or venue of thinking—the mind—inside our heads.

I try to show that, when the various figures of speech are properly unpacked, it can be seen that what the colloquial thinking vocabulary really refers to is not—as it seems when the vocabulary is taken literally—intracranial phenomena. Rather, the real, underlying subject matter is certain subtle actions and meta-actions that people perform. Specifically, it is what I describe in chapters 4–7 as *covert tokening of concerted activity* or *covert token concerting*.

The vernacular explanation for the covertness of covert tokening—in terms of its taking place in the person's head—is metaphorical. Thinking does not literally go on inside the head, any more than does watching a football match, carefully describing a traffic accident, or pretending to be a walrus.

I argue that cognitive scientists have taken the "in the head" metaphors too seriously. The apparent intellectual advance in going from mind to brain as the internal agent and/or venue of thinking really only cements the mistake in. Certainly the brain is real and can be studied, and its functions can be studied. If we want to study thinking, however, then taking the brain as the agent and/or venue of thinking, and going on to study the brain and its functions, is quite the wrong approach. The fact is that thinking has no internal agent and/or venue. It is something the person does.

The question whether lay folk make the same sort of mistake—whether they take the colloquial thinking vocabulary too literally, and believe there really are such intracranial phenomena as minds, beliefs, desires, and intentions—is more difficult to answer. Certainly the layperson may habitually visualize according to, and in response to, the colloquial metaphors. However, these visualizings are fragmentary, unsystematic, and extremely diverse, reflecting the diversity of the metaphors. No matter how inveterate these imaginings become, they can never approximate a theory. I suggest that it is unrealistic to think even of a folk "concept" of mind. The most earnest attempt to extract a concept or a theory from the colloquial vocabulary could result only in a kind of minestrone of extended and mixed metaphors. To find out what lay folk really believe about the mind, we can only go by what they say. And what they say is figurative. They hardly ever try to speak literally about the mind in the way philosophers do.

In chapter 10, I attempt literal paraphrases of several of the more important families of thinking metaphors—especially those associated with the noun *mind*. In each case, the metaphor can plausibly be read as intended to highlight some aspect of covert tokening of concerted activity, alias "thinking."

Finally, in chapter 11, I address the question I raised earlier: whether people's actions (including their thinking) can be reduced to or explained in terms of natural, and especially physiological, processes and events. Is action physicalism true? I provide two arguments that suggest it is not. I also briefly address some further questions: What kind of things are actions? Are they things in the world? If not, then is our knowledge of actions more basic or less basic than our knowledge of things in the world?

1   Action-Based Theories of Thinking (1)

In this chapter and the next I briefly review six action-based theories about thinking. They are not cognitivist theories, and they neither define thinking as a brain function nor conceive the brain as a computer-like information processor. But they are not actional theories either. They each define thinking as some function of actions, but not as itself an action. Despite the latter, the theories reviewed in these two chapters have all contributed insights to the actional theory I put forward in chapters 3–7, and they can be regarded as precursors of it.

Behaviorism

From early in the twentieth century until the 1970s, when cognitive science took over, the dominant theories in psychology and the philosophy of mind were behaviorist ones. Behaviorists believed as cognitivists do that popular talk of "mental" phenomena does not reflect the existence of non-physical processes and entities. Where cognitivism redefines mental phenomena as neural representations in and functions of the brain, behaviorism redefines them in terms of people's overt behavior. However, behaviorists do not say that thinking is itself a behavior. What do they say? There are several kinds of behaviorism.[1] I will summarize two.

Logical Behaviorism
Logical behaviorism, whose foremost representative is Gilbert Ryle, denies that there are any mental phenomena at all, whether these are conceived in the popular way, as ghostly entities and processes in the head, or in the scientific way, as neurophysiological entities and processes in there. Ryle denies, in addition, that there is any distinctive action or activity one could

call thinking—or remembering, believing, imagining, etc. In his best-known book, *The Concept of Mind*,[2] Ryle says that we come to believe in the existence of intracranial "mental" entities and processes, and to believe that there is a ghostly inner activity called thinking, because we mistake the "logical grammar" of our everyday vocabulary for talking about thinking. Despite appearances, the terms in this everyday vocabulary—verbs like *thinking, imagining, conceiving, believing, desiring,* and *remembering,* and the nouns derived from them—do not refer to unobservable intracranial processes, entities, or activities. Rather, Ryle claims, these terms register abstractions from or "logical constructions on" aspects of our ordinary observable activity. Ryle suggests that colloquial mentalist talk is really a way of talking about people's "dispositions and abilities" to do certain things—solve problems, write poems, display cheerfulness, make confident avowals, and so on. We describe and explain people's behavior in terms of the dispositions and abilities we observe and infer.

Although we may fancy otherwise (and, regrettably, some colloquial expressions and some philosophical doctrines encourage these fancies), none of these behavioral dispositions and/or abilities, Ryle says, are ghostly inner states. Nor are they flesh-and-blood behavioral or physiological realities. They are merely logical constructs, concepts we have devised to help us describe behavior. Thus, terms that apparently refer to ghostly intracranial phenomena in fact relate to dispositions and abilities to do things.

Emotion terms, for example, relate to dispositions toward particular kinds of emotionally demonstrative behavior. Personal attributes such as intelligence reflect tendencies to intelligent, thoughtful behavior and also certain abilities. To say that P has a certain belief about X is to say only that P has a disposition to say and do certain things in relation to X:

. . . to believe that the ice is dangerously thin is to be unhesitant in telling oneself and others that it is thin, in acquiescing in other people's assertions to that effect, in objecting to statements to the contrary, in drawing consequences from the original proposition, and so forth. But it is also to be prone to skate warily, to shudder, to dwell in imagination on possible disasters and to warn other skaters. It is a propensity not only to make certain theoretical moves but also to make certain executive and imaginative moves, as well as to have certain feelings.[3]

One objection to this account is that it is circular. Ryle has included, among the behaviors P is disposed to perform things such as "dwelling in imagination," "making theoretical and imaginative moves," and "having certain feelings." These are mental phenomena such as were to be explained in the first place. Ryle is relaxed about this, but it is hard to see why. In fact, it has been plausibly argued that, if any mental phenomenon is to be satisfactorily described in terms of dispositions to do things $X_{1 \ldots n}$, there must always be a mental component among those $X_{1 \ldots n}$. This would make any behaviorism that is based on dispositions circular and empty.

Other critics say that Ryle's having shunted mental phenomena off into the mythical (and/or the merely grammatical) leaves our actions and our dispositions unexplained. Common sense explains people's actions at least partly in terms of beliefs and desires. Performing an action presupposes that one has beliefs about the present situation and a desire to achieve some end. More generally, rational action presupposes, and is motivated by, previous or concurrent mentation of some kind. Ryle does not show that common sense is mistaken about this.

Methodological Behaviorism

Methodological behaviorism is a psychological theory that defined itself against the introspectionism that dominated experimental psychology up until 1920 or so. Introspectionism required the psychologist's subject to observe and report on the contents of his own mind. Methodological behaviorists such as J. B. Watson rightly rejected this method of research as unreliable and unscientific. If psychology is to be a science, Watson said, its data must be publicly and objectively observable, and verifiable. Following on from Watson, B. F. Skinner recognized only two kinds of subject matter for psychology: the external stimulus to which the organism is subjected and the ensuing overt behavioral response. Skinner claimed that by studying just these two scientifically observable variables, stimulus and response, and by establishing reliable correlations between them, the behavioral scientist can in principle find out all there is to know about human and animal behavior. Skinner believed that once law-like correlations between stimuli and responses were established, they would explain all the behaviors and aspects of behavior popularly attributed to internal mental phenomena.

Strictly speaking, methodological behaviorism neither asserts nor denies the existence of mental phenomena as popularly conceived. Because the supposed mental phenomena are unobservable, the existence question cannot be decided on scientific grounds and is thus outside the psychologist's field. So it never arises.

The attitude of methodological behaviorists to neurophysiology and brain science is also noncommittal. Although brain science cannot be dismissed as unscientific, most behaviorists wanted their area of study to exclude anything intracranial or even subcutaneous. Apart from the fact that brain science was young at the time and had come up with few findings of interest to psychologists, behaviorists were convinced that the important brain processes could all be determined indirectly, by inference from the laws of stimulus and response. Some behaviorists, including Donald Hebb, did speculate about neurophysiological processes; for most of them, however, the brain was of as little interest as the mind. The subject's head might as well be an unopenable black box.

The Problems with Behaviorism

All behaviorists face two problems. First is the cluster of essentially philosophical questions as to whether, and/or in what sense, mental phenomena exist—and, if they do exist, what kind of things they are. Logical behaviorists deny they are anything real, and this strikes many as just too implausible. Surely one *feels* the glee and the grief, and sees them in other people. Surely there are underlying causes or "categorical bases" for our dispositions and abilities, whether these underlying causes are mental or physiological. Methodological behaviorists effectively ignore the ontological questions, which is perhaps even less satisfactory.

Second, behaviorists have to make up their minds what "behavior" is, what "actions" are. Some behaviorists believe that people's actions are just physical events, the same for scientific purposes as biological events and processes. For these "action physicalists," behavior is describable solely in terms of objectively observable and recordable bodily movements—in terms of complex body-part trajectories, say. Other behaviorists believe that a behavior's external circumstances—the "stimulus conditions"—must be specified before we can define it. Others, including Ryle, concede that even specification of physical movements and external circumstances is not enough. In fact, the main opposition to behaviorism comes from philosophers who believe that our concept of behavior presupposes the very concepts—of belief, desire, intention, etc.—that the behaviorist is trying to do without.

There is some good in behaviorism though. For one thing, it highlights the important fact that, whatever thinking is, it is closely related to our abilities and dispositions to do things in the ordinary overt way. Behaviorism brings the relationship between thinking and overt action to center stage. Perhaps even more important, behaviorism contributes a salutary skepticism about the everyday mentalist vocabulary we have for talking about thinking. Wittgenstein, Ryle, and others warned about how the metaphors and grammatical false appearances in our everyday talk about thinking can affect philosophical talk about thinking. For example, look at the passages I quote at the end of chapter 8. Such warnings have generally been disregarded by cognitivist theorists. However, for better or worse, they prompted me to undertake the analysis of the rhetoric of mind idiom I present later in this book.

Behavior-Abbreviation Theories

In addition to the various behaviorisms, there is another kind of theory of thinking that defines thinking in terms of its relation to action. It is sometimes called *behavior-abbreviation theory* or *abbreviationism*. Many of the prominent behavioral psychologists (including Watson, Pavlov, de Laguna, Guthrie, Hull, Skinner, and Hebb) had versions of abbreviationism as add-ons to their respective behaviorist theories. Although it has never been as well known or as influential as behaviorism, abbreviationism has a much longer history.[4] Its first advocate is arguably the Scottish philosopher David Hume, who distinguished (mental) imaginings from (physical) perceivings on the basis of the latter's greater "vivacity" or "force and liveliness."[5] Abbreviationism survives as a theoretical orientation within neuroscience today.[6]

The abbreviationist idea is that what are popularly called mental phenomena are in fact ordinary overt behaviors that are occurring in greatly abbreviated form. The person is "performing" an action, but in so abbreviated a fashion that little or nothing of the performance is observable. The only indicators that the action is being performed (in the special abbreviated way) are certain micro-behavioral phenomena—vestigial muscle and/or gland activity, pulse rate changes, blushing or blanching, and so on. Such phenomena are overt in principle but are usually so subtle as to be difficult to observe without special instruments. Other manifestations of this radically abbreviated "behavior" are entirely internal and physiological—for example, vestigial neuron firing in sense organs, in the brain, and in muscles.

I argue later that the very subtle micro-behavioral and internal physio-logical phenomena on which abbreviation theorists concentrate represent only the subtle end of what is essentially a continuum. "Abbreviated" behavior is sometimes quite large scale and easily observable to the naked eye. Emotions, for example, are characterized by clearly visible facial expres-sions and other bodily agitations, sometimes including quite large gestures. Abbreviationists tend to look at just the very subtle and the internal mani-festations, those requiring special instruments and a white coat to investi-gate. They assume, too, that if mental phenomena are the quarry then "inside the person" is the place to look.

The various kinds of thinking (or mental phenomena) are thought to be or to be "physically underpinned by" the relevant abbreviated behavior. Watson[7] and Skinner[8] identify most thinking as abbreviated speech. And abbreviationists generally believe that, in the words of Durant Drake,

. . . in thinking, or in dreaming, we are reacting, though merely in slight, tentative ways, not visible to a spectator. Whatever we are conscious of (whether in perception or in conception, with our eyes open or in brooding reverie) we are reacting *to*. The behaviorists have dragged to light these multitudinous, minute, incipient reactions, and shown us that all organisms, and especially the higher organisms, are incessantly performing these delicate reactive movements, and, in that way, keeping in touch, as it were, with their world. . . . We might be content to call this incessant play of reac-tions, incipient and overt, the organism's consciousness of things. . . .[9]

Behavior-Abbreviation Experiments

The classic abbreviation experiments compare the micro-behavioral and internal physiological phenomena that appear when a subject is asked to imagine or think about X-ing against what happens during an actual per-formance of X. In most cases, it transpires that the phenomena that occur during thinking are, basically, abbreviations of the overt movements and physiological phenomena that would be occurring were the action in question being fully and/or actually performed. For example, if I am angry, although I may remain motionless, the program of physiological events going on in my body will be a miniature version of the program that would be occurring were I performing some overt aggressive act. If I don't actually make a fist, at least the relevant hand muscles will tense, say, and my adrenal gland will become active. Or, if I am thinking about making a bookcase, I will likely make tiny eye movements consistent with visually inspecting a bookcase, my larynx may exhibit slight muscular contractions as of speech (relating to bookcases), the muscles in my arm that would be involved in sawing and hammering may be vestigially active, and so on.

In the standard experiment, the subject S performs some simple action X and physiological events PX relating to the X-ing are concurrently recorded. S is then asked to just imagine X-ing; while S is doing this imagining, related physiological events PIX are recorded. Comparison of PX with PIX generally supports the abbreviation hypothesis. That is, PIX is found to be similar to, but a reduced version of, PX. Numerous experiments with this format have been and still are being published in the literature of psychology and neuroscience.

Edmund Jacobson's work is typical. His 1930–31 experiments culminated in an investigation of "imagination, recollection and abstract thinking involving the speech musculature."[10] Electrodes were inserted in the tongue and/or lower lip and electromyograph recordings (registering electrical activity of motor neurons in muscles) were made while various acts of speaking were both performed (sotto voce) and imagined. In addition, subjects were asked to "think of abstract matters such as 'eternity,' electrical resistance,' 'Ohm's law,' [and] 'the meaning of the word *incongruous*,'" and recordings were made. The results conformed to expectations, the electromicrograph readings showing significantly lower voltages for imagined speech than for actual whispered speech.

Richard Davidson and Gary Schwartz showed that EEG readings correlated with two different kinds of action—attention to a flashing light and finger tapping—may be identical to those taken when the respective actions are imagined.[11] Thus, brain activation occurring when S imagines seeing the flashing light or imagines tapping a finger is similar to that when S actually does these things.

As a third illustration, Jean Decety and co-workers measured heart and breathing rates concomitant with treadmill running and pedaling at different speeds.[12] They found that, as the speed of running or pedaling increased, so did these physiological indicators. Heart and breathing rates were then recorded during imagined running and pedaling, and these were found to vary in the same way—depending on what speed of running or pedaling was being imagined. As expected, absolute pulse and respiration rates were consistently greater with real exertion than with imagined exertion. For example, the heart and respiration rates of a subject imagining running at 12 kilometers per hour were the same on average as those recorded when the subject was actually walking at 5 kph.

A final example seems to suggest a physiological basis for empathy. Giacomo Rizzolatti and Michael Arbib researched monkeys and humans and found that grasping and manipulating activity is accompanied by a distinctive pattern of firing in special "mirror neurons" in the pre-motor area of the brain.[13] This pattern of neural activity is duplicated, minus corresponding overt activity, when the monkey or person is watching another monkey or person perform the same grasping and manipulating movements. On these results, observation of others' actions requires empathy—that is, oneself imagining doing what the other is actually doing.[14]

What Kind of "Abbreviation"?

Abbreviated behavior has many aliases: "tentative movement" and "incipient motor process,"[15] "implicit response,"[16] "the incomplete act,"[17] "inhibited response,"[18] "fractional antedating goal response,"[19] "readinesses" that "are not complete acts but . . . consist in tensions of the muscles that will take part in the complete act,"[20] "trace activity,"[21] "simulation,"[22] "anticipatory phases of activity" and "mental practice,"[23] "covert action," and "scaled-down action."[24]

Are abbreviated responses just physiologically weak versions of actions, too weak to produce overt movement? Or does the action start off at full strength, only to be immediately inhibited by countervailing neural activity? Margaret Floy Washburn, the pioneer of abbreviationism as a physiological theory, opts for weakness, but she despairs of certainty:

The precise nature of the physiological process which underlies a tentative movement, and the precise difference between this process and that underlying a full movement, it would be useless to conjecture. Is there simply a difference in the amount of nervous energy sent along a given motor pathway to the muscles, a less amount producing the very slight contractions of tentative movements; or do full movements require the action of more neurons than tentative movements do?[25]

B. F. Skinner construes abbreviation—in the case of verbal behavior, at least—in terms of how much energy is put into a performance:

The range of verbal behavior is roughly suggested, in descending order of energy, by shouting, loud talking, quiet talking, whispering, muttering "under one's breath," subaudible speech with detectable muscular action, sub-audible speech of unclear dimensions, and perhaps even the "unconscious thinking" sometimes inferred in instances of problem solving.[26]

Another alternative, in which behavior and its physiological correlate are activated in the normal way but then immediately inhibited, is proposed by Douglas Hofstadter:

It may be that imagery is based on our ability to suppress motor activity. . . . If you imagine an orange, there may occur in your cortex a set of commands to pick it up, to smell it, to inspect it, and so on. Clearly these commands cannot be carried out, because the orange is not there. But they can be sent along the usual channels . . . until, at some critical point, a "mental faucet" is closed, preventing them from actually being carried out. Depending how far down the line this "faucet" is situated, the images may be more or less vivid and real-seeming.[27]

In the same vein, Marc Jeannerod suggests that "simulating a movement is the same thing as actually performing it except that execution is blocked."[28] He points out that imagining often produces involuntary overt bodily agitations as "spillover." In these cases, some neural commands must be reaching motor neurons on muscles: ". . . the fact that muscular activity is only partially blocked during motor simulation emphasizes the delicate equilibrium between excitatory and inhibitory influences at the motoneuron level and suggests that motoneurons are close to threshold."

From a somewhat broader cognitivist perspective, Nico Frijda supports the equilibrium idea. Talking about emotion, he describes "the regulatory tuning of impulse by the reciprocal action of inhibitory and facilitatory mechanisms"[29] as working to fine-tune the intensity levels of both overt emotional behavior and suppressed "action tendencies." He concludes:

Regulation is an essential component of the emotion process. Emotion—outwardly manifest emotion, but equally emotion as experienced—is to be considered the product of excitation of action tendency of the one hand and inhibition of that same action tendency on the other. What is observed or felt depends on the balance between these two.

The emotion system should be viewed as a system governed by dual, reciprocal control. Dual control is rather usual in biological systems. It is found in movement control by the simultaneous action of antagonistic muscles, in autonomic response in the interplay of sympathetic and parasympathetic activity, in hormonal response, to name a few instances. Evidently, dual control permits finer tuning than does single-graded excitation.[30]

Function of the Abbreviated Response

There is general agreement as to the function of the abbreviated (or mental) response. This is consistently described as a "readying" or "priming" of subsequent actual performance. The readying effect is thought to apply whether the delay preceding action is long or short. The abbreviated behavior is a kind of interim, provisional response to an environmental stimulus, an internal dummy run or rehearsal before actual behavior. In cases where the stimuli that would normally trigger behavior X are incomplete, or where the situation is otherwise unfamiliar or ambiguous, the abbreviated response establishes a readiness to X which can be sustained until the situation clarifies. The readying enables quicker, more efficient X-ing if and when the stimulus situation does subsequently become propitious for X-ing. If it turns out that the situation becomes less propitious, at least the person or animal will not have made a faux pas initially.

Ulrich Neisser's version of the priming hypothesis is as follows:

If images are anticipations, they should facilitate subsequent perception. Perceptual readiness is not a minor by-product of visualizing, but its essence. . . . A subject who has just seen a given letter, say A, will identify another A as the same letter more quickly if . . . the subject is not shown but merely *told* what the coming letter will be, so that he can imagine it in advance.[31]

In many sports, "mental practice" is an important supplement to actual practice for improving the reliability and skill level of subsequent performance.[32] "Imagined movements," Neisser concludes, "have a real effect on subsequent overt behavior. Indeed imagined movement is often carried out deliberately in an effort to improve proficiency in a skill. Many athletes are convinced that 'mental practice' of this kind improves their performance, and a number of experimental studies substantiate that opinion."[33]

As the psychologist and philosopher Grace de Laguna notes, the readying may also ensure sustained effort once an action has begun: ". . . this tendency to anticipate the final stage of an act is not merely to prepare the organism, but to reinforce the course of action that has been initiated and to assure its being carried to completion."[34] The effects of readying a response in advance—quickness off the mark, skill, reliability, sustainedness of effort, etc.—can be pictured in terms of the action being "warmed up" in advance. The physiological mechanism now thought to underlie the warming-up is "synaptic facilitation." The abbreviated X-ing exercises and improves the connections between the neurons involved in actual X-ing, enabling them to transmit pulses faster and more reliably.[35]

Problems with Abbreviation Theory

Like behaviorism, abbreviationism is beset with logical and terminological confusions and uncertainties. Can we view abbreviated responses as purely physical events that are objectively describable in trajectorial and/or physiological terms? Or do they require a richer conceptualization—as "actions," perhaps? How do they "correspond to" or "correlate with" mental events? In addition to these uncertainties about the physical or actional status of abbreviated responses, and about how abbreviated responses relate to "mental" phenomena, there is also uncertainty as to how abbreviated responses relate to the behaviors of which they are abbreviations. The theoretical basis of abbreviation research—whether in psychology or physiology—has never been systematically spelled out.[36]

Few if any of the "aliases" mentioned earlier can be taken literally. And the technical term *abbreviation* on its own is no use. If an action is abbreviated to the point where little or no overt movement is occurring, then that action is no longer being performed at all. Notions of "silent speech" are often invoked in this connection—as with Skinner's "subaudible speech,"[37] Theodore Sarbin's "muted speech,"[38] and Daniel Dennett's "entirely silent talking to oneself."[39] Yet the expression *silent speech* is not only metaphorical but oxymoronic. Silent speaking is a contradiction in terms. Imagined X-ing is not literally a kind or version of X-ing. It is as much, or more, like a refraining from X-ing, as Ryle says (see chapter 2 below).

Many abbreviation theorists, aware of the hirsute nature of the abbreviation concept, appeal also to notions of "internalized" behavior, "inner" rehearsal, "inner" speech, etc. The fancy of someone's doing something inside his head is a very familiar and useful one. However, obviously, it is as figurative as *silent speech*. Only metaphorically may one do something inside one's head. There is no question of anyone's literally getting in there, let alone doing things in there once entry has been gained. Certainly though, the metaphor is apt. The "abbreviated" doing we are talking about is in some respects just like doing something behind the scenes, or doing it "under wraps." But it is only a metaphor. And "doing in the head" is just the kind of metaphor that invites back in those notions of goings-on in the mind that the abbreviationist, as much as the behaviorist, is so keen to evict.

Clearly, "abbreviated" behavior is a real and familiar phenomenon. Equally clearly, there are close relations between this "abbreviated" X-ing and both actual X-ing and imagined X-ing. However, none of the abbreviation theorists comes close to explaining, in literal terms, just what those relations are. All the same, abbreviation research has established that these questions are important. The nature of abbreviated behavior and its relations to actual doing and imagined doing are things that psychologists and philosophers of mind should think about.

Ryle's Adverbial Theory

In addition to his well-known dispositional account of mental concepts in *The Concept of Mind*, Ryle advanced two other theories of thinking, neither of which can be described as behaviorist. These are the "adverbial" theory and the "refraining" theory. Both identify thinking as not itself a kind of action but rather as a function of, or meta-operation on, actions. I discuss the adverbial theory here and the refraining theory in the next chapter.[40]

Thinking What One Is Doing

According to the adverbial theory, thinking is not a separate action or activity in its own right; rather, it is the performing of some ordinary activity in a distinctive "thinking" way. It is performing it "thinkingly." Ryle claims that the paradigm case of thinking is "thinking what one is doing." And "what one is doing" may be just about anything—anything, that is, that can be done in a thinking or a thoughtful manner, as opposed to unthinkingly or thoughtlessly.

One kind of thinking that looks as if it would be quite resistant to an adverbial analysis is the kind of motionless, absorbed thinking that Le Penseur is doing on his rock. Certainly, a behaviorist analysis does not seem promising. Here, if anywhere, thinking is an actually occurring activity or process, something that cannot be glossed in terms of dispositions, abilities, or other "logical constructs." The thinking is going on right now in front of us. On the other hand, since he is motionless, there does not seem to be anything that Le Penseur is doing "thinkingly," either.

The aim of much of Ryle's later work is to find out what is going on in the Penseur case. This makes it somewhat surprising that he opts for the adverbial theory, with thinking what one is doing as the paradigm of thinking. To all appearances what Le Penseur is doing is very different from, say, what the thinking tennis player intent on getting his shots right and outplaying his opponent is doing, and very different from what the absorbed conversationalist is doing—being thoughtful, inventive, amusing, polite. Le Penseur is conspicuously not doing anything—apart from thinking.

However, Ryle aims to explain Le Penseur's thinking on the same model, as also a case of thinking what one is doing. His aim is "to show that it is the notion of engaged thinking, like that of the tennis-player or the conversationalist, that is the basic notion, while that of disengaged thinking or reflecting, like that of Le Penseur, is supervenient. The notions of being pensive and having thoughts do not explain, but need to be explained via, the notion of intelligently X-ing, where 'X' is not a verb of thinking."[41]

Ryle claims that the conventional idea of thinking what one is doing is of person P performing some overt action and accompanying this external performance with a separate internal performance, which is the thinking. Making a chess move is doing one thing, and thinking about that move is doing another. Against this, Ryle insists that the thinking is not another (ghostly, internal) action performed in parallel with the moving of the chess piece. Rather, it is an adverbial quality of the chess move. The thinking is "higher-order" than or "parasitic on" the per se action—e.g., the chess move—but does not constitute a separate performance. Generally, the thinking agent "conducts his operation efficiently, and to operate efficiently is not to perform two operations. It is to perform one operation in a certain manner or with a certain style or procedure. . . ."[42] Thus, "to X, thinking what one is doing, is not to be doing both some X-ing and some separately do-able Y-ing; it is to be X-ing under a variety of qualifications, such as X-ing on purpose, with some tentativeness, some vigilance against known hazards, some perseverance and with at least a modicum of intended or unintended self-training. It is to X intentionally, experimentally, circumspectly and practicingly, and these by themselves are not additional things that he is doing or might be doing."[43] So thinking what one is doing is not a matter of doing two things in tandem—the overt X-ing, plus some interior thinking-about-X-ing. Instead, it is a matter of doing the one thing, the X-ing, in a certain manner. Just one action or activity is in question, not two.

Ryle claims *think* is really an "adverbial verb," like *obey.* One can "obey" only by performing some infra act of X-ing—washing one's hands, say, or getting one's feet off the table.[44] Thinking and obeying are "actions" only in a formal grammatical sense. They are not themselves doings. They need an actual, per se, infra action to realize them.

Doing X Heedfully

What manner of X-ing is the "thinking" manner of doing X? How does one do X "thinkingly"? The adverb Ryle singles out is *heedfully*. One performs X in a heedful way. There are other adverbial verbs of thinking,[45] but according to Ryle heed is implicit in all of them. And none of them names a per se action or activity. Their logical role is supra-actional and adverbial. Each marks a particular heedful or thinking manner of performing some infra activity.

Ryle says that we judge whether or not person P is doing X in the thinking, heedful way by using two kinds of criteria. First, does P have certain dispositions and/or abilities? To drive carefully or heedfully is to be prepared for certain emergencies, to be able to answer questions about the road, and so on. A connection is thus maintained with the dispositional account. But, second, to drive heedfully is also to exhibit, while driving, a certain disciplined and attentive demeanor. A driver's "readiness to cope with . . . emergencies would show itself in the operations he would perform, if they were to occur. But it also does show itself by the ways in which he converses and handles his controls even when nothing critical is taking place."[46] Although in his earlier writing Ryle has reservations about this kind of "concurrent behavioral evidence" of heed,[47] by 1979 he has decided on a criterial role for behavioral evidence, especially in cases where P is learning as he goes. If P's performance is improving, and/or he is appropriately admonishing himself for deficiencies in it, this is conclusive evidence of heed and thinking. Thus, "if someone is doing something on purpose and is exercising some ordinary care in doing it; and if, moreover, he is learning something, or at least being ready to learn something, however minimal, from his successes, failures, difficulties and facilities, so that he is in fact, if not in intention, tending to improve as he goes along, we shall not and should not hesitate to say that he is thinking what he is doing. He himself deplores some of his lapses, omissions, falterings and inadequacies in epistemic terms of abuse as mistakes, misestimates, muddles or at least stupidities."[48]

Doing X Self-Teachingly

Some kinds of thinking are more difficult and effortful than others.[49] Ryle is primarily interested in what Le Penseur is doing, and this seems to be at the more difficult, problem-solving, brow-knitting, pondering, calculating end of the spectrum. For Ryle, the essence of this kind of thinking is "teaching oneself" how to cope in the problematic situation. It is a matter of self-education. Problem-solving involves a "self-teaching" kind of heeding. "Thinking things out involves saying things to oneself, or to one's other companions, with an instructive intent."[50]

According to Ryle, in thinking one has to bring one's past experience as a pupil to bear. One's experience as a pupil helps prepare one to be a teacher, and to be one's own teacher. Thinking is more than the rote application of past lessons. A more sophisticated brand of heeding is required. Typically, the thinker must now apply previously acquired "heuristic techniques" to new problems and/or in new ways. Thus, "Le Penseur is tentatively, experimentally, suspiciously, and quite likely despondently trying out on himself expedients, routines, procedures, exercises, curbs and dodges of types which teachers do employ, not always successfully, when they want to teach things that they do know to pupils who do not. . . . Naturally my Penseur knows what it is like to be taught things that he does not know by teachers who do; and he knows what it is or would be like himself to be the teacher of some things he knows to others who do not. So now he experimentally applies to himself, just in case they may turn out to be effective, operations of the types that are often or sometimes employed effectively by live teachers upon live pupils."[51] Ryle suggests that "we might parody Plato and say that in thinking the soul is not just conversing or debating with herself; she is experimentally conveying could-be lessons to herself."[52]

But What Infra Action Is Le Penseur Performing?

If Ryle has satisfactorily characterized "thinking what one is doing," can what the motionless Penseur is doing be explained as a variant or derivative of it? In particular, what is the infra X-ing in the Penseur case? "I have," Ryle confesses, "said nothing about what Le Penseur is engaged in, that is, about the person who is engaged in the thinking of thoughts. He is surely so meditating, reflecting, pondering or thinking that the report "he is thinking" is *not* an unfinished adverbial report. . . . The notion of thinking what one is doing does not amount to any of the notions of for example meditating, reflecting, examining, deliberating, pondering or calculating. The telephone interrupts the typist's attentive and careful typing; but it interrupts Le Penseur's attentive and careful thinking."[53] He confesses that "we now seem to be stumped to nominate any . . . autonomous X-ing or X-ings such that Le Penseur must be X-ing more or less exploratively, tentatively, pertinaciously, pugnaciously, scrupulously or cannily."[54] However, he does suggest possible X-ings for Le Penseur to be doing. If Le Penseur is composing a tune or a speech, solving a problem of arithmetic, or preparing a chess move, then he may well be respectively fingering piano keys or humming tentatively, uttering or muttering part-sentences out loud, jotting down numbers, or moving a chess piece experimentally and without letting it go. On the other hand, these are straightforward cases of thinking what one is doing, to which the adverbial story straightforwardly applies. Tune-playing, speech-making, sum-solving, and chess-piece-moving are all overt actions, performed (albeit in fragments) tentatively, experimentally, mindfully, and self-instructively.

Certainly, Le Penseur might be doing such things and doing them heedfully. It is true that "the sealing of the lips is no part of the definition of thinking. A man may think aloud or half under his breath; he may think silently yet with lip-movements conspicuous enough to be read by a lip-reader. . . ."[55] And it is true that "the child, told to think again, is not disobeying if he mutters audibly, 'Seven times seven is forty-nine, nine and carry four.'"[56] However, it is also true that none of these are things the thinker must do while thinking. They are optional. The thinker might just as well, "as most of us have done since nursery-days, think in silence and with motionless lips."[57] At any rate, there seem to be no action fragments which the rockbound Penseur is heedfully performing.

Ryle offers other candidate X-ings—such as brow-knittings, beard-tuggings, cheek-scratchings, mouth puckerings, other facial expressings, chin-supportings, breath-holdings, sighings, groanings, gazings heavenward, and stayings stock-still. Certainly another Penseur might be doing things such as these. Only, for two reasons, they cannot be the X-ings that are being done heedfully and self-teachingly. First, far from being done heedfully, such behavioral epiphenomena of thinking are typically "done" at best half-consciously. Second, like the fragmentary X-ings mentioned above, they are dispensable.

In his final attempt to reconcile the fact that Le Penseur is thinking but conspicuously not doing any X-ing, Ryle is reduced to postulating intra-cranial X-ings, doings in the head. There is no other way he can identify an infra activity for Le Penseur to be engaged in thinkingly. He brazens it out: "It does not matter whether Le Penseur actually draws his diagrams on paper, or visualizes them as so drawn; and it does not matter whether in his quasi-posing his on appro [on-approval] Socratic questions to himself he speaks these aloud, mutters them under his breath, or only As-If mutters them on his mind's tongue."[58]

Ryle's use of the phrase *on his mind's tongue* suggests that he wants to make light of his appeal to the doing-in-the-head idiom. However, in the absence of any other likely X-ing for Le Penseur to be doing, he is having to rely on it.[59] Ryle well knows that talk of intracranial doings is metaphorical,[60] and he cannot say that "it does not matter whether" one does the X-ing overtly or in the head, as if there are two kinds of X-ing here. "X-ing in the head" is not a kind of X-ing.

Ryle's argument for the adverbial theory and the numerous examples he discusses at least establish that heed and self-teaching are of the essence in thinking what one is doing. And Ryle does establish that thinking what one is doing, heedful X-ing, is derivative of educative activity. Plausibly, heeding is originally a joint enterprise. And Ryle begins to answer the very important question of *how* this earlier educative experience is brought to bear in subsequent solo action. His suggestion that earlier lessons are somehow reprised in the heedful and self-teaching manner in which the solo agent is X-ing is a valuable initial contribution.

However, Ryle's application of the adverbial account to "just thinking" is not convincing. There is heedful X-ing and, some way down the road toward just thinking, there is heedful doing of fragments of X. Further down the road, the X-ing stops getting done in any form. At this point, Ryle resorts to metaphor and his adverbial analysis fails. Just thinking is not a special case of heedful X-ing. It is not a case of X-ing at all. The kind of thinking Le Penseur is doing on the rock consists in the performance—perhaps the heedful performance—of some *other*, unobservable, activity, which Ryle does not identify. Admittedly though, this other unspecified activity is in some obscure way *like* X-ing.

2   Action-Based Theories of Thinking (2)

Ryle's Refraining Theory

Here and there in *The Concept of Mind*, the idea is mooted that imagining is a species of refraining.[1] I have italicized parts of the following passage in order to illustrate the kinds of refraining Ryle has in mind:

> . . . fancying one is humming a known tune involves "making ready" for the notes due to be hummed, were the tune actually being hummed. It is to make ready for those notes in a hypothetical manner. It is not humming very, very quietly, but rather it is *deliberately not doing* those pieces of humming which would be due, if one were not trying to keep the peace. We might say that imagining oneself talking or humming is a *series of abstentions* from producing the noises which would be the due words or notes to produce, if one were talking or humming aloud. That is why such operations are impenetrably secret; not that the words or notes are being produced in a hermetic cell, but that the *operations consist of abstentions* from producing them. That, too, is why learning to fancy one is talking or humming comes later than learning to talk or hum. Silent soliloquy is a flow of *pregnant non-sayings*. *Refraining from saying things*, of course, entails both knowing what one would have said and how. . . .[2]

Visualizing Mount Helvellyn is also to be equated, somehow, with specific "non-seeings of" or "failures to see" it. Thus, "the expectations which are fulfilled in the recognition at sight of Helvellyn are not indeed fulfilled in picturing it, but the picturing of it is something like a rehearsal of getting them fulfilled. So far from picturing involving the having of faint sensations, or wraiths of sensations, it involves missing just what one would be due to get, if one were seeing the mountain."[3]

Negative "Actions"

In *On Thinking*, Ryle revisits this idea and sets out an analysis of refraining as a negative "action."[4] The refraining theory is to be added to his dispositional and adverbial accounts. The hypothesis this time is that the particular brand of logical construction we mistake for an ethereal and intracranial mental phenomenon is not a disposition to certain actions, nor a certain quality of action-performance, but rather a negative "action," a "refraining" from a certain action.

Ryle claims that refrainings—abstainings, forgoings, resistings doing, avoidings, waivings, desistings from, eschewings, etc.—are not "positive and witnessable actions." They are instead "non-actions" that "consist in the agent's intentional *non*-performance of some specifiable actions."[5] He is careful throughout the account in *On Thinking* to put scare quotes around *action* when it comes after *negative*. A negative "action" is no more an action than a decoy "duck" is a duck. It is no more an action than a disposition or ability, or a quality of action, is an action. And, like dispositions to act and adverbial stylings of actions, negative "actions" are logically parasitic on genuine actions. They are meta-operations on genuine actions. The logic of *refrain* is like that of *obey* and *heedful* in this respect.

Ryle admits that refrainings have some action-like features. They are intentional. And they are voluntary in the sense of being subject to the imperative: one can be asked to refrain from something. They are subject to moral evaluation. And they have duration, as many actions do. One can refrain for a time and then pitch in, just as one may pitch in for a time and then desist. Despite these action-like features, negative "actions" are not really actions at all. This is because, Ryle thinks, they are "circumstantially and behaviorally hollow."

Ryle's examples of refrainings include refraining from smoking, waiting for a train, and stopping for a rest during a mountain climb. He explains their circumstantial and behavioral hollowness in terms of what he claims is "a familiar point about negation in general,"[6] namely, "the factual hollowness of *denials* of existence, occurrence, performance, etc., in general. The reason why 'not at home' fails to fix the householder's actual location is the reason why 'waiting' fails to specify what in particular the traveler is actually doing."[7] That is, Ryle explains, there are no characteristic performances associated with negative "actions": ". . . there is nothing in particular by doing which I await the train."[8] A report that P refrained from X-ing implies nothing about what P actually did do. "The negativing title or description of a negative 'action' specifies only that one particular thing the agent is *not* doing, smoking, for instance, or moving away from the train's arrival platform, or continuing climbing; it is non-committal about what else in particular he is doing."[9]

Preconditions for Refraining

Despite Ryle's claims, refraining is neither circumstantially nor behaviorally empty. Certainly, it is only the negative fact that is explicitly specified when P is described as having refrained from doing such and such. But to describe P as having refrained from doing such and such is *appropriate* only if P is in one of a fairly limited range of practical and social situations. If a given refraining description is true, we can infer that a "refraining situation" applies. In this sense, P's refraining from X-ing certainly does bespeak facts about P's circumstances and what P actually does.

Refraining situations have five features: (1) there is some "positive and witnessable" action X from which P is refraining; (2) P knows how to do X; (3) P has an opportunity to do X; (4) something influences P toward doing X, at least to the extent that the thought of doing X occurs to P; and (5) by means of some effortful countervailing action, P successfully avoids X-ing.

Conditions (1)–(3) concern circumstances that must apply, and conditions (4) and (5) concern behavior that must be performed—things P must actually, positively do—before he can truly be said to have refrained from doing X. Ryle grants the first condition, that there be an action being refrained from, in his definition of negative "actions." The logic behind the second and third conditions is that, if P either doesn't know how to X or has no opportunity to X, then he is perforce unable to X and the question of his refraining from X-ing cannot arise. Ryle grants this: "Mentionings of abstainings, postponings and permittings specify things that could have been done but were not actually done."[10]

The interesting conditions are (4) and (5). Condition 4 is really a combination circumstance and behavior condition. P must be influenced toward doing X to the extent he thinks of doing X. To begin with, something must be influencing P toward doing X. For example, given opportunity, one can refrain from taking the last sausage roll, because we assume a natural tendency to take and eat sausage rolls. But one cannot, other things being equal, sensibly be said to "refrain" from hacking off one's own big toe, or "refrain" from misspelling every sixth word one types, or "refrain" from doing anything it would never occur to anyone to do. If there is no influence, there can be no refraining. The influence may be minimal. Custom or

mere habit can provide impetus of a suitable kind here. Or perhaps someone tells P to X. Others' hortations per se provide sufficient impetus to legit-
imize refraining talk. Doing X might even be something P just feels tempted
to do, has a hankering or impulse to do, or considers doing on a whim.
However, *some*—perhaps unspecified—influence is always presupposed.

In addition, the influence must be sufficient to make it occur to P that he
might do X. If it doesn't occur to P to do X, he cannot refrain from doing
it. Ryle implies condition (4): "A person who is . . . holding something back,
must be doing this consciously or wittingly. Indeed his doing it must incorporate in some way (*what* way?) the 'thought' of the very retort which he is
holding back, or the very bit of letter-writing which he is deferring until
later."[11]

Finally, there is condition (5): before P can properly be said to have
refrained from X-ing, P must have taken steps to avoid or prevent his doing
X. By citing refraining from smoking, waiting for a train and pausing during a climb as examples of negative "actions," Ryle effectively concedes this
condition too. Notoriously, refraining from smoking requires earnest self-
admonitions, effortful turnings-away, regretful declinings, and so on. And
hanging around the railway platform is doing something. Ryle says waiting
requires "only the simple circumstance of remaining near where the train
will come in and not going to sleep"[12]—but *act* or *expedient* would be more
accurate than *circumstance* here. Flinging down one's backpack and sitting
down for a while is doing something too. Again, in explaining what the
vegetarian and the confidant must do, Ryle mentions "devouring fruit" and
"tongue-holding," respectively. He also concedes behavioral implications in
connection with not stopping for a chat with Miss Bates: "Roughly, in this
particular context there is only the singular and perfectly specific answer to
the question, 'What *else* did I do than stop for a chat?,' namely, indiffer-
ently, 'I strode on to avoid chatting' *or* 'To avoid chatting I omitted to
halt.'"[13]

Granted that there is something, however minimal, inclining P to X, in
order to refrain from X-ing, P must somehow overcome this tendency. Even
though it is a matter of not doing something, refraining is an achievement—and achievements presuppose prior effortful strivings of some kind.
The nature of the striving may be so obvious as not to merit mention, or it
may be unknown, or it may be of no interest. Striving nevertheless must
have occurred. For refraining from X to be achieved, prior active counter-

vailing of the tendency to X is necessary. To refrain from X-ing, P must undertake some action that precludes, and is intended to preclude, X-ing. Ryle rightly says that refraining ascriptions do not in themselves specify just what countervailing action is involved. But he cannot deny that successful refraining presupposes some countervailing effort. Despite what Ryle argues, refrainings are neither circumstantially nor behaviorally hollow.

The necessary countervailing effort is in fact supplied by a class of actions that Ryle himself has carefully singled out. He distinguishes them from negative "actions" and calls them "nullifying actions." In Ryle's definition, nullifying actions are "positive and witnessable actions": "actions that we perform in order that things may *not* be the case which otherwise would or might be the case."[14]

So we can say, despite Ryle's claims to the contrary, and using his terminology, that refrainings are brought about by action-nullifying actions— where action-nullifying actions are actions performed to ensure that certain other actions are not performed. In short, refrainings are the achievements that action-nullifying actions bring about.

Rather than speak of a refraining achievement and separate task activity that effects that achievement, it would perhaps be more realistic to speak of two ways of specifying one and the same action. We can specify it by mentioning the achievement (I didn't say a word) or by mentioning the nullifying action (I bit my lip).

Is Imagining a Species of Refraining?

If imagining is a species of refraining, it must satisfy the five circumstantial and behavioral conditions of refraining I listed above. The first condition is fulfilled easily enough. There is always an infra action in the picture. Admittedly, we often speak of imagining things (such as Mount Helvellyn) other than actions. However, these cases can plausibly be described—as I describe them in chapter 6—in terms of imagined perceptual activity. In any event, plausibly, in cases of imagining the infra action in question is deliberately left unperformed.

The second condition applies with respect to imagining too. In order for P to imagine X-ing, he must know what it is like to X. Ryle puts it this way: ". . . we cannot say of a person in whose head a tune is running that he does not know how it goes. Having a tune running in one's head is one familiar way in which knowledge of how the tune goes is utilized."[15] Again, visualizing Helvellyn "is one utilization among others of the knowledge of how Helvellyn should look."[16]

The third condition, the need for P to have opportunity to X, if he is to refrain from X-ing, has no clear parallel in imagining. One of the main features of imagining is that you can do it when real X-ing is impossible. However, there might be a way out for Ryle. Elsewhere, Ryle often mentions active pretending or make-believe performances in connection with imagining, and he sometimes seems to be suggesting that imagining is a matter of inhibiting, or refraining from, overt pretendings.

Many cases of imagining don't involve resisting a tendency to do something so much as positively trying to imagine something. In these latter cases, one often engages in auto-stimulation, coaxing one's imagination by "making as if to" do X. This may involve actual movements, actual commencings, not of real X-ing but of make-believe X-ing. To help oneself imagine being a bear one might briefly commence an overt pretending-to-be-a-bear performance, or carry out fragments of such a performance. One always, other things being equal, has the opportunity to engage in overt pretending-behavior of this kind. So at least some imagined X-ing might be a matter of refraining from overt "as if" X-ing, rather than refraining from real X-ing. Thus, when real X-ing—my dining with Greta Garbo—is impossible, I can still nevertheless refrain, if not from dining with her, then from overtly pretending, in some active charade, to dine with her.

The fourth condition is an influence that brings about the thought of doing X. Deciding if this is applicable to imagining is tricky. To think of doing X is already to imagine doing X. Imagining is in this respect not an example of or similar to refraining but a necessary precondition of it. Given this, though, it is still useful to ask whether it is necessary in cases of imagining that P be influenced toward doing X, at least to some minimal extent.

The answer is probably yes. Very seldom if ever do we find ourselves imagining something just out of the blue—and even then we would suppose some influence we are unaware of. Normally, our imaginings are prompted by other imaginings, or by things we perceive in our environment, or by things others say—or else by pictures and other kinds of representation that are purpose-made to prompt imaginings.[17] Always there is some influence, and plausibly the influence is either toward actual X-ing or toward overt make-believe X-ing. The imagining is a substitute activity when we realize that an actual performance is not on.

Finally, there is the fifth condition. Are any countervailing exertions such as are required in refraining required in imagining? Is there anything in imagining corresponding to biting one's lip, averting one's gaze, or walking on by? There must be. If P has an impulse toward X-ing (or make-believe X-ing), yet stays motionless, then he must be doing something to stop himself X-ing. Despite his desire to refrain from any talk of actual doing, in connection with imagining, Ryle admits that "very likely . . . people who imagine themselves producing noises tend to activate slightly those muscles which they would be activating fully, if they were singing or talking aloud, since complete abstention is harder than partial abstention."[18] And, although he adds "but these are questions of fact with which we are not concerned," Ryle is clearly conceding some active nullifying effort on the imaginer's part.

The Usefulness of Ryle's Refraining Theory

By scratching the surface of Ryle's portrayal of refraining as negative "action," mere absence of action, we bring to view a special type of positive action the task of which is to nullify impulses or tendencies to perform specific infra actions. When we compare one of the central varieties of thinking—imagining—to refraining, we see that, like refraining, imagining is twofold. It involves an initial impulse to action and some countervailing action that nullifies that impulse.

We would be wiser about both refraining and imagining if we could say with confidence what kinds of things "impulses to action" are. In the context of the refraining theory, Ryle does not tell us. And we don't need to hear any more about dispositions. In some places in Ryle's other writing, though, it is possible to construe him as saying that an impulse to action may amount to an actual, if minimal, commencing of the action in question. For example, in the passage just quoted he speaks of imaginers' activating "slightly those muscles which they would be activating fully." On this understanding of *impulse*, refraining and imagining would both be twofold actions. Imagining would involve both incipient action and rapid or simultaneous curtailment of that incipient action. Ryle also describes being distracted—and a distraction is just a troublesome imagining—as "the conjunction of an inclination to behave in a certain way with an inhibition upon behaving in that way."[19] Such a twofold action reminds us of the physiological process of sequential or simultaneous initiation and inhibition of a response speculated by Hofstadter, Jeannerod, and Frijda.

Vygotsky: Internalization of Speech-Mediated Social Activity

According to the developmental psychologist Lev Vygotsky, thinking is not a natural process but a cultural phenomenon. As Vygotsky's colleague Alexei Leontyev says, "consciousness is not given initially and it is not generated by nature. Consciousness is generated by society; it is produced."[20]

Vygotsky explains intellectual abilities as "internalized" social abilities. The social abilities are established in the child's repertoire first. They consist of abilities to participate, in both follower and leader roles, in a variety of speech-mediated cooperative activities. The child subsequently learns to "engage in" such social activity, and especially the speech transactions involved, in a special abbreviated and internal (intracranial) way. Vygotsky is most illuminating in connection with the nature of social abilities, how speech acquires its mediating role, and how the child learns the trick of rehearsing social exchanges while alone. Unfortunately, his descriptions of the final stage of internalization and of internal speech don't get past the "doing in the head" metaphor.

Speech-Mediated Social Activity

Infants acquire some elementary practical skills naturally—hand/eye coordination, different kinds of grasp, ability to visually track moving objects, balance, locomotion, etc. This foundation is built upon in demonstration-and-imitation sessions with caregivers (usually the mother). Infants have a natural and powerful tendency to imitate actions performed in front of them. By imitation, and with the support and encouragement of the mother, the infant can learn behaviors he could never have picked up on his own. Vygotsky calls this encouraging cooperative learning context that mothers and others provide for infants the "zone of proximal development."

Among apes, even the best imitators are unable to transcend their current skill level in imitation sessions, at least not in the way infants can: ". . . primates can use imitation to solve only those problems that are of the same degree of difficulty as those they can solve alone. . . . Children can imitate a variety of actions that go well beyond the limits of their own capabilities. Using imitation, children are capable of doing much more in collective activity or under the guidance of adults."[21] Furthermore, "the cleverest animal is incapable of intellectual development through imitation. It can be drilled to perform specific acts, but the new habits do not result in new general abilities. In this sense it can be said that animals are unteachable. In the child's development, on the contrary, imitation and instruction . . . lead the child to new developmental levels. . . . What the child can do in cooperation today he can do alone tomorrow."[22]

A variant of the demonstration-and-imitation transaction then develops in which the mother gives only a token demonstration of the action to be imitated. She merely gestures—that is, performs just the very beginning of the action, or some other distinctive fragment of it. These token performances come to have the same imitation-inducing effect as a full performance would have. Granted, the term *imitation* is now not strictly appropriate, since the demonstrator is merely making a gesture, but the responder is performing the whole action.

Apes also seem to be capable of this streamlined form of demonstration and imitation:

Usually a chimpanzee will *begin* a movement or an action he wants another animal to perform or to share—e.g., will push him and execute the initial movements of walking when "inviting" the other to follow him, or grab at the air when he wants the other to give him a banana. All these are gestures *directly* related to the action itself. Kohler mentions that the experimenter comes to use essentially similar elementary ways of communication to convey to the apes what is expected of them.[23]

As Alexander Luria (another colleague of Vygotsky) reports, speech first appears as a means of directing the child's attention during demonstratings or gesturings of actions. Specific speech is associated with and distinctive of a specific activity. Its function is to focus the child's attention—usually on some object involved in the activity. Eventually, speech used by the mother in this way, as an ostentator of a demonstration or gesture, gives way to speech used by itself as a means of getting the child to do things:

The mother communicates with the child and gives him/her instructions with the help of speech. For example, she draws his/her attention to objects in the environment (e.g., *Take the ball, Lift your arm, Where is the doll?* etc.), and the child carries out these spoken instructions. What is the mother doing when she gives the child these verbal instructions? As we have already said, she is drawing his/her attention to something, she is singling out one thing from among many. With her speech she organizes the child's motor acts. Thus the child's motor act often begins with the mother's speech and is completed with his/her own movement. Vygotsky pointed out that initially the voluntary act is shared by two people. It begins with the verbal command of the mother and ends with the child's act.[24]

With speech installed as a means of cueing specific actions on the child's part, the development of speech-mediated social activity is completed. The child's behavior is now "social" in the sense that it involves participation in cooperative interactions with others, and in the sense that it was learned in demonstration-and-imitation sessions with other people. The child's behavior is also "speech-mediated" in the sense that it can be initiated, and controlled while in progress, by others' speech.

Internalization

By dint of the mediating or regulating effect that others' speech has on a child's activities, the culture gradually "appropriates" the child. The culture provides the speech forms and speech-mediated cooperations, or language-games, to which the child's behavior increasingly cleaves. However, the child also appropriates the culture—by "internalizing" it. Vygotsky explains:

> . . . the process of internalization consists of a series of transformations: An operation that initially represents an external activity is reconstructed and begins to occur internally. Of particular importance to the development of higher mental processes is the transformation of sign-using activity. . . . An interpersonal process is transformed into an intrapersonal one. Every function in the child's cultural development appears twice: first, on the social level, and later, on the individual level; first, between people (interpsychological), and then inside the child (intrapsychological). . . . The internalization of socially rooted and historically developed activities is the distinctive feature of human psychology.[25]

Although the final "into the mental" stage is the crucial one, there are two preliminary stages in the internalization process. First, the child learns to take the initiative in cooperative undertakings. That is, after a lot of practice in the role of follower—having his behavior mediated by others' speech—the child learns to use speech and gesture to prompt others into action too.

When the child is experienced in both passive and active speech-mediating roles, he can proceed to using speech to influence his own behavior. This is the second stage of internalization. The "egocentric speech" (thinking out loud) characteristic of this stage is at first simply a general self-prompting and self-motivating ploy, providing added impetus to action when the child is not being engaged with or is alone. It is a bit like whistling in the dark. Later, the speech is more specific and strategically timed, cueing particular phases of activity in advance. The child's now considerable skills at controlling others' actions with speech are borrowed to control his own actions.

Egocentric speech can plausibly be regarded as an abbreviation of ordinary interpersonal speech. Both interpersonal and egocentric speech involve actual saying and hearing of words. From the child's point of view, what is missing from his solitary, make-do performance is perceivings corresponding to the presence and participation of an interlocutor. However, despite the missing perceptions, the remaining cues, which the child is producing himself, have a residual motivating and guiding ("mediating") effect on his actions.

I have not mentioned Vygotsky's account of the transition from controlling others' behavior with gestures (qua substitutes for whole performances) to controlling others' behavior with speech. This is the transition accomplished in stages (3) and (4) in the following list. However, I shall return to the topic of the transition from gesture to speech more than once later in the book.

Vygotsky's account of the speech-mediating of actions and of the first two stages of internalization can be summarized as follows:

(1) The demonstrating of action X by caregiver M naturally induces her audience P to do X too, because of P's natural tendency to imitate.

(2) After suitable training, an abbreviated demonstration (mere gesturing) of X by M comes to have a similar X-ing-inducing effect on P.

(3) Demonstratings and gesturings of X by both M and P are typically punctuated with speech unique to X-ing.

(4) Later, speech by itself, without demonstration or gesture, acquires action-inducing and action-regulating effects similar to those of a full demonstration or mime.

(5) P's solitary egocentric speech represents a further streamlining of the original demonstration-and-imitation transaction that nevertheless retains residual action-mediating effects on P.

The important thing for Vygotsky is that egocentric speech is necessarily preceded by, and has its form and function determined by, social speech. Egocentric speech gives the same kind of assistance in practical action as is provided by social speech:

The greatest change in children's capacity to use language as a problem-solving tool takes place . . . when socialized speech (which has previously been used to address an adult) is turned inward. Instead of appealing to the adult, children appeal to themselves; language thus takes on an intrapersonal function in addition to its interpersonal use. When children develop a method of behavior for guiding themselves that had previously been used in relation to another person, when they organize their own activities according to a social form of behavior, they succeed in applying a social attitude to themselves. The history of the process of the internalization of social speech is also the history of the socialization of children's practical intellect.[26]

As the child gets more used to doing things on his own, egocentric speech gradually becomes more sketchy and perfunctory. The third and final stage of internalization is reached when egocentric speech becomes "silent" and "internal." Instead of talking out loud to himself before and during action, the child can do the talking "silently" and/or "internally."

Like every other writer I have read on this topic, Vygotsky talks about "inner speech" as if it were a *kind* of speech, different from audible speech only in that it is silent and performed inside the person's head. As I have mentioned, silent speech is a logical impossibility and intracranial speech must be, at best, exceedingly difficult. The expression *inner speech* is a metaphor for some real learned skill of the person, but that learned skill is not a special kind or way of speaking. The child who no longer needs to think out loud can now just imagine saying things to himself. That is, he can just "think" those things and *not* say them.

Vygotsky is free in his use of terms like *intra-psychological, intra-mental* and *psychological plane*. These terms have a clear connotation of "mind" and "mental" in the traditional Cartesian sense. The effect is to give us the picture of speech gradually fragmenting and abbreviating, right down to the point where no audible (or otherwise perceptible) speaking is being done at all. At that point the speech slips out of view (as it were) and into the mental: ". . . when egocentric speech disappears from view it does not simply atrophy but 'goes underground,' i.e., turns into inner speech."[27] At the vanishing point, the mental reaches out and takes the speech—like the Lady of the Lake's hand grabbing Excalibur. One infers that the speech is still going on, only now internally and mentally.

A passage from Leontyev is often quoted as evidence that Vygotsky's notion of the intrapsychological does not presuppose any Cartesian-type mental domain—and as evidence that, for Vygotsky, the mental is a purely actional and developmental concept. What Leontyev says is that "the process of interiorization is not external action transferred onto a pre-existing internal 'plane of consciousness'; it is the process in which this internal plane is formed."[28] This is usually taken as meaning that the internal psychological plane is nothing over and above the internalization process.

Alternatively, the psychological is in some sense the product of that process. However, all we are told in the passage is that a psychological world, or "plane"—of a very Cartesian-looking kind—does not precede but rather follows the (still undefined) internalization process. The idea of an internal plane is still presupposed by the internalization concept.

In fact, Vygotsky does usually write as if internalization is the stashing away of "external," social abilities into an already-existing "internal" and "private" repertoire. In any event, even if the internal repertoire is somehow constituted by the material delivered to it, or brought into being by the delivery process, we still need to be told what kind of thing the inner repertoire or plane is. We are not told this, and Vygotsky's "intrapsychological plane" still looks very like Descartes' "mind."

Hampshire's "Inhibited Display" Theory of Emotion

The philosopher Stuart Hampshire writes about the relation between emotional behavior and the feeling of emotion.[29] The popular conception of emotions, and mental phenomena generally, has them existing prior to, and underpinning, their overt behavioral expression: the internal mental phenomenon determines the character of the outer behavior, and we describe emotional displays by nominating which ulterior emotion is involved. Hampshire believes that the logical dependencies actually go the other way. He claims that the real logical priorities are represented in the developmental sequence in which we acquire abilities to feel and express emotions. He says that abilities to perform the expressive behaviors come first, and that the feeling of emotions results from our learning to "inhibit," "abbreviate," "control," or "interiorize" these expressive behaviors.

Hampshire is not saying, as Ryle might, that the inhibited version of the emotional behavior (the version Hampshire says is equivalent to feeling the emotion) is a purely grammatical entity—a "non-behavior" perhaps, or a mere disposition to behave. For Hampshire, emotions are actualities and not abstractions:

At a particular moment I may want to laugh, or I may be inclined to weep, I may have an impulse to run away, or need to restrain myself from striking the man in front of me. These are primary dispositions to act that I feel, and that occur as episodes in my biography, no less than my sensations and actions. Even though they remain unexpressed, as episodes in my inner life, not perceptible by observers, they are accounted episodes, occurrences, not possible happenings only.[30]

Emotions are "behavior at its vanishing point"[31] or "inner perturbations"[32] or "residues"[33] resulting from the inhibition of overt behavior. Or they are "incipient behaviors."[34]

There is an essential ostentatious and theatrical element in the expression of emotion. It is always display. Hampshire thinks there are few naturally given emotional behaviors. For the most part, the child must learn what to display, and learn the techniques of display, by imitation. Although they are behaviors, or mini-dramas, the various customary patterns of emotional display have a constancy and objectivity comparable to that of familiar objects. The child will "engage in imitative play, deliberately and at will, and knowing what he is doing. He assumes the expression and posture of an angry father, or of a frightened child, distinguishing this fiction from fact. The success of the imitation, as imitation, carries its own satisfaction with it, as truth-telling carries its own satisfaction with it. They are both cases of making or doing something which matches, and which is in its own medium an equivalent of, an independent reality. The making, or discovery for oneself, of such an equivalence is at once the source and the evidence of an adequate grasp of the reality. The making of an equivalence may be taken as a kind of mastery of the independent reality, a reduction of it to our own terms. . . ."[35] On this account, "having the concept" of a given emotion is being able to accurately imitate its expression. Despite the similarity with objective knowledge, knowledge of emotions is a performer's or participant's knowledge, and the name of an emotion is not so much a label on a thing in the world as a cue for a familiar routine.

If Hampshire's theatrical concept of emotional display is correct, customary patterns of emotional expression should tend to become abbreviated. The aim of theatrical display is to get the audience to imitate or empathize, and the law of least effort dictates that the minimum performance that reliably achieves this will become the norm. Full-scale emotional displays are readily replaceable for communicative purposes by much-reduced versions, mere gestures: "Posture, gesture, facial expression are immediately legible by others, as signs of an inclination to behave in a specific way, when they are the last vanishing vestige of a familiar and classifiable pattern of behavior. So the man who looks daggers at his neighbor has cut off the action of aggression, and the vestige of it remains in his glance. . . . The truncated action is legible as a sign. . . ."[36] Conventional and abbreviated expressions of feeling have an artificial, stylized aspect. About fist-brandishing as a token of aggression, Hampshire says: "If a movement is seen effectively to serve some evident and familiar human need or purpose, its significance as gesture is lost. The behavior generally needs to be uneconomic and useless, as action, in order to be taken as a sign."[37]

To help explain the role of speech in the feeling and expression of emotion, Hampshire requisitions Wittgenstein's "replacement" theory of pain avowal.[38] The full behavioral expression of an emotion (or pain, in the replacement theory) will naturally include vocalizing of one kind or another. With streamlining, stylizing, and standardizing of displays, some standard vocal element will evolve that is distinctive of this display. As the original full display gets streamlined, this vocal-*cum*-verbal element tends to remain and to take on much of the expressive and evocative burden—albeit with assistance from residual facial expression, mien, etc. Hampshire agrees with Wittgenstein that the words *I am in pain*, etc., can be said to "replace" natural expressions of pain.[39] In the same way, he says, an avowal of emotion, along with vestiges of expression, comes to do duty for a full emotional display. Usually in adult life, if observers want to know what another person is feeling, they "must rely primarily on the subject's avowal."[40]

In Hampshire's account, as with Vygotsky's, there is emphasis on the role of imitation in teaching the child how to participate in social transactions in the first place. Vygotsky's "cooperative practical activity" is equivalent to Hampshire's "theatrical displays of emotion" in this respect. Speech is given an initial attention-directing, imitation-abetting role at the initial social-activity-learning stage. When the activity is subsequently abbreviated down to gesture for communicative purposes, speech is the most persistent residue of the original full-blown version. Again as for Vygotsky, when familiarity, ease, and interpersonal expediency have boiled the activity down, so there is little more than speech left, we approach the departure point for "the mental."

In this final developmental stage, the last vestiges of overt emotional behavior and the speech both disappear. The person just feels the emotion. Where Vygotsky uses the terms *abbreviation* and *internalization*, Hampshire uses *inhibition* and *interiorization*. As I will tirelessly repeat, notions of "abbreviation" and "inhibition" are useful only up to the point where the behavior (speech, for example) disappears entirely. Then the behavior is no longer occurring. *Interiorization* is a metaphor. Really, Hampshire doesn't tell us what the mental is, or how we get there, either.

In recent writing, Hampshire continues to allude to "the social origins of mental acts (propositional attitudes), which in any person's experience are first encountered as observable interpersonal business."[41] This time the prototype public activity up for interiorization is not emotional display but the kind of practical adversarial discussion that characterizes moral, legal, political, and managerial decision making. As when he was talking about emotions and emotional displays, Hampshire thinks the conventional assumptions as to priorities are wrong:

Descartes presented the paradigm of thought as a process in the inner consciousness of the solitary thinker, sitting beside his stove. . . . I suggest that the Cartesian paradigm should be reversed, and that the paradigmatic setting and circumstance of intellectual thought is not the solitary meditation by the stove but the public arguments for and against some claim publicly made: the supposition is that we learn to transfer, by a kind of mimicry, the adversarial pattern of public and interpersonal life onto a silent stage called the mind. The dialogues are internalized, but they still do not lose the marks of their origin in interpersonal adversarial argument.[42]

As to how these public, interpersonal proceedings get to be internally rehearsed, Hampshire is no less poetic or more specific in 2000 than he was in 1960. He says, "Mental processes in the minds of individuals are to be seen as the shadows of publicly identifiable procedures. . . ."[43] He says, ". . . we learn to transfer . . . the adversarial pattern of public and interpersonal life onto a silent stage called the mind. The dialogues are internalized. . . ."[44] And again, ". . . the mind is the unseen and imagined forum into which we learn to project the visible and audible social processes that we first encounter in childhood: practices of asserting, contradicting, deciding, predicting, recalling, approving and disapproving, admiring, blaming, rejecting and accepting, and many more."[45]

Hampshire turns in the direction of a literal description when he talks about imitation in connection with the internalizing process. He speaks above of the child's learning to transfer the public transactions onto the private stage "by a kind of mimicry" and he also speaks of "a solitary imitation of these exchanges."[46] He suggests that imitation has some fundamental role in thinking. In a personal communication to the author he contemplates "inhibited (or concealed) shared action, as a person who follows 'in his mind' a tune through many harmonic distractions participates in singing the tune 'under wraps' as it were. This is the point at which imitation becomes central. I think *mimesis* in Plato and Aristotle embodies . . .

[the] concept of shared action (participated in) rather than copying."[47] However, mimesis is still on the overt and interpersonal side of the ledger. We need a concept that can explain the unobservability and "privacy" of just thinking and just feeling.

Other "Internalized Social Activity" Theories

Theories of thinking as internalized social activity are developmental theories. They assume that, although not itself a learned action, thinking is a process—some sort of quasi-natural intracranial process—that becomes possible only after certain actions and activities have been mastered by the child. Prominent among these actions and activities are such interpersonal transactions as speech-expedited practical activity, demonstrating and imitating, educative activity of other kinds, showing, exhorting, dramatic portraying, emoting, miming, conversing and discussing, reporting and describing, and graphic representing. Such are the activities said to be internalized by the developing child. Vygotsky and Hampshire are clearly in the internalized-social-activity camp. Ryle has a foot in it too. His adverbial account sources heedful doing in previous educative activity, and he says things like the following:

> Much of our ordinary thinking is conducted in ordinary monologue or in silent soliloquy. . . . This trick of talking to oneself in silence is acquired neither quickly nor without effort; and it is a necessary condition of our acquiring it that we should have previously learned to talk intelligently aloud and have heard and understood other people doing so. Keeping out thoughts to ourselves is a sophisticated accomplishment.[48]

Grace de Laguna is a pioneer internalized-social-activity theorist. In *Speech: Its Function and Development*,[49] she says that "the form of conversation from which thought springs is the discussion, which has for its end agreement among the participants regarding some specific conditions of common action. . . . Thinking is the internalization of this form of conversation and its independent practicing by the individual."[50]

A better-known representative of the tradition is the social psychologist George Herbert Mead. In *Mind, Self and Society*,[51] Mead too claims that thinking originates in social, communicative transactions: "The internalization in our experience of the external conversation of gestures which we carry on with other individuals in the social process is the essence of thinking. . . ."[52] Mead says that he "accounts for the existence of minds in terms of communication and social experience; and by regarding minds as phenomena which have arisen and developed out of the process of communication and of social experience generally—phenomena which therefore presuppose that process, rather than being presupposed by it. . . ."[53]

After Vygotsky's death in 1934, the Vygotskyan approach was continued for a time in Russia—particularly by Leontyev. "Consciousness," Leontyev wrote, "is *co-knowing*, but only in the sense that individual consciousness may exist only in the presence of social consciousness and of language that is its real substrate."[54] And Leontyev has been quoted as asserting that "the higher specifically human psychological processes can only emerge in the interaction between men, that is, they can only be interpsychological, and only later are they performed by the individual independently, some of them losing their initial external form, becoming intrapsychological processes."[55]

Many of the internalized-social-activity writings are somewhat rambling and woolly. Perhaps this is due to their reliance on the internalization metaphor. The final significant contribution I will mention is "Imagining as muted role-taking: A historical-linguistic analysis,"[56] an admirably concise paper by the psychologist Theodore Sarbin.

For Sarbin, imagining is an active, learned performance, itself an action—not merely a "logical take" on action (as it is for Ryle) or an action that has been "internalized" (as it is for Vygotsky and Hampshire). Like Vygotsky and Hampshire, Sarbin puts imitation in a foundational role. Imagining is "a skill, dependent upon concurrently acquired skill in role-taking and in imitating"[57] and "an active form of conduct, a performance, a doing, that has its origin in the practice of imitating with models present and with models absent."[58]

Sarbin's descriptions of the act of imagining involve various combinations of the adjectives *attentuated, muted,* and *as if,* and the nouns *behavior, role-taking,* and *imitation.* His explanation of imagining as "as if" behavior is reminiscent of Ryle's discussion of pretending[59] and of Ryle's refraining theory. Sarbin's notion of attentuated and/or muted speech is similar to Vygotsky's and Hampshire's notions of silent and/or abbreviated speech and is subject to the same difficulties. This vitiates Sarbin's avowedly actional view of imagining. If imagining is as an action impossible to perform, as muted speech is, then it may as well be an impersonal process. At least, refreshingly, Sarbin does not resort to the word *internalization.*

In Sarbin's account, the development of the imagining skill has three stages. The first is ordinary face-to-face or side-by-side imitation. Second, the child learns to imitate in the absence of the model. Sarbin calls this delayed or deferred imitation "role-taking." He stresses the importance of make-believe games or "suppositional hypothetical behavior" in mastering this stage. For example, "a child may set up a tea table with limited stage props; she may pour fictional tea into ephemeral cups and talk to an unoccupied chair as if it were holding a guest."[60] Arguably, to attribute pretending behavior of this complexity to deferred imitation leaves too much unexplained. Sarbin's third developmental stage "is concurrent with another achievement of early childhood: the muting of speech. To talk to oneself rather than aloud at first requires only the skill in controlling the volume of air that passes over the vocal cords. With practice, the child learns to inhibit most of the obvious muscular characteristics of speech. At the same time that he acquires the skill in muting his speech, the child learns to attenuate his role-taking actions, to reduce the amplitude of the overt responses that compromise his 'let's-pretend' roles. For this third stage—muted, attenuated, role-taking—the word *imagining* is appropriate."[61]

As will be clear by now, the main difficulty with internalized-social-activity theories, as with abbreviation theories based on the physiology of individuals, is that the concepts of abbreviation and internalization remain undefined. However, the social-activity theorists have further problems, which the physiology-based abbreviationists do not have. How can an individual on his own reprise or rehearse a transaction that is essentially social and necessarily involves other people?

The problems social-internalization theorists face are evident in the following passage, in which Janette Lawrence and Jaan Valsiner attempt to clarify just what is internalized:

With internalization, what was originally in the interpersonal (or inter-mental) domain becomes intra-personal (intra-mental) in the course of development. However, this general concept of internalization is not sufficient for elaborated theoretical use, nor is it helpful in deriving empirical research methodologies. To go beyond generalities it is necessary to specify what "materials" are imported from society into the intra-personal world of any individual, and *in what ways* this process operates. The first question can be answered here in generic terms. In human internalization, the materials involved are of a semiotic nature.[62]

The vagueness about what is internalized results in other imponderables. For example, what exactly is the process that Mead glosses as "taking the role of the other"?

Internalized-social-activity theory faces another kind of problem too. One success of the abbreviationists is their plausible account of the function of abbreviated responses as readying the individual for action. However, the internalized-social-activity theorists cannot chalk this one up to their team. Even if an individual is able to in some sense internally rehearse social interactions, it is impossible to believe that such solo exertions could thereby ready a social interaction. I mean, how could it ready the contributions of the other participants?

3 Concerted Activity

A Sunday school teacher once led all his children out of the stuffy church, where they were distracted and uneasy, and off to the woods. There he blindfolded every one and had them just sit on the ground and feel, without being able to look at, the pebbles, the plants, the earth. Not a word was said . . . and when the blindfolds eventually came off, the children were startled to discover that every hand was in the tight clasp of another's.

—Richard Taylor, *With Heart and Mind*[1]

. . . mimesis forms the core of an ancient root-culture that is distinctively human. No matter how evolved our oral-linguistic culture, and no matter how sophisticated the rich varieties of symbolic material surrounding us, mimetic scenarios still form the expressive heart of human social interchange.

—Merlin Donald, *Origins of the Modern Mind*[2]

My account of thinking in the next five chapters is primarily a developmental one. I attempt to describe the activity of thinking by describing how infants and children learn how to do it. Undertaking a developmental explanation of a skill is similar to any other kind of productive investigation. It involves an ongoing interaction of theorizing and research. One must have some theoretical basis to start from—so that one may begin to make sense of the empirical data—but, from then on, the data must be allowed to influence the theory. In the case of a developmental approach to thinking, one requires a preliminary notion of what kind of activity thinking is, what are its component actions, how they might combine, what use is the activity, and so on. The initial data as to what children learn and when can then be interpreted accordingly. However, it is also necessary that the empirical findings be used to improve the theory. To a large extent we have to find out what thinking is by seeing what and how children learn when they learn to think. My contribution is at the earliest stage. I am offering the bones of a theory about what general kind of activity thinking is. I cite and quote the research I do solely to establish some provisional credibility for the theory I am suggesting. Should the theory be judged promising, that will only get us to square one as far as thinking is concerned. The serious investigation would still be to come. However, there might be some who would agree that, in the case of thinking, even getting to square one would be very worthwhile.

In my view, thinking can be explained as a synthesis of just two kinds of action, both of them reasonably familiar. The first is a form of social inter-action, the *concerting* of actions. Concerting is two or more people doing the same thing—acting "in unison," as it were—with each aware of the partici-pation of the other(s). Concerting has important practical, educative, recre-ational, and ritual roles in our adult lives. For the infant learning to think, concerting is of primary importance.

The other main contributing activity in thinking is what I call the token performance or *tokening* of actions. To produce a token performance of an action, one commences performing it but then aborts one's performance. One "commences and aborts" the action. And one ends up giving a mere "token" performance of it. Tokening can be overt—that is, deliberately made observable to others. Or tokening may be done covertly, in which case the token performance may be so subtle and rapid as to be difficult or impossible for anyone else to observe. My theory is that thinking is a spe-cial combination of concerting and tokening. I say that thinking is "the covert tokening of the overt tokening of concerted activity." This is not as complicated as it might sound. At any rate, first things first. I talk about concerting in this chapter and tokening in the next.

We are too late, probably by more than a million years, to undertake an empirical study of the advent of hominid thinking. Our best currently avail-able source of evidence for a developmental account of thinking is modern infants learning to speak and think. Their situation is different from that of the first hominid thinkers in that, whereas the hominids had to gain the rel-evant abilities and techniques by themselves, modern infants are shown them by people who can already speak and think. The infants' task is, as Andrew Lock puts it,[3] the "guided reinvention" of speech and thought. In any event, recent research in developmental psychology has produced a wealth of reliable information directly germane to my theory that thinking derives from concerting and tokening. In this chapter and the next, I frequently draw on the findings and the words of leading developmental psychologists.

The proto-cognitive behavior of chimpanzees is also relevant, and I quote evidence from researchers in this field too. Research has shown that some important early developmental stages are achieved in the same way, and just about as quickly, by chimpanzees as they are by human infants.[4]

In what follows, experts contribute the developmental facts. I interpret and arrange these facts in a way that opens up one plausible view of what general kind of activity thinking is.

Defining Concerting

We tend to think of imitation as a solo action. However, in many contexts—and normally in mother-infant interactions—achieving successful imitation is more of a cooperative undertaking. The person being imitated (the model) becomes "demonstrator" and, by smiling and encouraging, facilitates the imitator's efforts. The demonstrator may also highlight parts of the action being demonstrated—by giving them a distinctive vocal accompaniment, say, or by performing them in an ostentatious way, such as by slowing their performance down.

Even in contexts where no such assistance is necessary, where one party just effortlessly falls in with what the other is doing, the model will usually be aware of being (successfully) imitated and will display this back to the imitator. The "acknowledgment of success" display might consist of a smile and/or a meeting of gazes, and performance of the action might become more enthusiastic. Furthermore, the imitator will be aware when his imitation is successful and may produce a similar success display. So the model's "you are successfully imitating me" display will typically be met by the imitator's "I am successfully imitating you" display, making the success display mutual.

Where imitation has this cooperative element and/or where it is successful and success is mutually acknowledged by some display, we can speak of *concerted* performance. However, "imitation consummated by a mutual success display" is not the only kind of case. It sometimes also happens that concerting occurs without there being a clear model and a clear imitator. Imitator and model roles can alternate or merge, with the result that a free-wheeling inter-conformity of action is sustained. Here, rather than arising out of imitation, concerting occurs spontaneously as "joint" activity, with the parties side by side in it, acting as one.[5] For now, a very simple definition will do: concerted activity is two or more people doing the same thing and being mutually aware of doing so.

We engage in concerted activity often in everyday adult life. It has four main applications.

Practical concerting exploits the "all hands to the pump" or "many hands make light work" principle, as when people join forces to lift a heavy suitcase, quell an enemy, or pick fruit. Some theorists have argued that the defining feature of personal action in social contexts is its being rule-governed.[6] If this is so, and rule-following is the essential feature of social interaction, then the practical importance of concerting is enormous. Following a rule is a kind of concerting. People "follow a rule" by deliberately concerting the portion of their behavior that the rule covers.

Educative concerting involves a teacher demonstrating an action and a pupil copying, hopefully more and more efficiently, until a dance step, a bowling motion, or a way of solving an equation has been got right.

Recreational concerting occurs in dancing, in singing, in attending sporting or cultural events, and in lovemaking.

Ritual concerting is exemplified by mutual smiling, by concerted facial expressions of other kinds, by greetings (formal kisses, hugs, handshakes), and by eating or drinking together.

Admittedly, the division into just four roles for concerting is somewhat arbitrary, and it is hard to classify some cases. Arguably, the recreational function is the original, dominant one. At any rate, concerting per se seems to have, for most of us and especially for children, a distinctive, powerful, and near-inexhaustible charm.

Infants' Innate Abilities

. . . the instinct of imitation is implanted in man from childhood, one difference between him and the other animals being that he is the most imitative of living creatures and through imitation learns his earliest lessons.
—Aristotle, *Poetics* IV

The infant's ability to engage in concerted activity (typically with the mother) presupposes imitative abilities. In fact, as Colwyn Trevarthen reports, "babies less than a month old are capable of imitating facial expressions. Indeed, with some babies, it is easy for a mother to see for herself that her new-born, just minutes old, may watch her mouth intently if she pro-trudes her tongue or opens her mouth wide, then move his mouth and appropriately poke out his tongue or open wide his mouth. The model is accurately copied. Expressions of happiness, sadness or surprise are also imitated. With calling vocalizations, a similarly prompt imitation can be obtained, when the baby is a few weeks older. Imitation of movements of the hands opening or coming together has also been seen."[7]

To be able to imitate, the infant must first possess certain subservient abilities. At least four come to mind.

First, perceptual abilities are required: ability to fixate objects such as his own hands, and the faces and hands of others, ability to track his own and others' movements, ability to hearken at vocal sounds, etc.

Second, some basic motor skill is required, including ability to make hand, limb, and head movements and to form facial expressions (especially of emotion) and to make simple vocal sounds. That very young infants normally possess such perceptual and motor skills is well documented.[8]

Imitation also requires an ability to match up perceptual and motor performances. Perceptions of another's behavior bring about performance of that same behavior. As I mentioned in chapter 1, Rizzolatti and others have discovered a possible physiological basis for such an ability—groups of "mirror" neurons in the brain. These neurons fire similarly when the subject is performing a certain manual action and when he is merely observing someone else perform it: "Taken together, human and monkey data indicate that, in primates, there is a fundamental mechanism for action recognition. We argue that individuals recognize actions made by others because the neural pattern elicited in their premotor areas during action observation is similar to that internally generated to produce that action. . . ."[9]

A fourth set of abilities is required if imitation is to develop into concerting. As an imitator, the infant must be able to recognize when his imitation is successful and be able to display this awareness. The leading contemporary researcher of neonate and infant imitation, Andrew Meltzoff, finds that "imitation is an end in itself. Infants struggle to match the adult, self-correct if they do not get it right, and smile upon producing a matching behavior. Human infants derive joy in matching per se."[10] Furthermore, when in the model role, the infant must be able to recognize when his own behavior is being successfully imitated by another, and be able to display this awareness. Meltzoff confirms the recognition ability: ". . . infants not only imitate others, but can recognize when the form of their own behavior is being matched."[11] And Jerome Bruner reports that infants are in fact very responsive to being imitated: ". . . smiling and vocalization can be greatly increased in the infant by like responses in an adult."[12] Thus, very young infants can both judge when imitation is successful and register success by displaying pleasure.

Taken together, these four areas of skill, which are all necessary for concerting, seem to constitute a significant repertoire of perceptual, motor, and interpersonal mastery. And we are granting the infant these skills before he first experiences concerting. This seems to constitute a problem for my approach. My concept of thinking, broad as it is, would presumably include the abilities we are now attributing to young infants. That is, it would include perceiving others' actions, it would include recognizing when one behavior is the same as another, and it would include feeling and displaying pleasure. I have claimed that concerting follows and develops out of imitating, and that thinking in turn follows and develops out of concerting (and tokening). To make matters worse, I will argue below that an individual's ability to perform "actions" also must follow, and cannot precede, his ability to engage in concerted activity. This means that the infant's having, from birth or near enough, what look very like abilities to perform actions— actions, moreover, of the "thinking" kind—is problematic. If the infant can think and act from the start, my attempt to derive thought and solo action from concerting must be circular and futile. My way out is to claim that, despite appearances, infants' early imitatings (and their apparently actional ingredients) are not actions; they are something else. One could say the relevant perceptual and motor skills are biological (perhaps "macrophysiological") phenomena. And here one would be viewing the infant as an organism rather than as a person capable of doing things. For several reasons, I am unenthusiastic about this recourse. However, the alternative seems even less palatable. I do not want my accounts of thinking, individual action, and personhood—all of which I claim are developmental descendants of concerting—to go by the board.

The situation may not be grave. After all, we have no difficulty in putting the baby's reflex sucking, its burping and puking, and perhaps its mewling and bellowing in the "physiological process" bag along with breathing, digesting, and excreting. Why shouldn't gaze-following and imitative smiling, waving, and cooing go in there too? Rizzolatti has suggested a possible mechanism for some of these. I am inclined to bite the bullet and accept that, for theoretical purposes, infants are best viewed as organisms incapable of performing actions. Our everyday concept of action requires that actions be learned, that they be biddable (or voluntary in some other sense), and that they be morally evaluable—and none of this applies to what the infant "does." Maybe we should confine all the infant's "behavior" within scare quotes and require that the infant refrain from being a person, refrain from performing actions, and refrain from anything that might count as thinking, until concerting has been mastered.

None of this bears on how we should regard infants in practice: it is psychologically impossible for us to withhold empathy. We are constitutionally incapable of viewing an infant as an organism. Infant (and even much animal) "behavior" irresistibly elicits empathy from us, and talk of "him" or "her" "doing things." Thus, although it may be impossible to philosophically justify regarding infants as people and regarding what they "do" as "actions," this is how we do and will continue to regard them. This is just as well. It is largely due to our constantly treating the infant as a personal agent—talking to him, showing things, imitating, empathizing, smiling, and being responsive generally—that he becomes one.[13]

First Concertings

I will not address the question of how, if at all, the concerting we do is related to concerting-like behavior seen in animals. Cetaceans and great apes appear to be able to concert their behavior in ad hoc practical and recreational ways much as we do. Several carnivorous mammals rely on concerted attack of prey. The herding behavior of grazing animals is arguably a kind of concerting too, possibly akin to the group nomadism of our ancestors. A flock of sheep may, for no apparent reason apart from recreation, suddenly begin racing around their field as one, leaping high in the air as they run. The sometimes amazing gyrations of starling flocks in the evening, the seemingly concerted darting of herring shoals, and the mid-air "endless fountain" displays of small flying insects in summer gardens all suggest a primeval biological origin for concerting. The biologist Rupert Sheldrake[14] has done pioneering research and theorizing in this area, and his concept of "morphic resonance" may constitute the beginnings, albeit the very beginnings, of an explanation.

Whereas an infant is imitating and being imitated within days (even within hours) of birth, it is likely that he first participates in truly concerted activity at around six to eight weeks of age. Presumably it takes the infant this long to master imitating not only the action being demonstrated but also the considerably subtler success display. At any rate, it is around this time that the infant's excitement in imitating seems to suddenly increase.[15] Commonly, a mother who has up until this time been "acting as if" her infant is a person will feel for the first time that the infant really is a person—"not just a puppet to be animated by a miming mother," as Trevarthen puts it.[16] Thus, true concerting and the mother's first sense that the infant is a person seem to arrive roughly together, at around two months. As Meltzoff and Gopnik report, "Imitative games between parent and child have been recorded in widely differing cultures. Do they serve any psychological function over and above the shared enjoyment that is experienced? As one parent expressed it to us: 'After playing these games I feel so happy—like I've been able to reach my baby and communicate with her.'"[17]

The infant first experiences concerting, usually with the mother, in such simple forms as meeting the other's gaze, mutual smiling, sharing other facial expressions, vocalizing the same, laughing, waving, kissing, cuddling, touching faces, holding and playing with hands, shared contemplation and manipulation of objects, and various of these in combination. Normal infants quickly become addicted to concerting, especially in games and other recreations.

Concerted action is just as likely to be initiated by the mother imitating the infant as by the infant imitating the mother. As Meltzoff notes, "In humans, imitation is a bidirectional activity. Human adults not only adopt an explicit 'do what I do' pedagogical style (which requires infant imitation to be fulfilled), they are also rabid imitators of their young for the first several years of an infant's life—sliding objects when their infants slide, banging when their infants bang, and cooing when they coo."[18] Whoever initiates the session, what starts out as unilateral imitation ends up, with the addition of mutual success displays, as *concerted* action. There is some kind of merging of agency. Stern puts it this way: ". . . in imitative interactions, the behavior of the other may be isomorphic (similarly contoured as far as intensity and vitality affects are concerned) and often simultaneous or even synchronous with the behavior of the infant. One might expect that these experiences are the ones that come closest to the notions of merging or of dissolution of self/other boundaries. . . ."[19] James Baldwin uses the term *participation* in this connection.[20] Stern also reports that early concertings are often engaged in with great enthusiasm: ". . . in smiling interactions the dyad can increase by increments the level of intensity of the affect display. One partner increases a smile's intensity, eliciting an even bigger smile from the other partner, which ups the level yet again, and so on, producing a positive feedback spiral."[21]

Stern and Trevarthen both speculate a connection between early concerted activity and lifelong matters of love, trust, allegiance, and community morale:

Moments of self/other similarity tend to occur at times of high arousal and retain throughout life their ability to establish a strong feeling of connectedness, similarity or intimacy, for good or ill. Lovers assume similar postures and tend to move toward and away from one another roughly simultaneously, as in a courting dance. In a political discussion that divides a group into two camps, those of the same position will be found to share postural positions. . . . Mothers and infants, when feeling both happy and excited, will tend to vocalize together. This has been given several different names: coacting, chorusing, matching and mimicking.[22]

Trevarthen thinks that, as well as honing imitative and interactive skills, early concerting establishes a fund of *communitas* that is drawn on much later, during long and sometimes arduous adult sessions of practical concerting:

In adult society, working beliefs and relationships of trust needed for practical cooperation (doing tasks together) appear to be strengthened by exuberant . . . expressions of pleasure in moving and experiencing with others—in art, sport, theatre, carnival, festivals of all kinds. The essential quality of sharing happiness and vitality, and the solidarity of purpose that it creates, is already apparent in the games of 6 month olds. Their actions already have a purpose in building and testing their relationships of trust with identified others.[23]

Kenneth Kaye believes recreational concerting is tied to educative concerting. He separates "cognitive" and "social" reasons for imitating, but shows their interrelation:

. . . imitating and being imitated have important effects upon interpersonal relationships. . . . The child has a motive for continuing to imitate some very familiar or very silly kinds of actions, when doing so will create or maintain a mutual attraction with a parent, interesting adult, sibling, or peer. . . .

These two motives are closely related, once infant and parent move into the period of shared memory. . . . An infant's ability to make optimal use of imitation for cognitive development, by being presented with salient models on the frontier of his existing repertoire of skills, is facilitated by greater dyadic experience with adults who know where his frontier is.[24]

By enjoying the "very familiar or very silly" stuff too, the child cements ties with those adults (especially parents) best placed to teach him behaviors at or near his developmental level. To speak as Trevarthen does of the infant's "purpose" of fostering trust, or to speak as Kaye does of the infant's "motive" of improving his own chances for education, imputes too much. More likely, the infant just has an overweening urge to behave in concert with others, and familiar others provide more opportunities for this.

Educative Concerting

How else do things work always unless by imitation bred of the passion to be like? All the processes of society are based on it, all individual development.
—Doris Lessing, *The Memoirs of a Survivor*[25]

With the advent of the human, zoological evolution may have reached a plateau. The distinctively human part of the human repertoire—including the behavior that ensures our survival—is determined not by genes but by culture. The chief means of our acculturation, I claim, is educative concerting, that is, demonstration and imitation culminating in concerted performance. The only genetic endowment (apart from the usual primate gear) that the human neonate needs is a susceptibility to concerting. John Macmurray claims that, for the infant, "the impulse to communication is his sole adaptation to the world into which he is born."[26] Merlin Donald elaborates on what is involved in acculturation:

Much of the education of children in simple societies is still mimetic in nature. The basic vehicles of such training are reciprocal mimetic games and the imitation and rehearsal of skills. Children mime adults in every respect, including mannerisms, posture and gesture, they learn the customs and scenarios associated with each principal arena of action, and they acquire the manufacturing and survival skills essential to the tribal way of life. In addition, children learn a series of subtle limitations on impulsive behavior in a variety of contexts; this very basic type of learning is difficult to achieve in primates. . . . The period of child-rearing was already being extended with the australopithecines, but it surely would have become even more extended with *erectus*. A capacity for pedagogy in adults would be crucial in guaranteeing the child's acculturation into a mimetic society.[27]

As I hope to show in the next few chapters, so far as acculturation is concerned, modern infants and their caregivers still rely primarily on concerting—and on various derivative and make-do versions of concerting.

If a teacher knows roughly what a pupil's level of development is, the main tasks then become (1) to get the pupil to attempt to perform the action in question and (2) to assist the pupil with the performance as necessary. The best way to get another person to attempt an action is to demonstrate it and invite him to join you in a concerted performance of it. The demonstrator can then best assist the pupil by making demonstrations of actions ostentatious, inviting, unambiguous, detailed, patient, and repetitious, so as to best exploit the pupil's desire to engage in concerted activity. If the pupil is an infant or a child, this desire is often strong.

Why is concerting such an efficient means of teaching new behaviors? At an immediate and bodily level, it could be that the distinctive excitement of concerting has to do with Rizzolatti's mirror neurons. If these neurons fire both when P is witnessing behavior X and when P is himself performing it, then it could be that they fire considerably more rapidly when P is both witnessing and performing X—as happens during concerting. Marco Iacoboni seems to have found evidence that this does in fact happen.[28] This might help explain concerting's effectiveness as an educative recourse. The special kind of excitement that concerting generates might well make the new behavior more memorable—might, as it were, etch it better into the repertoire, or into the cerebral cortex.

Early concertings establish a joint repertoire of concerted activity for the primary caregiver and the infant. Much of this joint repertoire will be nuts-and-bolts-type concertings common to all caregivers and infants and common to most of their shared undertakings. Take, for example, concerted smiling (and some other facial expressions), intermittent mutual observing and gaze-meeting, and mutual gaze-following culminating in joint perception of objects. All these are concertings in their own right, and all are ingredients in almost every other kind of concerting mother and infant engage in. Such ground-floor concerting is more or less constantly in session, or at least is sustained for long periods, when the other is present.

In addition to the basics, most mother-infant teams will have their own private repertoire of more ambitious concertings—little games and other rituals they have arrived at. Familiar concertings of both the nuts-and-bolts kind and the games-and-rituals kind constitute the set scene, the proto-culture in which mother and infant operate. The mother is constantly introducing novelties into this secure zone.

Novelty is incompatible with simultaneous performance, and one early adaptation of concerting is what Meltzoff calls *reciprocal imitation*. Here imitation immediately follows demonstration rather than being simultaneous with it: "Dyads often engage in long bouts of reciprocal imitation at the highchair or kitchen table—first the infant performs an act, then the parent, then the infant, and so on."[29] Reciprocal imitation is probably the most important form of educative concerting. Stern lists a dozen or so researchers into what he calls the "enormous and important" role of reciprocal imitation in mother-infant interaction, and comments:

If the infant vocalizes, the mother vocalizes back. Similarly, if the infant makes a face, the mother makes a face. However, the dialogue does not remain a stereotypic boring sequence of repeats, back and forth, because the mother is constantly introducing modifying imitations . . . or providing a theme-and-variation format with slight changes in her contribution at each dialogic turn; for example, her vocalization may be slightly different each time.[30]

The mother is constantly accustoming the infant to following where she leads, and to combining and adapting existing skills.

One important application of immediate-but-not-simultaneous imitation is to situations that are problematic for the infant but in which he has the good fortune to be accompanied by the mother. According to Russell Meares, the infant finds out how to react to the situation by looking at what the mother is doing and copying that: ". . . the mother is playing with soap bubbles. She blows these bubbles into the baby's face, where they burst. The baby is startled and does not know how to respond. The mother laughs, so the baby laughs too, knowing now that this is fun. It is as if the mother shapes, affectively, the baby's experience."[31]

As Bruner and Meltzoff report, infants are aware when their behavior is being imitated and find this strongly rewarding. To imitate a certain behavior of the infant's, whether that behavior is fully performed or just nascent, is to reward the infant for performing that behavior and help fix it in the infant's repertoire. The behavior-molding potential of this selective imitation is put to good use by the mother. As well as demonstrating new responses for the infant to imitate, the mother will often selectively imitate desirable behaviors the infant just happens to come up with. Or, Meares says, she uses selective imitation to educe as yet inchoate behaviors from the infant: "The mother's response is selective, determined, at least in part, by her own personality and experience. . . . Some mothers would signal anxiety and others would encourage daring."[32] The selective imitation technique is used to improve the infant's speech: ". . . [the mother] is much more likely to echo sounds which resemble the beginnings of language rather than nondescript crying noises. The mother is not simply a mirror. In her responsiveness to the infant, she gives back some part of what the baby is doing—but only some part and not all—and also gives him something of her own."[33]

In many cases, the mother is partly demonstrating something new and partly coaxing out and clarifying something the infant is already, if indistinctly and incompetently, doing. Meares reports that mothers use selective imitation to improve the infant's humor too: "She does not, for example, mimic his crying. (Although she may frown and even moan a little bit.) However, when the baby's affect is positive, the mother's response is characteristically to 'mirror' it. When the infant is content, for example during feeding, she is content; when the child is interested, she too shows interest; when the child is happy she behaves like the child, escalating the happiness."[34]

Hanus and Mechthild Papousek point to a variation in which the mother imitates at the start of the action but is demonstrating the desired outcome by the end.[35] Kaye summarizes the mother's role in educative concerting:

When the mother imitates, it is much more than a mirroring of her baby. She pulls him from where he is in the direction of her own agenda for him. For example, there is *maximizing* imitation: baby opens his mouth and mother exaggeratedly opens her own mouth. We can read her intention even without hearing the kind of remark which sometimes accompanies such behavior: "Yeah, come on, you can do it." Or there is *minimizing* imitation: baby begins with a cry face and mother responds with a quick cry face that lasts only an instant and flows back to a bright expression. We are seeing the mother flash to where her infant is, and attempt to draw him back to where she wants him to be. Again, sometimes a vocalization will serve as a gloss on this behavior: "No don't cry." Finally there is *modulating* imitation: baby whines "waaaah" and mother responds with the same pitch, intonation and duration but mellows it to a sympathetic chanting "awwwww."

There is an important truth here about imitation. It is never a perfect match, always a variation, in the direction of an individual's personal style, a learner's incompetence or an instructor's agenda.[36]

Vocalizing and Speech in Educative Concerting

Speech is a natural ostentator of action. Like any irrupting noise, a vocally produced sound will attract attention naturally. Even neonates are susceptible: "Tests show that new-borns will turn in the direction of a loudspeaker behind a curtain, orienting not only the head and ears but the eyes as well, as if searching to see the person who calls."[37] If you speak, people will look at you and, if you are doing something at the time, they will look at what you are doing.

Most of the speech and pre-speech between caregiver and infant takes place in a context of actual or incipient concerted activity. Carpenter et al. report that "the vast majority of all conventionalized acts (mainly gestures and words) by both infants and their mothers were produced when they were jointly engaged with an object."[38] And Bruner confirms this: ". . . the child, in using language initially, is very much oriented towards pursuing . . . action being undertaken jointly by himself and another."[39]

Vocalizing is fun, interesting to listen to, easy to do and to imitate, and easy and satisfying to concert, either on its own or as part of other shared doings. Voices in unison blend satisfyingly. Vocalizing has more practical virtues too. It broadcasts well, and there is no shortage of different and easily discriminable vocal sounds. Attending to what the other is doing is a big part of concerting and, because it is such an efficient and reliable attention-director, vocalizing makes this part of concerting easier. Thus, apart from its being a source of pleasure, vocalizing has a significant early usefulness as a teaching aid for the caregiver.

Most of the mother's action demonstrations are garnished with vocals. She uses them both to advertise her whole performance and to highlight particular phases of it. Generally, the behaviors or behavior phases a demonstrator accompanies with vocals will be those the demonstrator thinks the pupil should be mastering at the time. Adding the vocal to the performance of a behavior has an ostentating effect similar to that achieved by performing the behavior in an exaggerated or an artificially slow manner. Moves flagged by a distinctive vocal will be better heeded at the time, and better remembered. The vocalizing adds another dimension of sharing, and another source of excitement, to the concerting already going on.

Thus, a distinctive vocal associated with a given behavior has a baptizing effect. The behavior in question is "marked" by the vocal, and its memorableness is increased. As E. Sue Savage-Rumbaugh and her colleagues find, "caretakers unconsciously utilize frequent and sometimes exaggerated postural, gestural, and verbal markers when engaging in interactions with very young children. . . . (When these markers occur in the vocal domain, they are referred to as 'motherese' because of their exaggerated style.) The markers are critical from a communicative standpoint because their purpose is to amplify or make obvious the signals of transition between various components of a given routine or changes from one routine to another."[40]

The first mother-infant interactions in which vocals play a useful marking role are extremely simple ones—such as waving, with the vocal consisting of *hello there!* or *goodbye, goodbye*. . . . In order for mother and infant to achieve more complex concertings, the activity in question needs to be standardized. Both standardizing and repetition are necessary to help guarantee successful concerting—so the activity in question becomes a reliable enough source of pleasure to lodge it in the repertoire. For maximum pleasure, the form of the activity needs to be invariant and both parties need to be very familiar with it. Thus, as Bruner puts it,

. . . mothers seek themselves to "standardize" certain forms of joint action with the child—mostly in play but also in earnest. This usually consists of setting up standard action formats. . . . The principal form of signaling is MARKING THE SEGMENTS OF ACTION. Most usually it begins by the use of terminal marking, the use of what might be called a COMPLETIVE. . . .

The notable thing about video records of young children's behavior is that, in fact, they are so continuous, so "seamless" and without definite beginnings and ends. The use of completives provides a finite structure that permits reproducibility. And reproducibility there is, for it would seem as if both infant and mother take particular pleasure in repeating acts (with variation) for which a definite completive has been agreed upon.[41]

It is in supplying the "completives" and other markers needed to standardize new concertings that vocalizing (and later, speech) comes into its own. Most of the formatting of new shared behavior is achieved by vocal means. This role for vocalizing is prepared for in the mother's early baby talk:

In visible records of the sounds of baby talk the overall effect is that of repeating patterns as in simple music. Apparently baby talk is regulated to create short dramatic episodes of action, with controlled change of intonation to a short succession of marked climaxes. The same may be said of the mother's playful movements of the head and face, of her touching with the hands and of her singing or nonsense syllables to create voice games.[42]

Sooner or later, proper speech will predominate over raw vocals. That is, sooner or later, most of the vocal sounds being uttered by mother and infant for action-marking purposes will—by a process of stylization and standardization directed by the caregiver—come to approximate recognizable words of English, Urdu, or Mandarin. At the early stage we are concerned with, even words that are recognizable as such have no other function than the kind of action marking I am describing. As Joel Wallman puts it, "The first words may not *have* any meaning in the conventional sense. Instead, their utterance may be merely a ritualized part of recurrent activity contexts, only nominally more linguistic than the nonverbal behaviors that also define these contexts, or it may be an attention-directing behavior, or both."[43] At this stage, words are just convenient items for the mother to use as distinctive vocal sounds for action marking. They mean no more or less than the feral vocals or ostensive gestures that are used for the same job.

Speech has as important a role in frivolity as it has in educative doings. Many games for one- to three-year-olds exhibit the regulating, disciplining influence on action that speech has. These speech games have stereotyped forms of words counterparting and accentuating virtually every physical move in the game. Pat-a-cake is one example. Another is *Round-about, round-about went a wee mouse* (chanted slowly, finger tracing slow circles round the child's palm) *round-about, round-about* (more circular tracing) *and . . . into his wee house!* (rapidly and loud, with fingers scampering up the child's arm into the armpit). In such games, the predictability of the proceedings is important. It prepares the child for the repetitive, ritual nature of much everyday activity.

As usual, the border between recreational and educative activity is vague and shifting. In both recreational and educative concerting, the infant or child gains invaluable experience of speech in the action-marking role. The child is constantly hearing (and imitating) speech used to mark out activities—to differentially flag different activities and phases thereof, and to thereby help initiate, segment, order, time and terminate concerted performances of those activities. As I have been keen to establish, the verbal component of concerting has educative benefits, in that it helps the child remember details of the activity and thus enables him to participate more efficiently. But it has recreational benefits too. As I said near the beginning of the section, efficient participation is a considerable source of pleasure to both mother and child. Savage-Rumbaugh et al. speculate that the "pleasure in efficient concerting" motive is paramount for both parties. They suggest that vocal marking "is driven, not by the mother's desire to increase the child's competencies, but by the *joint need* of the mother and the child to coordinate interindividual interactions within routines. To the degree that the mother unconsciously is scaffolding or ratcheting the process, it is not out of a conscious desire to teach the child. Rather, these behaviors emerge because they are necessary to make the inter-individual interactions with the child . . . 'successful' in the sense that they are coordinated and that both participants act smoothly together. It is the verbal and nonverbal segmental markers that allow this coordination to take place."[44]

The effect of marking is to increase the *heed* the pupil devotes to specific aspects of the activity and to foster the pupil's subsequent memory of those aspects. How does speech achieve these effects? Presumably, what happens is that the vocal or speech increases the pupil's excitement at just the moment when he is attending to the relevant stage or juncture in the activity. This grafted-on excitement could be partly due to the vocal sound being an attention-attracting noise, partly due to the vocal's being an intervention by a person (and hence also naturally attention-arousing), and/or the excitement could be partly due to the vocal's providing new raw material for concerting.

Done simply as an attention-attracting noise, the vocal effects the kind of marking done by drum or by cymbals' decision and emphasis, accomplishing ostentation "by association." Yet much of the mother's vocalizing is more than just an accompaniment to the concurrent action or action feature. She often attempts a kind of onomatopoeia, or "vocal representation," of the action. The effective ingredient in this latter kind of vocal marking is non-verbal. Stern calls it "affect attunement." Rather than simply juxtaposing vocal and action, the mother uses the vocal to, as it were, reach right into the action and seize it for the joint repertoire:

An eight-and-one-half-month-old boy reaches for a toy just beyond reach. Silently he stretches toward it, leaning and extending arms and fingers out fully. Still short of the toy, he tenses his body to squeeze out the extra inch he needs to reach it. At that moment, his mother says, *uuuuuh . . . uuuuuh!* With a crescendo of vocal effort, the expiration of air pushing against her tensed torso. The mother's accelerating vocal-respiratory effort matches the infant's accelerating physical effort.

A ten-month-old girl accomplishes an amusing routine with mother and then looks at her. The girl opens up her face (her mouth opens, her eyes widen, her eyebrows rise) and then closes it back, in a series of changes whose contour can be represented by a smooth arch. Mother responds by intoning *Yeah,* with a pitch line that rises and falls as the volume crescendos and decrescendos: *Yeah.* The mother's prosodic contour has matched the child's facial-kinetic contour.

The mother's vocal marks the host action more intimately and powerfully than mere temporal association could. But the aim is still to help the child focus on the action and to master particular aspects of it. In the above cases, variations in the vocal's loudness and tone work to differentially modulate effort in the relevant segments of the action.

The Matrix

Early in this chapter I refrained from labeling as "actions" the imitatings the infant does before his first experiences of concerting. Because it is reasonable to accord personhood only to one who can perform actions, I also withheld personhood from the pre-concerting infant. I later reported that mothers often feel, during the first concertings, that the infant has now become a person. To accept this is to accept that the ability to participate in sessions of concerted activity coincides with personhood. However, I would delay personhood still further. In my view, the infant's early contributions to concertings do not yet qualify as actions. They are not that advanced. By "actions" we generally mean solo actions, things the person does on his own. In the account that follows, solo action is a development that follows concerting and in fact requires considerable experience of it.

However, if we delay agency and personhood until after first concertings, a terminological problem arises similar to the one that arose in connection with neonatal "abilities." In describing (or even witnessing) concerted activity of a mother and an infant, we cannot help but think in terms of the two parties deliberately conforming their actions. The concept of separate individual agents—who act "jointly" or "in concert," who each "participate," who "imitate each other," and who "share in" behavior—seems indispensable in describing concerting. Yet to define concerting in these terms implies that individual agency is logically and developmentally prior to concerting. I am claiming that concerting is prior.

The problem is not just that we cannot help but see the infant as already a person but also that, in our everyday vocabulary and in the thinking that underpins this vocabulary, concepts such as action, agent, person—and arguably speech and thinking (or consciousness)—are *basic*. They are the irreducible, given concepts in our lives, the ground on which everyday language and thought walk. In the context of everyday speech and thought, there is no room for an explanation of individual action, speech, thinking, etc. This makes my view of concerting as the matrix—existing prior to and giving rise to solo action, speech, and thinking—impossible to state in everyday terms. In the view I propose, concerting is ineffable.

However, even if the idea of concerting qua matrix is indefinable in words, we can still imagine it—"behind" actions, persons, language, and mind. Words fail, but concerting is still definable ostensively, by demonstration. The kind of understanding that such a demonstration makes possible is the "understanding what it is like to do" that is achieved by imitation, or by empathy standing in for imitation. In this book I bow to necessity and continue to refer to and describe concerting in the everyday expressions we understand—expressions such as *participate, contribute, imitate, mutual awareness,* and *concert their actions.* Although my use of these expressions is, strictly, circular, it is justifiable insofar as it is underwritten by the possibility of actual demonstrations—of the form "this game is played."

The writers I quote above (and below) all acknowledge an important developmental role for concerting. However, few if any of them would regard concerting as I do—as the be-all and end-all. I claim that concerting is the font of solo action, personhood, language, thought, and consciousness. I claim these are, essentially, just *modifications* of concerting. We have glimpsed two very early modifications of concerting. In reciprocal imitation, the respective contributions are no longer simultaneous but are nevertheless closely sequential. In selective imitation, parts of the model's demonstration are deliberately omitted from the imitator's version. But how are such variants arrived at? By increments of what kinds of change does concerting eventually give rise to solo doing and to speaking and thinking?

4   The Tokening of Concerted Activity

I start out of my chair with an indignant cry, raise my hands in preparation for strangling, and stride purposefully toward my accuser. Then, with my fingers inches from his throat, I freeze, red-faced, eyeballing him. Generally, such a start-stop, irresolute, or inconclusive performance is a response to an ambivalent situation. One perceives something that would normally trigger X-ing—the accusation is insufferable, say, and "strangle him now" is implemented. But at the same time one perceives things that would normally preclude X-ing—for example, perhaps my accuser and intended victim is very old and is my professor. Or perhaps the situation changes while the action is in train. While advancing, I notice that the professor has drawn a handgun. In such an ambivalent situation, a natural but crude way of responding—which might be called, ironically, the *faux pas strategy*—is to commence doing X but then abort the performance before X-ing is accomplished.

Like any action, the faux pas response becomes more efficient with practice. Once one has more experience of commencing and then aborting particular actions in particular ambivalent situations, and more experience of commencing and then aborting actions generally, the commencing and the aborting can each be done with less fuss and bother. I can abort my "attacks" on the professor earlier and earlier as I become more accustomed to his outrageous accusations and heartless jibes. The second time it happens, say, rather than going right up to him I might stop in the middle of the room. Or I might stay in my chair, grip the arms of the chair, and glare ostentatiously, perhaps loosing a derogatory remark or two about his age and physical appearance.

Such closely sequential commencing then aborting of a performance of an action can be called *tokening* of the action in question. Tokening is thus a twofold action. Or, it is a sequence, or combination, of two different actions. It consists of both the commencing of a performance of an action and the aborting of that performance before it is completed. Tokening is also a "meta-action": an action performed on or with respect to another action. It represents an ability over and above the ability to perform the original action right through. It is an ability to perform bits of an action.

The infant's early acquisition of this kind of meta-actional ability reflects both innate ability in this area and the caregiver's propensity to teach some concerted activities bit by bit. As Trevarthen reports, "Two-month-olds can stop and start activity, a capacity which is essential for reciprocal exchange."[1] One of the things the infant learns in early concerting sessions is to perform actions *on cue*. There is a cue for the beginning (the caregiver starts the action) and a cue for the end (the caregiver stops). As we saw in the last chapter, these termini may have some additional gestural or vocal marking. To establish the further ability to commence and abort, it is only required that the infant learn to stop a performance prematurely, that is, before the usual endpoint. There are various ways premature stopping can be taught by example too.

I call the performance "tokening," rather than staying with the more descriptive but clumsier term *commencing and aborting*, partly for brevity and partly because *token* has welcome connotations of *token performance* and *token gesture*. My use of *token* as a verb is unusual, but it should not be difficult to get used to. The verb use is anyway salutary, insofar as it helps remind us that it is an action being talked about.

Tokening Done to Initiate Concerted Activity

In the original faux pas scenario, tokening is just damage control and can hardly be said to have a function. However, tokening soon becomes hugely important as a means of initiating and expediting concerted and coopera- tive activity. In chapter 3 we saw that the infant's natural ability and pro- clivity for imitation find him soon addicted to doing things in concert with the mother and/or others. A repertoire, or culture, of concerted activities develops between mother and infant. By various judicious adjustments of her contribution to concertings—including the use of vocal sounds to flag important phases and junctures in the proceedings, and to modulate effort—the mother is able to maximize concerting's educative effect on the infant. She constantly both exercises and extends skills the infant already has and establishes new skills. In the process, a foundation of delight in shared doing is laid down.

The infant is dependent for concertings on a willing and patient caregiver. Fortunately, adults are, as Meltzoff puts it, "rabid imitators" of the very young. With a parent present and attending, much of what the infant does will be imitated anyway. But in addition, from the beginning, the infant has means of attracting attention. Crying out is the main one, but, as Trevarthen reports, he may also gesture for attention: ". . . the infant may move to recover communication if the mother fails to display affection. The infant makes forced, abrupt and large gestures which attract attention, then shows passivity and sadness or grimaces and gestures of distress."[2]

To begin with, the infant enjoys concerting when it happens, but the only way he has of proactively initiating concerted activity is to begin a demonstration of the relevant movements. The demonstration will typically be laced with "large gestures which attract attention." These vocal and other gestures are either natural, as I presume are those Trevarthen refers to above, or they are copies of the gestures that the mother has used in the past to highlight or "mark" her own demonstrations of this activity. Meeting, or attempting to meet, the other's gaze is a ubiquitous and important ingredient in these ostentatious "invitatory" demonstratings.

The demonstration may fail to attract the participation, or even the attention, of the other, and so be abandoned halfway. An unsuccessful demonstration is much the same as a tokening of the faux pas type. As the infant becomes experienced at invitatory tokening, his efforts will become more efficient. The overall ostentatious and invitatory aspects must be retained, but any distinctive fragment can come to serve as an effective token of the activity in question. Often, the initial phase of the activity will be suitably distinctive.

The token demonstration may at first be vague and in need of refinement. For a very familiar and/or recently enjoyed activity, even an inchoate and perfunctory effort might work. Bruner reports that "at the outset . . . [the child's] mode of signaling for the recurrence of the action is usually to show a typical level of excitement or a generalized vocative in an appropriate context, or by performing some portion of the desired action (e.g., pumping up and down on the adult's knee to produce a recurrence of 'Ride-a-Cock-Horse')."[3] In chapter 2 I quoted Vygotsky reporting Kohler's finding that "usually a chimpanzee will *begin* a movement or an action he wants another animal to perform or to share." Konrad Lorenz corroborates chimpanzees' ability in this area:

In the Yerkes Laboratory two chimpanzees were given the task of pulling up a basket by means of a piece of string threaded loosely through the handle. The two animals had to pull the ends of the string at the same time. When one of the chimpanzees saw how to solve the problem, he took his companion to one end of the string and made him hold it in his hand; he then ran quickly to the other end, picked it up and mimed the action of pulling it.[4]

The common feature in the above examples is the infant's or ape's giving a token demonstration of, or "tokening," an activity, in an attempt to initiate a joint session of it. We do just the same thing when, as an invitation, we mime drinking from a glass. One commences the activity, or performs some distinctive part of it, but then discontinues the performance. Or one makes as if to perform the action, but in a deliberately abortive way—for example, with no glass in hand. One performs the action in a token way. And the tokening is done in an ostentatious and invitatory manner. It is token *concerting*, after all.

How this kind of invitatory tokening originates, and whether it derives from faux-pas-type tokening, are unclear from the literature.[5] Certainly, the infant learns the tokening technique at least partly by copying what adults do when they solicit his own participation in an activity.

Speech Replaces Other Types of Tokening

. . . the routinized interactions in which an infant and its caregiver engage are the seed from which language grows. Dyadic interactions between . . . infants and their caregivers are initially effected by the use of sounds and gaze to establish and maintain joint attention, and are then supplemented by natural gestures and then sounds to initiate or coordinate inter-individual routines. The infant starts to look where its caregiver wants and starts to attend to objects and situations. Soon afterwards the infant begins to use gaze and gestures to direct its caregiver's attention, and then to use gestures and conventionalized sounds to initiate exchanges.
—E. Sue Savage-Rumbaugh, Stuart Shanker, and Talbot Taylor[6]

How is it that, simply by speaking, one can get another person to do something—pass the salt, say? In my view, the power of speech to effect and affect others' behavior can be traced to just two sources. The first is people's natural disposition to concert their actions (albeit often of necessity in a token way). The second is the power token performance of an action has to ready a person for actual performance of that action.

Tokening done to solicit others' participation in an activity will often include gestures that the caregiver has used as markers when teaching that activity, or that distinctive phase of that activity. That is, invitatory tokening will often consist of exaggerated movements and onomatopoeic and/or conventional vocal sounds. In the child's experience, such markers are part and parcel of the original activity and are thus available as raw material to use for invitatory tokening.

As I say, experience in invitatory tokening makes it more efficient. Markers that are easier to perform, have good attention-directing potential and broadcast well, and are distinctive of the relevant activity will tend to remain in the final, streamlined and efficient version—at the expense of markers that are more laborious and/or not so distinctive. If an activity has been well marked out by speech initially, a combination of facial expression, tone of voice, and spoken words is usually the most efficient means of tokening it. That is, speech, delivered in a certain way, becomes the easiest and most distinctive and compelling way of tokening desired joint activity.

Vygotsky believes that invitatory tokening evolves in the child's repertoire by a gradual process of essentialization or abbreviation. The child moves from full demonstration with markers to mime and gestural markers (with or without speech), and then to speech pretty much by itself (with minimal other gesturing). Vygotsky reports experiments involving children at play that show speech gradually replacing mime and gesture:

Whereas some children depicted everything by using movements and mimicry, not employing speech as a symbolic recourse at all, for other children actions were accompanied by speech: the child both spoke and acted. For a third group, purely verbal expression not supported by any activity began to predominate. Finally, a fourth group of children did not play at all, and speech became the sole mode of representation, with mimicry and gestures receding into the background. The percentage of purely play actions decreased with age, while speech gradually predominated. The most important conclusion drawn from this developmental investigation . . . is that the difference in play activity between three-year-olds and six-year-olds is . . . in the mode in which various forms of representation are used. In our opinion, this is a highly important conclusion; it indicates that symbolic representation in play is essentially a particular form of speech at an earlier stage. . . .[7]

The point is that speech is an improved method of doing something— which I call "invitatory tokening of concerted activity"—which the child can already do, albeit not as efficiently, by other means. As Macmurray puts it, "Long before the child learns to speak he is able to communicate, meaningfully and intentionally, with his mother. In learning language, he is acquiring a more effective and more elaborate means of doing something which he can already do in a crude and more primitive fashion."[8] There is a considerable literature on how speech develops from gesture.[9] In this literature, the fact that speech is itself a kind of gesture seems to have escaped notice. *Gesture* is just another name for invitatory tokening. A gesture is unilateral "token concerting" of an activity done to solicit the other's participation in an actual concerted session of the activity. Speech is token performance in the same sense and it is done for the same purpose. With speech, the fragment of the activity that is selected as a token just happens to be the verbal marker part. Speech replaces other means of tokening simply because it is easier to do, it is less ambiguous, and it broadcasts better.

Hampshire is specifically interested in the tokening of emotional behavior. Full-scale emotional displays are readily replaceable for communicative purposes by much-reduced versions. Earlier I quoted Hampshire saying that "the man who looks daggers at his neighbor has cut off the action of aggression, and the vestige of it remains in his glance . . . the truncated action is legible as a sign."[10] Hampshire believes that "the child's responses to meaningful gestures, and his imitation of them, are the earliest phases of a continuous history, which ends with the use of language."[11] He says, accordingly, that "when Wittgenstein suggested that the *words* 'I am in pain' can be said to replace a cry of pain, he concentrated an immense transition, a whole history, into this single word 'replace'."[12]

Savage-Rumbaugh and her colleagues have researched the development of verbal tokening in children and apes. For the ape, the verbal act involves either the ape itself or the caretaker pointing to a lexigram. The research reported below concerns a joint routine that involves blowing bubbles. The researchers sum up how the child's or ape's attempts at tokening the routine improve:

. . . once a routine and its markers are understood, the child or ape can begin to use the latter to initiate the routine and thus play a part in determining the course of events. At first, such initiations will be limited and "primitive" in the sense that they are usually action based and context dependent. For example, the child or ape may see the bottle of bubbles among other toys, pick it up, and look at the caretaker. By selecting the bubbles from other things, she conveys a desire to execute the "bubble-blowing" routine. Later, she may simply point to the bubbles and look at the care-taker. Still later, she will say *bubbles* or point to the *bubbles* lexigram and turn to the caretaker.

In so doing, children or apes begin the move from the role of a responder during routines to that of primitive initiator and then to that of a symbolic communicator capable of announcing their intentions to another party. . . . This appears to happen more rapidly with routines that are most clearly structured and effectively marked.[13]

Covert Tokening

Even tokening done in faux pas mode becomes streamlined with experi-ence. One's physical assaults on one's intellectual superiors will eventually diminish beyond staying put in one's chair and bawling or muttering insults. At a still more mature level, one may just blush slightly and tense one's arm muscles. And one's eyes may darken for a second. After a whole semester in which to improve my response to my professor, I may evince no sign of being in attack mode, though I still am. Now, when the profes-sor points at me, sniggering, I just nod and smile politely. Let us call such mature, subtle, facile, inconspicuous commencing and aborting *covert* tokening.

Neither "Abbreviated" nor "Inner" X-ing

To begin with, we can look just at the intermediate and still overt stages. I am halfway across the room, say. But is it in any sense abbreviated, incom-plete, or truncated strangling that is going on? Well, no, not literally. I have not strangled anyone, even "in an abbreviated way." I have not half-strangled the professor, nor have I even so much as 1% strangled him. I have not touched him. It is true that, at least in the very early cases, when I first leap out of my chair I might not know what I am doing. It looks as if I really am about to strangle the professor. Perhaps I am about to. Who can say? But I end up not doing it—that is, not strangling anyone—to any extent.

I have done something. Literally, I have overtly commenced and then aborted a strangling attack Or, you might say, I have done some deliberately aborted or abortive X-ing. Or, I have "made as if to" X. Similar but more sophisticated variants of overt tokening can be described as "mock" X-ing or "pretend" X-ing. The point is that it is the *tokening* of action X that I am doing—and doing 100%—and no actual X-ing at all. There is no actual X-ing in the picture.

Now we can look at the case of covert tokening, where the tokening is done so subtly and quickly as to be unobservable. At least, it is not observable without very close scrutiny of the person and/or without using special recording instruments. Can we speak literally of inner or internal X-ing here? We cannot. Just as there is no X-ing of any degree or kind going on in the overt case above, neither is there any going on in the covert case. Even less, one is tempted to add. And this is true apart from the incomprehensibility of people literally doing things inside their heads.

More useful, at first glance, is the question whether not the X-ing but the *tokening*, the token X-ing, when it is covert, can be truthfully described as being done inside the person. Here we do come up against the incomprehensibility of "doing inside the body." Covert tokening is an action, no different in principle from its overt counterpart. It may be extremely subtle, even "behavior at its vanishing point" in Hampshire's phrase. (I repeat, it is the X-tokening that is at vanishing point, not any X-ing.) However, no matter how subtle, the tokening is still, like any action, done in the place where the person happens to be at the time. The smallest place where covert tokening can occur is the smallest place a person can fit into—a cupboard, perhaps, or a large sack. There is no question of fitting a person inside anyone's head, let alone his own.

The Mechanics of Covert Tokening

Just as overt commencing requires some effortful bodily adjustment on the person's part, so does the corresponding subsequent or simultaneous aborting. It is not important for our purposes what kind of bodily exertion is required to effect the aborting, only that some effort is required. Probably the nature of the exertion varies, depending on what action is to be aborted and on how far the commencing has gone. The aborting might be achieved by the person selectively relaxing the muscles involved in the commencing—and this relaxing would require a specific kind of effort. Or, perhaps, the commencing could be stymied by activation of muscles that work in opposition to the commencing muscles, counteracting them.

Presumably, the same applies to covert commencing and abortings—the main difference being that, in the covert case, the muscular activations (etc.) required for the respective commencings and abortings will be more subtle. Training and practice will be necessary before the covert response becomes quick and easy. As we saw in chapter 2, Ryle is keen to remove anything muscular or otherwise bodily from the concept of imagining, and he describes the refraining or desisting element in imagining as a negative "action"—an absence of action, a species of inaction and not an effortful doing at all. However, if covert tokening is merely a more efficient and subtle form of overt tokening, as I claim, and if overt commencing requires effort to abort, then Ryle is wrong here. As we also saw, he concedes that "complete abstention is harder than partial abstention,"[14] and he concedes that "the trick of talking to oneself in silence is acquired neither quickly nor without effort."[15] That is, some active exertion must be required even when the commencing and aborting is covert. The point is long-windedly but effectively made by the literary critic Kenneth Burke:

. . . the *action* is delayed precisely because one has trained the body to undergo certain physiological *motions* of a sort designed to forestall the kind of motions ordinarily following such a stimulus when it is received uncritically. The body during the state of delay does not cease to exist. The mental *attitude* of arrest must have some corresponding bodily *posture*. The very delay of action is thus maintained by motions. . . . There is at least as much neural motion going on in the body that hesitates before sitting down as in the body that sits down without hesitation. Mentally to look before one leaps has its equivalent in internal bodily motions quite as leaping does.[16]

There is another thing. Covert tokening does eventually become, in many instances, so easy as to be apparently effortless and automatic. However, as I argued in the introduction, *effortless* is hyperbole when applied to an action. It does not mean that the action is done literally without effort, only that it is done with minimal effort. *Automatic* is also, though apt, figurative. It does not mean that the tokening is not an action of the person. It does not mean, for example, that the person's brain is doing it, so the person does not have to.

I imply above that covert tokening is just a matter of the relevant muscular exertions, involved in the commencing and the aborting, being more subtle. However, I don't mean to rule out the possibility of commencing and aborting being accomplished at a pre-muscular, neural level. After suitable training, a person might become able to voluntarily initiate the particular program of neuron firings appropriate to a given muscular performance—or to initiate some abbreviated, weak, or inhibited version of this firing program—without activating any of the relevant muscles at all.

Overt tokening may be either an episodic action, like striking a match, or a continuous, durational one, like keeping the matchbox in your hand. There are also intermediate cases—actions that are episodic and durational, as when one holds the box briefly in one's hand. Speech and mime are episodic doings, but postures and facial expressions generally have duration. Again there are intermediate cases. Covert tokening, similarly, can be episodic and/or durational. Presumably, there are, correspondingly, two kinds of aborting or inhibiting: a knocking-on-the-head episodic type and a maintaining-a-tight-grip-on durational type. Dr. Strangelove's compulsive saluting illustrates both episodic and durational tokening. His right arm shoots up in salute (episodic commencing), and he immediately grabs it with his left hand and pulls it down (episodic aborting). Then a struggle ensues as the saluting arm attempts vainly to rise (durational commencing) while gripped and held down by the other hand (durational aborting).

Tokening could all be episodic. One could, in theory, account for duration in terms of constant repetitions of episodic commence-and-abort cycles. On the other hand, much tokening does seem to be of the maintaining-a-tight-grip-on sort, in which the commencing effort is continuous, and continuously held in check.

Suppose tokening does come in different episodic and durational varieties. For the episodic variety, the tokening is covert when the aborting follows the commencing so closely that very little or no overt movement results. The commencing and the aborting may be almost simultaneous. In durational tokening, on the other hand, the commencing and the aborting must be simultaneous. Durational tokening is covert when the aborting effort so precisely and comprehensively counteracts the commencing effort that very little or no overt movement results.

The concept of the covert tokening of an action is anyway not difficult. Covert tokening is just an efficient, sophisticated, discreet version of overt tokening—which is, approximately, "commencing X-ing to the extent of performing observable acts consistent with X-ing, but then aborting before X-ing is achieved." For experienced adults, the act of covert tokening is not difficult, either. It is second nature to us, and we do it practically all the time. We even do it periodically while we are asleep. For the infant first learning to token actions covertly, however, it is difficult. It requires training and practice: as Ryle says, "the trick of talking to oneself in silence is acquired neither quickly nor without effort." I will discuss how the infant or child might learn the covert tokening trick in the next-to-last section of this chapter.

The Uses of Covert Tokening

It also helps us see what general kind of action tokening is if we consider why we do it—that is, what use it is. In its original overt, faux pas form, tokening is just damage control and can hardly be said to have a function. However, as we have seen, overt tokening quickly acquires huge importance as a means of initiating and expediting concerted and cooperative activity. Covert tokening is also indispensable, but for other purposes.

Although faux pas tokening is more an inability than an ability, once the infant graduates to essentializing and covertizing his commencings and abortings we can start talking about abilities and usefulness. Covert tokening done in advance, before overtly commencing an action, often enables the agent to avoid a likely or possible faux pas in a problematic situation. In fact, this proactive, testing-the-waters type of covert tokening is so often useful that, as I said above, we do it all the time and it becomes second nature to us.

The usefulness of proactive covert tokening is not limited to damage avoidance in ambiguous situations. It is not just the defensive, inhibiting, aborting, delaying side that is important. The positive, commencing, preparing aspect of tokening is just as often the salient factor. The positive effect of covert tokening (as with overt tokening) is to *ready* or *prime* the person for a performance of the action being tokened, enabling a quicker and more efficient performance subsequently. This is the function that the physiological abbreviation theorists all found, in animals as well as people, for their abbreviated or incipient responses.

Faced with an ambiguous or as-yet-unresolved situation, a person can covertly token behavior X and, by doing so, simultaneously ready himself to perform X and delay the performance (or delay total abandonment of the performance) until the situation clarifies. In addition, the covert tokening enhances the person's attentiveness and perceptual abilities during the wait. A person who is covertly tokening X-ing is much more likely to notice things and events relevant to X-ing than someone who is not.[17] The covert tokening confers a directed alertness on the person's demeanor.

The readinesses to act and to perceive relevant things are achieved, and can be sustained indefinitely, without any commitment to overt action. This is in situations where immediate overt action might be not only unsuccessful because of being premature, but possibly laborious and/or risky as well. Effort and risk are minimized, yet the chances of a subsequent well-timed, prompt, and efficient response—when the situation does decisively improve or deteriorate—are greatly increased. In addition, covert tokening has a readying role within actions. As I quoted de Laguna saying, later phases of an action are covertly tokened in anticipation during performance of earlier phases, thus "ensuring the action is carried to completion."[18]

The ground-floor, prototype way of getting good at doing something, or readying oneself for doing something, is by means of overt practices, rehearsals, dummy runs. In theory, such practices and rehearsals would qualify as "overt tokenings" of the action in question. So, I must belatedly mention a large and important category of overt tokenings—mock-doings, shadow-boxings, leapings out of the starting blocks, etc.—the function of which is not to solicit another's participation in some activity but to ready the tokener for his own action. The degree of actual movement required for an overt token performance of X to adequately ready the person for X-ing will vary according to how experienced at X-ing the agent is and how suitable the current situation is for X-ing. The more experienced an agent is and the more suitable the situation, the less wholehearted an overt rehearsal needs to be—and the more it can tend to the abbreviated, perfunctory, and covert. In practice, covert tokening is the minimum tokening performance necessary to ready a fairly experienced agent for a fairly unproblematic action in a fairly suitable situation. In colloquial terms, the distinction is between "physical" practice or rehearsal and "mental" practice, and this is how the physiological abbreviationists draw the distinction too. What I am suggesting is that the difference between physical and mental practice is a matter of degree—of effort, readiness, experience, ability, and so on.

I have given overt tokening three roles: faux pas, self-readying for action (as above), and invitatory or other's-participation-inciting. I have given covert tokening a single self-readying, faux-pas-minimizing role. In life, intricate mixtures of overt and covert tokenings, with corresponding mixtures of functions, often occur. Covert tokening may combine with overt, invitatory, empathy-inciting tokening. The smile, frown, or bereft expression flitting across someone's face may indicate incompetence or laxness in his covertizing of some tokening, or it may be for public consumption. In cases of other kinds, overt tokening done for another's benefit as a demonstration or invitation may, fortuitously, simultaneously ready the person doing it for action. Or a conspicuous overt faux pas may solicit participation, help, and/or instruction from others. Overt tokenings may become covert as a situation changes, and vice versa. Like the situations to which they are responses, our tokenings may be multi-leveled, ambivalent, and changing.

How Covert Tokening Is Taught

If we look at the adult's powers of covert tokening, we note the great speed, subtlety, complexity, versatility, and durability of adult tokenings. We note the fact that in many situations these powers appear to be exercised automatically, without voluntary effort of the person. We might well be tempted to attribute these powers not to the person but to a special supernatural or natural agency inside the person. On the other hand, we can, if we work at it, trace the adult's tokening skills back to the first bumbling efforts of the infant, back to benighted overt commencings and abortings in ambivalent situations. We can see then how these early efforts are subsequently—in small increments and over years, via innumerable teachings by example on parents' and others' parts—trained up into the rapid and sophisticated covert responses of the adult. Then the impression of supernatural (or other) goings-on in people's heads is considerably diminished. It is still pretty amazing how good we get at covert tokening. But once we recognize the beginnings for what they are, and appreciate some of the teaching methods, it becomes easier to see thinking as something we do, and have to learn to do.

For the philosopher of mind, the most interesting part of what the developmental psychologist has to say about the infant's and the child's intellectual progress is not how the infant learns to participate in joint activities, or learns efficient means of overtly tokening joint activity. What is most interesting is how covert tokening is learned.

Is there a natural, perhaps "genetically built in," basis for covert tokening? Above, I supposed some initial natural ability to—with practice—covertize faux-pas-type overt tokening. This is consistent with what Ivan Pavlov found in dogs.

In Pavlov's experiments, a dog was conditioned to the sound of a buzzer being followed by meat powder administered directly into its mouth.[19]

Later, the buzzer was sounded without the meat powder being delivered. On hearing the buzzer, the dog commenced "meat-powder-chomping" (it salivated and moved its jaw muscles), but when the meat powder failed to arrive this response was inhibited. In subsequent trials, if the sounding of the buzzer was only sometimes (and unpredictably) followed by meat powder, creating an ambivalent stimulus situation for the dog, the commencing-and-inhibiting reaction persisted, but at a low level of activation.

Does the training that human infants receive serve to install a covert tokening ability they did not have before, or does the training merely improve a pre-existing ability? More important, what is this training? Because what is to be taught is covert tokening, it would seem impossible to teach by the usual method of demonstration and imitation. However, covert tokening can be taught this way. Like other activities, covert tokening can be done in concert.

Learning How to Cope Quietly with Delay

One important teaching strategy seems to be as follows. First, a delay period is (apparently perversely) introduced into a familiar joint activity. The teacher stops in mid-performance, say. Second, when the infant responds with invitatory tokenings of the next stage in the proceedings, the teacher refrains from imitating or otherwise confirming these tokenings. With repeated experience of a delay interrupting this activity, the trend will be for the infant's invitatory tokenings to be aborted earlier and earlier, and eventually become covert. However, before the overt aspects of the tokening disappear, the teacher ventures the kind of corroborative gesture (smiles, nods, *mm-mm* sounds, etc.) normally used as success signals in concerting. This gesture confirms and rewards the less overt, more patient waiting display the infant is now producing. After repetitions, in which the teacher reserves the smile-nod-*mmm* success signal for progressively more restrained overt tokenings on the infant's part, the teacher will end up making the signal in association with fully covert tokenings by the infant.

In one common form of the game peekaboo, an object being jointly observed is made to disappear and reappear—with considerable ostentation and vocalization marking the disappearings and reappearings. The educative benefits of this game are at least threefold. First, the infant is getting practice in concerted performance of the perceptual behavior associated with this object. The appearance-disappearance method of presentation of the object is as efficient as pointing in delimiting just what perceptual behavior is to be shared. The behavior is defined by a temporal frame. Second, the infant is getting practice in the rapid starting and stopping of an action (in this case, a perception recipe) and this is beneficial in refining overt tokening skills. But third, peekaboo of this type enables the sharing of specific *covert* tokenings. The appearance-disappearance strategy creates a frame not just for the perceptual behavior being shared when the object is visible, but also for what is happening while the object is invisible. When the object is invisible, both parties are covertly tokening the imminent perceptual behavior. In colloquial terms, while the object is obscured, mother and infant are nevertheless "imagining" or "visualizing" it. They are readying themselves for seeing it—suddenly and soon. This covert tokening, this excitement-packed "non-seeing" of the object, is shared—and confirmed with vocals and smiles, and exchanging of glances—just as enthusiastically as the subsequent fully performed perceptual behavior is shared, when the cover is lifted again.

Another, related way of introducing covert tokening to the child is as a covert response to overt tokening by the other party. So far, I have concentrated on invitatory tokening's role in inciting actual, overt concerted activity. This is its most important early function for the infant but, for the older child and adult, overt tokening—and particularly speech—is more important as a means of inciting *covert tokening* on the other's part. In this new transaction, the teacher/speaker overtly tokens doing and perceiving certain things and the pupil/hearer does his best to covertly token doing and perceiving those things. For example, the speaker talks about something and the hearer does his best to imagine it. The transaction may be in preparation for some actual undertaking, involving one or both parties, in the near or distant future. Or the transaction may be engaged in for pleasure.

We can imagine how the infant might come to master this kind of transaction. To begin with, the adult invitingly tokens some activity, say dinner, well in advance. The tokening involves speech and eating noises, perhaps. Although he sees no other sign of dinner, the infant may reciprocate with an abbreviated reprise of the adult's overt tokenings. The infant makes a chewing movement, say—a mini-tokening confirming the adult's display—and smiles at the adult, who smiles back. What is being engineered—and confirmed by the exchange of smiles and the mini-tokenings—in this period immediately after the initial invitatory tokening is the concerting of the adult's and infant's respective covert tokenings of future dinner-eating.

We are still looking at a delay scenario. Invitatory tokening has been done and acknowledged, but of the full-scale concerted activity (dinner), which would normally be imminent after such tokening, there is no sign. Because the other cues necessary for dinner-eating are absent, the invitatory tokening cannot *initiate* dinner-eating but only *ready* the hearer for it. In response to the adult's announcing and miming dinner-eating, the infant "commences" dinner-eating but then, because of the otherwise unpropitious cue situation, aborts this performance. The infant's situation is perhaps similar to that of Pavlov's dog. A faux pas commencing and aborting is—after repeated experience of the ambiguous cue situation that triggers it—refined into more streamlined tokening. In the absence of food, the adult's premature dinner signaling has an effect on the infant analogous to the effect the ambiguous cue situation devised by the experimenter has on the dog. Only, in the human case, the overt tokening and the covert response are parts of an interpersonal, communicative transaction.

The task in a delay scenario is to maintain some minimal tokening of (hence readiness for) activity X over the period in which X-ing is impossible. In the interests of least effort, the long-haul tokening may as well be covert. However, in cases like the adult and infant awaiting dinner, the infant's covert tokening task can be made as easy or difficult as desired. The adult can always intervene, if necessary, with another *overt* tokening of dinner. This will temporarily relieve the infant of having to continue covertly tokening it.

The adult's and the infant's covert tokenings are in a very real sense being concerted and being successfully mutually demonstrated. Immediately after overt tokening, and/or in the intervals between any subsequent refresher-type overt tokenings, the parties are still exchanging "mini" second-order confirmatory imitations (of the overt tokening), and exchanging confirmatory smiles. This expressive microbehavior (mini-overt-tokenings, smiles, etc.) "supports" the mutual covert tokening.

Make-Believe Games

Waiting for dinner is one of several kinds of scenario that encourage concerted covert tokening. The infant and child get used to progressively extended delays between overt tokenings and the real thing—from "imminent" (as in peekaboo) initially, to "in a while" (as with dinner above), to "someday, perhaps" (as with going to the zoo). After these, there are "yes-terday" and "not really" to be learned. Mother and infant spend a lot of time in make-believe. Probably, the make-believe type of overt tokening has an important educative role, serving to give the infant experience in con-certed covert tokening. Only secondarily does it serve to hone verbal and theatrical skills. In the make-believe that Paul Harris describes, joint atten-tion is as much on what is patently left undone as on what is done:

Playful acts with some of the features of pretense can be seen towards the end of the first year. Thus, infants will proffer an object or food to an adult but teasingly with-draw it at the last moment. . . . Here, we see in embryonic form the same pattern that is extended and elaborated in the second year. The infant engages in a familiar, goal-directed sequence but deliberately stops short of the standard terminus for that sequence. Thus, the infant holds out an object or a spoonful of food, but omits to hand over the object or let the food be eaten. In the course of the second year, simi-lar behaviors are produced but with the terminus suspended in an even more radical fashion. For example, Lucienne at 19 months pretends to drink out of a box and then holds it to the mouths of all who are present.[20]

The overt tokening—"pouring the tea" or growling like a bear—cues and orchestrates the main event, the concerted covert tokening. The overt cues the covert. Experience children gain of teasing and being teased, of lying and being told lies, and of tricking and being tricked also provides invalu-able assistance in mastering covert tokening.

Apes are not as good at aping as we are, but they are not miles behind. A human-like interplay of overt and covert tokening—with the overt being used to buoy the covert—is evident in the make-believe games Savage-Rumbaugh's chimpanzee Kanzi initiates:

His favorite pretend game centers around imaginary food. He pretends to eat food that is not really there, to feed others imaginary food, to hide such food, to find it, to take it away from other individuals, to give it back to them, and to play chase and keep-away with an imaginary morsel. He will even put a piece of imaginary food on the floor and act as if he does not notice it until someone else begins to reach for it, then grab it before they can get it.[21]

Props and Prompters

Children are eventually able to overtly and covertly token complex social scenarios and long action sequences within these scenarios. Diverse inter-personal transactions involving concerted covert tokening become familiar and easy. Such transactions include sustained make-believe games with and without toys, doing things on request and making requests, telling and hearing endless stories and descriptions of what people did, viewing and showing pictures and other representations, seeing films, and so on. Many objects are purpose-made for encouraging covert tokening.

Presenting a doll or other toy is a way of overtly tokening the perceivings that the real thing would normally occasion. The appropriate response to the presentation is to covertly token (imagine) the relevant perceivings. As Kendall Walton puts it, "dolls, toy trucks, and representational works of art contribute to social imaginative activities by assisting in the coordination of imaginings."[22] For Walton, the raison d'être of toys and pictures is as "props" and "prompters" of imaginings: "Prompters are obviously a boon to collective imaginative activities. A toy truck or a well-executed snowman induces all who see it to imagine approximately the same things—a truck or a man of a certain sort. It coordinates their imaginings. . . . Moreover, it is probably obvious to each participant that the others will imagine what he does."[23] Concerted covert tokening of quite complicated perceptual behavior can be initiated by the showing of pictures. I will discuss the concerting of perceptual behavior, and our response to pictures and other representations, in chapter 6.

Conventional gestures, including facial expressions, are another kind of overt tokening done to elicit covert tokening in response. Many of these conventional gestures are abbreviated mimes—kissing at a distance, shaking one's fist at someone, expressing surprise with one's eyebrows, showing the length of a fish, showing attentiveness or pain. An interesting example is the above-mentioned nod-and-*mmm* of agreement in conversation. This probably is a stylized abbreviation, a mini-tokening, of "what the speaker has just said." With his nod-and-*mmm*, the hearer is saying "I am covertly tokening what you have just overtly tokened and, to prove it, I am ready to repeat your overt tokening back to you, and here's a start. . . ." The nod-and-*mmm* is intended to elicit from the speaker a reciprocal mini-tokening of the hearer's mini-tokening of the speaker's original overt tokening (of whatever it was). So the speaker may nod-and-*mmm* back.

Overt tokenings are "inadequate cues." They "demonstrate" an activity, or "re-present" it. But they do so in drastically abbreviated and/or stylized form. The responder is torn between joining in with the (largely unperformed) activity or inhibiting this impulse. So he does both, in the sense that he commences *and* aborts, that is, "tokens" the activity in question.

Because it is already clear from initiator's performance what activity is being tokened, and because the initiator has no doubt the responder is now covertly tokening this activity, the responder's tokening can stay covert.

We learn to respond, with rapid and sophisticated covert tokening, to overt tokenings of many kinds and to complicated series of them. We concert our covert tokening with the overt tokening the initiator is doing in front of us. This overt tokening may be in the form of a mime or a gesture, or speech, or presentation of a prompter (a toy, a picture, a text, a mathematical formula, a film or television image).

The Notion of "Expressing" Thoughts and Feelings

The adult's covert tokening abilities are exercised more or less constantly, and constitute a permanent backdrop or chorus behind his everyday overt actions. Hampshire remarks, in connection with feelings of emotion, that, although feelings arrive in the repertoire as inhibited versions of emotional displays, children "gradually acquire an inner life of unexpressed feeling, which becomes more and more distinct from their overt behavior."[24] As the child becomes an adult and overt displays of emotion become rarer, "the notion of the mental states that lie behind their behavior and expression, as something distinguishable from them, becomes more and more definitely applicable."[25] Priorities have changed. For everyday practical purposes, the covert tokening, the feeling, is now where the action is as far as emotions are concerned.

This constant covert tokening, or thought, as it were "behind" everyday overt saying and doing, encourages a certain view of how the thinking is related to the saying and the doing. In this view, the inner mental phenomenon is there first. The outer emotional behavior is a product or expression of the inner mental state, and something that may or may not result from it. In this picture, most thoughts and feelings occur without corresponding behavior but, when there is behavior, it is the mental state which has caused and which explains it. The picture is of the mental state as logically primary, with behavior flowing from it (or not).

This popular picture seems to capture well the role of covert tokening (thinking, feeling, etc.) relative to everyday adult behavior. We do lots of covert tokening that is not subsequently actioned. We ready ourselves in a token way for things we never do. And when we do things, the doings are mostly preceded by covert tokenings of them. The popular picture is not so helpful, however, when we are trying to see the relative developmental and logical priorities of covert tokening and behavior. Being convinced by the popular picture makes it difficult to concede or even understand Hampshire's claim that thinking is developmentally and logically derived from doing.

Hampshire puts his claim this way: "The expression of a sentiment or emotion is not something that is extrinsic to the sentiment or emotion itself, as something that may or may not be added to it. On the contrary, that which we call the natural expression is originally constitutive of the sentiment or emotion. . . ."[26] Logically and developmentally, what I call the "covert tokening" of an action is not something that precedes, or is a necessary constituent or precondition of, that action. Rather, it is a special, derivative, covert doing-and-not-doing of the action itself. Our window for seeing the truth of this is small: a year or two in the early life of the child. The view we get through the larger window of adult life—of the thinking "underlying" our actions and our speech—is useful for everyday purposes, and it is appropriate that our colloquial vocabulary for talking about thinking should be geared to this image. However, to see what thinking was originally, hence what it essentially is, we must look through the small window.

5 Derivation of Solo Action from Concerting

If you go off alone into the wilderness you take with you a mind formed in society, and you continue social intercourse in your memory and imagination, or by the aid of books. This, and this only, keeps humanity alive in you, and just insofar as you lose the power of intercourse your mind decays.

—Charles Horton Cooley, *Human Nature and the Social Order*[1]

The Developmental and Logical Roots of Solo Action

In the introduction, while provisionally distinguishing actions and natural processes, I suggested that the concept of performing an action, in the everyday "learned and voluntary personal action" sense, is a social concept. I suggested that the concept of performing an action is inseparable from concepts—such as demonstrating, being-requested-to-do, and being-morally-responsible-for—in which the social, interpersonal relevance is obvious. An action is by definition "that which may be demonstrated" and/or "that which one may be requested to do" and/or "that which one is responsible for." In other words, you don't get "actions" until you have already established institutions of demonstrating-how, requesting, and being personally responsible.

In my account, the institutions of demonstrating, requesting, and taking responsibility all develop out of the concerting procedure. The concerting comes first; the rest are subsequent adaptations of the concerting. The infant's part in concerting is not yet the performing of actions. It is only once the infant has mastered these later modifications of concerting that we can speak of the infant performing actions.

For example, we cannot consider the infant to be performing actions until he is capable of having an action demonstrated to him. In the very first concertings, the mother's contribution is as instinctive and ineffable as the infant's. However, after several weeks, the mother's contributions begin to look like demonstrations of actions she wants the infant to perform. The infant's slavish responses begin to look, correspondingly, more and more like proper actions. Later on, the infant attempts what deserve to be described as demonstrations of actions he wants the mother to imitate.

My point is that the earliest true actions are essentially social, interpersonal gambits; they are plays in games. There has to be a game, such as reciprocal imitation, to create a logical space, as it were, for personal action to inhabit. Educative concerting not only founds the infant's ability to perform actions developmentally (and physiologically), it also generates the social procedures (of demonstrating, requesting, cooperating, etc.) that define what an action logically is. That is, while particular demonstrations define—even "create"—particular actions, and assist the infant to perform them, the institution of demonstrating prescribes what actions are in general; it creates the whole concept of action. It is in at least two senses that educative concerting "enables the infant to perform actions."

I mentioned earlier, in connection with the idea of expressing emotions, that the feeling of emotions is more common and thus of more practical importance in everyday adult affairs than fully overt emotional displaying. Feeling is the paradigm. The overt displaying has come to be thought of as derivative of or logically parasitic on the feeling. It comes about that we are able to construe the overt display only as inner feeling that has been "expressed" or "revealed." However, the fact that feeling has greater cultural importance than overt emoting does not invalidate Hampshire's claim that feelings are developmentally and logically derivative of overt displays.

An analogous situation exists with regard to concerted, as against solo, action. In everyday adult life, solo action is more obvious, more common, more culturally important and more often topical than concerted action. In both everyday and philosophical discourse, solo action is the paradigm of action. It is what we mean by the word *action*. Because solo action effectively monopolizes the word *action*, when we want to talk about concerted action, we cannot help but describe concerting in terms of the putting together, "in concert," of separate acts of individuals. Because *action* immediately implies solo action, we have no way of expressing the primacy of concerting. Yet it remains true that solo action is developmentally and logically derived from concerted action.

Make-Do Concerting

Although we frequently touch base with concerting in small-scale interactions—such as handshakes, kisses and smiles, recreation such as sport or dancing, or running into the surf with one's partner (holding hands and laughing gaily), or in ritual religious or football observance—fully realized concerted activity is not very common in everyday adult life. Far more common, so common it might be said to constitute everyday life, is concerted activity that is compromised in some respect—activity that falls short, in one or more ways, of being fully realized concerted activity. Some accessory thing(s) or person(s) is/are absent, or some contributing action(s) is/are for whatever reason unperformed; yet the participant(s) press on with the activity anyway, making do.

The "doing without" is a matter of continuing with the activity as normally as possible in the absence of a given accessory. Instead of performing that portion of the activity that would have been performed had the absent accessory been present, that portion is merely tokened by the participant(s). For one kind of example, imagine two people playing tennis without a ball. Because they want the exercise, our mock-tennis players overtly token, or mime, hitting the ball. The recipient player anticipates where the ball would have gone with that kind of stroke, and runs there as if in pursuit, and so on.

In other kinds of make-do concerting, covert tokening will suffice. If the missing accessory is a person, say, one covertly tokens the perceptual and interpersonal behavior one would perform were the person present. Though P is absent, one maintains an orientation and readiness for him. One acts *as if* P were present, or in the wings. In one's make-do, compromised performance the covert tokenings substitute for the activity that would have been performed had P been present.

In this chapter, I look at abilities that are fundamental in our everyday lives—solo and solitary action, empathy, and soliciting and engaging in cooperation. I suggest how each of these might have derived, via the kind of making-do process sketched above, from prototype, fully performed concerted activity. Insofar as there is a developmental progression in the abilities I discuss, the progress is from concerted to solo action. The chapter can be taken as a very brief (and unsystematic and impressionistic) sketch of how, and to what extent, the individual becomes an autonomous agent.

Early Solitary Action

Developmentally, concerting is the mother of agency. Being able to join in with teachers' demonstrations of actions, and being able to be guided and helped in other ways to do things, is a necessary condition of being able to do things by oneself.

While alone, the infant attempts activities he has previously engaged in only in with the caregiver. In the following passage, Stern discusses the fact that an infant accustomed to concerted rattle play with the mother will, when solitary, respond to the sight of a rattle with the kind of excitement characteristic of concerted play. The infant imagines the mother to be present and participating with him. The "social episode" or "interaction generalized" Stern refers to below is equivalent to my "familiar concerted activity." In this case the activity is shared rattle play. The deficit in the present situation, which the infant compensates for with covert tokenings, is the absence of the mother. In Stern's terms, the mother is the infant's fellow-participant or "self-regulating other" (the self being regulated is the infant's). The infant's tokening of perceptual and other behavior that would be due were the mother present and participating is what Stern calls the "evoking of a companion":

Evoked companions can also be called into active memory during episodes when the infant is alone but when historically similar episodes involved the presence of a self-regulating other. For instance, if a six-month-old, when alone, encounters a rattle and manages to grasp it and shake it enough so that it makes a sound, the initial pleasure may quickly become extreme delight and exuberance, expressed in smiling, vocalizing, and general body wriggling. The extreme delight and exuberance is not only the result of successful mastery, which may account for the initial pleasure, but also the historical result of similar past moments in the presence of a delight- and exuberance-enhancing (regulating) other. It is partly a social response, but in this instance it occurs in a nonsocial situation. At such moments the initial pleasure born of successful mastery acts as a retrieval cue . . . resulting in an imagined interaction with an evoked companion that includes the shared and mutually induced delight about the successful mastery. It is in this way that an evoked companion serves to add another dimension to the experience, in this case, extra delight and exuberance. So that even if actually alone, the infant is "being with" a self-regulating other in the form of an activated memory of prototypic lived events. The current experience now includes the presence (in or out of awareness) of an evoked companion.[2]

Stern thus begins to make my general point about abstractions from a prototype concerted interaction being compensated for by covert tokenings. How could the infant learn this kind of making-do? One possibility is that no learning is necessary, that the infant's excited rattling when alone is just faux-pas-type overt tokening of concerted rattle play, an abortive attempt at it. Alternatively, the ability to covertly token the mother's being there, or to token any other action or accessory missing from the present situation, is something the infant is taught how to do by the mother. But how could the mother teach the infant to do something in her own absence?

The Teacher Unilaterally Disengaging

It could be that solitary performance derives from concerted performance via a series of intermediate stages in which the teacher progressively decreases her contribution to the proceedings and eventually retires altogether. If a mother is teaching her infant something he eventually needs to be able to do by himself, like eating with a spoon, she will typically begin by demonstrating it, in the special ostentatious, inviting way. When he imitates her, she will continue participating—by continuing to use the spoon herself or by physically assisting his efforts. In either case she will insert speech at strategic points. Thus, the infant's first experience of eating with a spoon is of it qua concerted activity.

Once he has got the hang of the perceptual and motor skills, and some of the accompanying verbals, and is participating enthusiastically, the mother can begin to extricate herself from the proceedings. The disengaging is an ancillary technique, an add-on to the educative concerting itself. During a session, she stops physically helping the infant. Or, if she has been eating with him, she begins miming some of the eating movements rather than actually performing them. Then she just perfunctorily gestures them. Subsequently, she stops making the large movements altogether, but perhaps continues with the speech, using her voice to dramatize the exertions, phases and consummations in the infant's performance. At this stage, she is still very much a party to the proceedings. For one thing, although the performance is no longer, strictly, concerted, she continues to exhibit the excitement characteristic of participation in a concerted performance.

She then withdraws further, by restricting the vocals to an occasional approving noise; and perhaps she smiles when he happens to look up— as he still often will. At this stage she is participating only to the extent that she is still there attending to what he is doing. Concerted activity has become "solo performance for an audience." But the solo perform- ance is still literally a social occasion. The performer still plays to the audience, and the audience, though mostly motionless, still contributes now and then with sympathetic looks, nods and other vestiges or relics of participation.

Finally, the mother/instructor can physically absent herself—at first by withdrawing further and further physically and then, once she is out of sight, staying out for longer and longer periods. Perhaps, she pops back from time to time to check he is still performing well (and is appreciative when he is). Once this is possible, the infant can be said to have mastered not only solo but solitary performance.

This pattern—of the mother teaching an activity in concerted sessions and then unilaterally withdrawing, gradually—could be repeated across a variety of new actions and activities. As a pedagogic strategy, it would eventually streamline and reduce to just one or two demonstrations, with appropriate verbal marking, being followed by a more or less competent solo performance, or deferred imitation, on the child's part. The new skill might have at no stage been exercised in a concerted way, yet its solo per- formance by the child still in some good sense developmentally presup- poses concerted performance. Presumably, the child will for some time accompany his subsequent solitary performances of that action with covert tokenings of (perceivings of) the teacher's original demonstratings and related speech.

Empathy

... our view [is] that the whole nature of intelligence is social to the very core—that this putting of one's self in the places of others, this taking by one's self of their roles or attitudes, is not merely one of the various aspects of intelligence or of intelligent behavior, but is the very essence of its character.

—George Herbert Mead, *Mind, Self and Society*[3]

The infant's solo performances for a progressively withdrawing audience presuppose complementary abilities, on the part of the audience/instructor, to empathize. Empathy is, roughly, attending to the other's behavior and covertly tokening it, while refraining from actually joining in. Spectator empathy thus fulfills the requirements for being a make-do or compromise "form of" concerting. The "concerting" proceeds in a form where the contribution of one of the parties is done without and is substituted for by covert tokening.

As well as being useful in the latter stages of disengaging from educative concerting in the course of teaching infants to perform actions solo, empathy is indispensable elsewhere. Arguably, this particular compromise version of concerted action determines the form of all our awareness of other people and their behavior. The empathic "interested spectator" or would-be fellow-participant mode is our primary heuristic recourse with respect to others' actions. It is our primary means of identifying and understanding what other people are doing. One imagines oneself in the other's position, perceiving the things he is perceiving and performing the actions he is performing. In addition, as part of this imaginative performance, one covertly tokens the verbal aspects of the activity. One "mentally describes to oneself" the action one is looking at. Often, empathizing enables one to anticipate what the other person is going to do next and thus enables one to adjust one's own behavior accordingly.

Perhaps the infant or child learns to empathize by another—this time naturally occurring—kind of gradual withdrawal from a concerting session. For example, the infant might drop out of a recreational concerting session from fatigue, his contribution gradually diminishing, until even the perfunctory overt tokening done to show willing (such as smiling and catching the other's eye) gives way to entirely covert tokening. The infant remains attentive, however. He is still empathizing, still covertly tokening the behavior he would be performing if he were to join in again.

Alternatively, the infant could learn how to empathize by copying what the mother does at the relevant stage of the disengaging-from-educative-concerting procedure. The infant might be able to master the basic principles of disengagement by copying her.

Perhaps it just happens that, while they are side by side eating their breakfasts one morning, he stops eating and looks at her. She is eating her breakfast, using her spoon, just as he does. Then she looks at him, sees what he is doing, and smiles; and he sees her doing this, and smiles. The role of spectator, the practice of empathy, is thus officially concerted, consecrated, by them. Empathy now becomes a recognized action, a thing to do, to be included in their shared repertoire.

Hortation

One of the social practices descended from concerting—one that (I suggested at the beginning of the chapter) provides necessary logical stage-setting for the appearance of individual actions—is the social practice whereby people request other people to do things. This institution may be called "use of imperative speech to get people to do things," or more simply *hortation.*

The *Oxford English Dictionary* calls hortation "the action of exhorting or inciting." We can assume that hortation is by definition verbal. In its customary usage, the term *hortation* relates primarily to solo action of individuals, and only secondarily and on occasion to concerted action. I will abide by this usage. I want *hortation* to cover the case where Q is being verbally incited by P to do something on his own, that is, to solo-perform some action.

We have seen speech used as a marker—that is, as an ostentator and memory aid ancillary to the demonstrating and concerting of actions. And we have seen speech used for invitatory tokening—in the form of an overt verbal inception of concerted activity X—done to induce hearer participation in activity X. Either of these functions would amply justify including the speech skill in the repertoire. However, their usefulness is insignificant compared to the usefulness of hortation. Hortation exploits our enthusiasm for concerting and enables the behavioral technique that has ensured human survival: the trick of verbally expedited (hence subtle, reliable, versatile and rapidly implementable) *cooperation.* As I explain in the next section, cooperation is a derivative of concerting in which—somewhat paradoxically, at first glance—the participants do different things.

The marker and invitatory applications of speech are the developmental precursors of hortation. The marker function makes the invitatory tokening of concerted activity possible, as described earlier, and the invitatory tokening function in turn makes hortation possible. Hortation is a matter of the speaker's using speech to invitingly token an activity but then refraining from participating in the activity herself. In the meantime, the words have done their work and the hearer is off doing what ever it is, on his own. It is a bit like a trick.

Hortation could evolve from educative scenarios in which P successfully verbally tokens a session of concerted X-ing with Q, but then herself desists/refrains from X-ing, so Q is left X-ing on his own. The basics of the hortation transaction are anyway already prepared in the solo-performance and spectator-empathy scenarios above. The child is accustomed to carrying on a performance while the other watches. The hortation itself, the speech—the *Go on, eat your dinner*, or whatever—is the residue of the verbal and other tokens of participation the mother leaves as sops in the course of her retreat into spectator-only.

In a passage quoted in chapter 2, Luria describes a learning situation in which the mother's use of speech seems to be intermediate (and ambiguous) between the vocal marking-out of an action and hortation encouraging the child's performance. In the situation described, a gradual transition—from full concerting with verbal markers, to invitatory (verbal) tokening, to hortation and solo performance—is clearly possible. Luria says that "initially the voluntary act is shared by two people. It begins with the verbal command of the mother and ends with the child's act."[4]

"Solitary" performances are solo performances without an audience. Presumably they constitute a further developmental advance, a further departure from prototype fully realized concerted activity. Whereas the solo performer interacts (albeit sometimes minimally) with an audience such as an instructor or admirer, the solitary performer merely covertly tokens such interaction. The child doing something by himself covertly tokens perceptual behavior and speech such as would be performed were the instructor present. In the passage quoted earlier, Stern links the evoking of a companion to "extreme delight and exuberance, expressed in smiling, vocalizing, and general body wriggling." The older child doing chores as commanded is unlikely to display body-wriggling enthusiasm, but the motivating effect of imagining the instructor to be present remains strong.

Julian Jaynes says that acting on instructions delivered by "inner voices" is the first real evidence of mind. In Jaynes's account, the inner admonitions at first have something of the quality of hallucinations: ". . . the presence of voices which had to be obeyed was the absolute prerequisite to the conscious stage of mind in which it is the self that is responsible and can debate within itself, can order and direct, and . . . the creation of such a self is the product of culture."[5] Jaynes implies, in the phrase "the presence of voices" and elsewhere in his book, that the normal child's covert tokening of others' hortations is an impersonal process, something that happens in the child's head. In my account, the covert tokening of companions and/or advisors and their speech is an action that requires effort and which the child must learn how to perform. The regulating influence the covertly tokened hortations (or "inner voices") have on the child's solitary actions is thus not an impersonal influence, as it were coercing the child. The covert tokening is a method the child employs to ready and to motivate himself.

Cooperation

The everyday term *cooperation* covers such concerted practical activity as lifting a heavy suitcase together, or everyone making a noise to scare the spider away, but it would probably not include concerted activity that is purely formal (like hand-shaking in greeting) or purely recreational (like dancing or wrist-wrestling). For an activity to be cooperative it has to have a practical aim. The *All hands to the pump!* has to be because we are taking on water.

More important, we would probably choose, as paradigm cooperative activity, activity that in one sense is not concerted at all. The paradigm would be two or more parties working together to a common goal but contributing in different ways. The waiter and the cook are engaged in the same enterprise but do different things. They coordinate their actions but do not concert them. Mostly, cooperation implies division of labor. And the divided-labor type of cooperation is what we spend most of our waking lives engaged in.

We could make cooperative activity "concerted" by definition. Job descriptions could remove all divisions of labor in advance. Cook and waiter could be equally "feeding the guests." There is something to be said for this approach but we will learn more if we see division of labor as a real and significant departure from prototype concerting.

Some writers assume that divided-labor cooperation—henceforth just "cooperation"—is developmentally prior to concerting. Certainly, there seem to be examples of spontaneous (in the sense of innately determined) mutual coordination of behavior in the very early mother-infant repertoire and in the behavior of other mammals. I suggest we throw the term *proto-cooperative* over these cases and forget them.

Plausibly, true cooperation, the standard kind of cooperating that people do, is based on mutual understanding. Both parties are aware (however dimly and/or mutely) of the situation-description, goal, methods and rationale, role allocations, etc. And they jointly commit to acting on this joint awareness. In my terms, "mutual understanding" is concerted covert tokening—initiated, and anon refreshed, by overt invitatory tokening.

It would be difficult to prove that all cooperative-looking behavior that occurs after the agents have mastered concerting is true cooperation in this sense. It would be difficult to prove that the participants are concerting their covert tokenings. On the other hand, proving that the earliest mother-infant cooperations do not involve concerted covert tokening would also be difficult.[6] Realistically, we should make acting on a shared understanding a necessary feature of cooperation. Accordingly, we should source cooperation in concerting.

The present-day infant's first participation in truly cooperative undertakings would presumably be fully engineered by the caregiver, with the nature of the infant's contribution being determined by the caregiver's hortations. However, derivation of cooperating from concerting might have taken place prehistorically, among hominids or earlier primates, as an ad hoc adjustment of concerted activity that involved more than three or four participants. Suppose that, in the course of some ongoing concerted activity, one or two individuals are allocated (by hortation) different tasks, the performance of which will increase the efficiency of the activity as a whole. That is, everybody starts off doing the same thing, but the solo performances of certain individuals are then modified, by hortations directed to those individuals, in ways that will more efficiently expedite the concerted activity going on around them. In this picture, cooperation developmentally presupposes hortation. The latter must have already independently evolved from the concerting prototype. Cooperation would result when hortation is mixed back in, as it were, in concerting.

There are, no doubt, several plausible origin scenarios for verbally expedited cooperation. (I prefer the term *verbally expedited* to the internalization theorists' term *verbally mediated*.) The qualifier *verbally expedited* registers the fact that that all these scenarios presuppose hortation. Cooperation is not so much a matter of making-do in the absence of some feature of concerted activity. Rather, it is concerting that is augmented by the addition of complementary solo or solitary action.

Cooperation, and the hortation it involves, is perhaps the most important generative context for solo and solitary action. Most of our adult solo and solitary actions are directly or indirectly cooperative and are performed in response to hortations.

Autonomous Solitary Action

Even after the child is able to respond appropriately to hortations—that is, do what he is told—a further developmental advance is necessary before he is capable of autonomous solitary action. Action in relation to which the child has had no specific instructions is more difficult to perform because here the child's task is not just to remember instructions. The child must self-instruct, must covertly token instructions of his own devising. This is Ryle's "self-teaching" or "thinking" manner of action-performance.[7] The child is able to covertly token actions a teacher might perform. Like Le Penseur, in problem situations "he experimentally applies to himself, just in case they may turn out to be effective, operations of the types that are often or sometimes employed effectively by live teachers upon live pupils."[8] Even though the child—or now, person—is no longer acting on identifiable hortations of identifiable instructors, it is still hortation that he is covertly tokening. However, he has more tokening to do, because he is at an even further remove from concerted doing. In the present problem situation, there are even more deficiencies to be made up for. He may never have been with a teacher in this situation.

Whether bidden or autonomous, solitary action seems to be a large and decisive step away from concerted action. In fact, it seems in many ways the opposite of concerted action. Yet it is a developmental descendant and in a good sense an abbreviated form, or make-do version, of concerted action. At least two components of concerted performance—the other's presence and participation, and corresponding hortations and other verbals—are done without and are perforce covertly tokened.

The category of "other"—Stern's evoked companion or Mead's general-ized other—is flexible. It may be an instructor, a fellow participant, or an empathizing spectator that the agent is imagining to be present. Typically, a child doing anything by himself will be concurrently covertly tokening perceivings and interpersonal responses appropriate to *some* other party to the proceedings. Stern says that "various evoked companions will be almost constant companions in everyday life."[9] The covert tokening of compan-ions, onlookers and interlocutors is inveterate in the solitary portions of adult life too. As Cooley says, "it is as true of adults as of children, that the mind lives in perpetual conversation."[10]

The Motivation for Solo Action

I have speculated about the logical dependence of solo action on contexts of concerted and cooperative action and I have stressed solo action's developmental dependence on educative concerting. It seems that our natural enthusiasm for concerting ensures some inherent motivation even in such vestigial "versions" of concerting as solitary action. The agent's covert tokening of companions regenerates some of the magnetism of actual concerting. The make-believe energizes solo action and keeps us going.

Concerting is *magnetic* in the sense that, from early infancy, seeing P doing X is a powerful natural inducement to join in and do X too. Concerting is also *educative* in that seeing P doing X invites performance of not just the vague motions but the details of action X. Concerting motivates and readies us to do things generally and to do particular things. Even the etiolated make-do forms of concerting typical of everyday adult life—forms in which the participants merely token certain aspects of the activity rather than actually perform them—retain much of the magnetic and educative power of prototype concerted doing. Concerting is the mother ship of our personal lives. Overt and covert tokening are lifelines or fuel lines back, enabling us to venture out on our own.

What Is Learned before What

Presumably, infants and children master the various adaptations of concerted activity I talk about in this chapter and the next. Probably, but not necessarily, the less there is left of full concerting, the more difficult the make-do version is to learn. It is in principle more difficult for the child to perform a given action silently and alone than it is for him to perform the action while overtly tokening it (thinking out loud) or while being instructed how to do it by another person.

I am inclined to think there is a single action-technological and developmental progression, albeit with numerous complications, all the way from prototype concerting—via invitatory tokening, hortation, spectator empathy, solitary action, etc.—to thinking. There are other clear priorities too. Some skills can only be mastered if certain other skills have been mastered first. Visualizing presupposes seeing. Does covert tokening presuppose mastery of overt tokening? It doesn't seem necessary that invitatory tokening be mastered before covert tokening. It isn't clear which is the more sophisticated ability. At any rate, there are separate questions of logical presupposition, relative action-technological sophistication, relative ease or difficulty of mastery, optimum order of learning, and actual developmental chronology. Some are for the philosopher to answer and some are for the developmental psychologist.

The child's mastering of the main meta-actional skills—concerting, overt and covert tokening, solo-performing, etc.—may be orderly or disorderly. However, once they have been mastered, new infra actions may be encountered at any meta-actional level, from "full-blown concerted performance" to "solitary covert tokening." We may imagine doing things we have never done before, and never heard tell of. With regard to many actions, adults and older children need no coaching, nor any hortation (including auto-hortation) nor anticipatory miming, to be capable of solo covert tokenings or even efficient actual solo performances of them. Not every solo action needs preparation in concerted doing. However, probably, the ability to perform actions of a certain general type does, and, as I have been saying, the general ability to solo-perform actions does.

6 Concerted Perceiving and the Tokening of It

The primitive triangle, constituted by two (and typically more than two) creatures reacting in concert to features of the world and to each other's reactions, thus provides the
framework in which thought and language can evolve. Neither thought nor language,
according to this account, can come first, for each requires the other. This presents no
puzzle about priorities: the abilities to speak, perceive and think develop together, gradually. We perceive the world through language, that is, through having language.
—Donald Davidson, "Seeing through language"[1]

In this chapter I illustrate my central thesis—that solo action, speech and
thinking derive by adaptations from the prototype practice of acting in
concert. I use the example of our perceptual abilities. I hope this chapter
will both clarify my claims and show how plausibly they apply to one
important category of actions.

Perception is of considerable interest to philosophers, especially in connection with epistemology—the study of what knowledge is and how we acquire
it—and much has been written about it over the last two thousand years. My
account differs from orthodox philosophical theories of perception. In the
course of the chapter I will say, necessarily very briefly, what the standard line
is on the relevant issues and why I have chosen not to follow it.

Perceiving Is a Kind of Doing

Perceiving things is an activity of the person and not an impersonal process.
Strictly speaking, as Ryle has pointed out, perception is an achievement
rather than an activity, and achievements are not themselves activities; they
are what activities (if they are successful) bring about.[2] However, achievements necessarily imply prior active strivings, and perceptual achievements
are no exception.

The prevailing approach to perception in philosophy and cognitive science is similar to the approach to thinking. Perception is seen as basically an impersonal physiological process, with a few, relatively unimportant, learned and voluntary aspects. The picture is as follows. Perception is the process by which the brain acquires information about reality. Information impinges on the respective sense organs and, transduced into neural pulses, is conveyed into the brain. From this information the brain forms neural representations that model features of the outside world in terms of neuron structures and firings. New representations are processed in various ways and stored. Patricia Churchland and Terrence Sejnowski explain it as follows: "Constrained by transducer output, the brain builds a model of the world it inhabits. That is, brains are world-modelers, and the verifying threads—the minute feed-in points for the brain's voracious intake of world-information—are the neuronal transducers in the various sensory systems."[3] Thus, perception is the process via which the brain automatically "digests" reality using the various sense organs. The brain and the sensory mechanisms are the effective agents of the perceptual process and the person is merely its host or vehicle.

I will argue a general case against attempts to explain actions in physiological terms in chapter 11. As far as perception is concerned, I believe I supply, in the rest of this chapter, sufficient argument and evidence to establish at least a prima facie case that perceiving, and especially visual perceiving, is a learned and voluntary action. I do not deny that perception has some features of, and looks quite like, a natural process. Once the right habits are established, perceiving soon becomes so skilled and rapid as to appear automatic. However, what I wish to argue in this chapter is that perceiving has sufficient of an actional component for (1) concerted perceiving to be possible, for (2) perceivings to be verbally or otherwise "marked" in the same way as other actions are, and for (3) the markers to be subsequently useful in soliciting repetitions of particular concerted perceivings. If perceiving has these actional features, then explanation of the basic facts of perception and of some philosophically important linguistic matters seems relatively straightforward.

A growing number of philosophers and psychologists accept that the person has an active role in initiating and expediting the perceiving process.[4] Mead puts forward the basic idea:

The process of sensing is itself an activity. In the case of vision this is most evidently the case. Here the movement of the eyes, the focusing of the lens, and the adjustment of the lines of vision of the two eyes require a complicated activity which is further complicated by the movements of the eyes which will bring the rays of light coming from all parts of the object upon the center of clearest vision. The process of perceiving an object through the eyes . . . is thus an activity of considerable proportions.[5]

Perception involves a range of small-scale to large-scale behaviors. One recent textbook distinguishes seven different kinds of eye movement employed in visual perceiving other than opening and closing.[6] These kinds of movement include focusing, convergence for distance perception, saccadic scanning, smooth tracking movement, movement compensating for changing body position, and coordinated combinations of the above. Apart from the small-scale, eye-movement-type skills, there are medium-scale skills: squinting, peering, head-turning, etc. And there are also large-scale investigative or heuristic skills—such as putting oneself in a position to see things by manipulating objects, moving to vantage points (or successions of them), conducting experiments, and using measuring devices.

We have to learn how to perceive the things in the world. Perceiving something of a particular type is a particular skill. Different categories of thing—objects, substances, life forms, processes, events, states of affairs, properties of things, geographical features, etc.—must be inspected in different ways. Each category has its characteristic "perception-recipe," and these must be learned. Identifying and inspecting particular things within the categories requires correspondingly more specific perceptual skills. Specific things call for specific perceptual tactics. David Noton and Lawrence Stark demonstrate that people use particular patterns of saccadic eye movement, particular inspection techniques, which are distinctive of what is being viewed.[7]

Researchers classify these patterns of oculomotor saccades as learned, voluntary, motor skills like any other. One learns how to visually inspect or "read" particular scenes and objects as one learns other strategies and tactics of movement. One has to learn how to see a cat, for example, and learn how to recognize when it is on a mat, and when someone is throwing a bucketful of water at it. Even the most basic things in the world must be effortfully visually extracted, one by one. The perceptual tactics we mark by *cat* are different from those we mark *possum*. Those marked *brown cat*, *mother cat*, *angry cat*, and *small animal* are different again. It takes years for a child to learn the techniques required to harvest adult-size crops of things from everyday visual fields, and to do the harvesting with the adult's ease.

Harvey Schiffman says that adequate eye movements take a long time to learn: "Efficient eye movements involve skilled muscle movements that appear to improve with practice."[8] Schiffman concludes that "as with the acquisition of skilled motor habits in general, preschool children have not yet learned efficient oculomotor control and, accordingly, have not yet acquired the specific motor skills necessary to perform effectively. It is reasonable to assume that developing efficient eye movements is a skill acquired gradually, with practice and experience extending well beyond the preschool years."[9]

A case reported by the neurophysiologist Oliver Sacks vividly illustrates the active, learned nature of seeing. A fifty-year-old man, Virgil, who had been blind with cataracts since childhood, had his cataracts successfully surgically removed. Sacks documents Virgil's experiences of learning, painfully and painfully slowly, how to see again, and comments:

One does not see, or sense, or perceive, in isolation—perception is always linked to behavior and movement, to reaching out and exploring the world. It is insufficient to see; one must look as well. Though we have spoken, with Virgil, of a perceptual incapacity, or agnosia, there was, equally, a lack of capacity or impulse to look, to *act* seeing—a lack of visual *behavior*. Von Senden mentions the case of two young children whose eyes had been bandaged from an early age and who, when the bandages were removed at the age of five, showed no reaction to this, showed no looking, and seemed blind. One has the sense that these children, who had built up their worlds with other senses and behaviors, did not know how to *use* their eyes.[10]

Learning New Perceptual Behavior

Because sense-perception is learned so early in life we are very apt to forget that it has to be learned at all; so that we talk of it as though the power to perceive a world of objects were born in us, and that its "immediacy" is an original datum of human experience. This is not so. Perceiving by means of the senses is an acquired skill.
—John Macmurray, *Persons in Relation*[11]

We learn how to perceive things in general, and particular things, by being shown how. Typically, teachers demonstrate new perceptual behavior to infants and young children by ostentatiously picking up the relevant thing, feeling it, turning it over and looking at its various aspects, pointing at parts of it, etc. A certain pattern or recipe of perceivings is being demonstrated. All the time during the demonstration, the teacher marks this perceptual behavior overall, and/or differentially marks the various phases and achievements in it, with attention-attracting vocal sounds.

The teacher might then hand the object to the child and invite him to do the same. The child imitates the sequence of perceptual behaviors as best he can, attempting to duplicate the teacher's way with the object and the vocal sounds she employs. Success is achieved when the perceptual behavior is shared—that is, when it is performed in concert or in close sequence by the parties, along with the correct speech. This is the main way of teaching perceptual skills. As with other abilities, initial grasp is achieved by demonstration and imitation culminating in concerted performance. Adults share perceivings using abbreviated forms of the same procedure.

Eventually, the older child will be equipped with most of the stock heuristic strategies we employ to simplify, order and organize our perceivings. These strategies include, for example, seeing parts in wholes, moving things to reveal other things underneath, moving from one object to another, counting, describing the outline of something, comparing sizes, waiting for an event to follow another, etc., etc. The perceptual moves such inspection strategies involve, along with their customary verbal markers, must be taught. And they are taught by example. However, we are getting ahead of ourselves. Mastery of these strategies for perceiving is quite a sophisticated achievement. We should look first at the beginnings of the perceptual repertoire.

From very early on, mother and infant are all the time embarking on concerted (and reciprocal and cooperative) perceptual behavior. They are all the time giving each other things to look at, palpate, listen to, taste, bite, manipulate, etc. Bruner mentions "the speed with which mother and infant follow each other's line of regard and come to attend jointly to common, concrete foci [and] . . . the mother's tendency to follow the child's line of regard and to comment on what the child is thought to be observing."[12]

Glyn Collis has shown that in many situations mothers constantly monitor their infant's direction of gaze.[13] Tracking the infant's gaze enables a mother to anticipate (and facilitate, or otherwise participate in) what the infant is about to do. And it enables her to vocalize in a way that reinforces the particular attending behavior the child—and now she—is/are engaged in. Bruner reports that although at first it is invariably the mother who takes the lead in joint perceptual activity, she will also encourage the infant to take the lead. For him to be able to do this, the activity must have already become somewhat ritualized:

Typically, mothers then seek to dissociate act from agent, and they follow a surprisingly regular pattern. It consists of dramatizing or idealizing the [perceptual] act itself with some kind of serial marking. Handing the child a desired object, the mother will move it slowly towards him with an accompanying sound increasing in pitch or loudness as it approaches the child, or changing sounds with steps in the approach. Over a period of days this will be repeated as a game, until the child begins to show an anticipatory act, usually at the end of the approach, taking hold of the object rather than having it placed before him. In the process, the agent and the act are being differentiated, attention shifting from the former to the latter. The child next becomes the agent in a reciprocal process of handing the object back to the mother, the mother becoming the recipient of the action.[14]

According to Stern, it is not until the age of 7–9 months that infants first learn to respond appropriately to pointing. They stop looking just at the mother's pointing hand and look in the direction it indicates. "Infants of nine months, however, do more than that," Stern continues. "They not only visually follow the direction of the point but, after reaching the target, look back at the mother and appear to use the feedback from her face to confirm that they have arrived at the intended target. This is now more than a discovery procedure. It is a deliberate attempt to validate whether the joint attention has been achieved, that is, whether the focus of attention is being shared."[15]

George Butterworth found that "infants at 6 or 9 months were as likely to fixate the pointing hand as the designated target. If babies at 6 to 9 months succeeded in fixating the target, they did so in two steps, pausing first at the adult's hand, then alighting on the target, whereas 12-month-old babies looked to the target rapidly and smoothly. Indeed, it has sometimes been noted that mothers go to a great deal of trouble, with exaggerated hand movements, to lead the young infant's gaze from her hand to the target."[16] According to Butterworth, infants are initially unable to identify the target of another's gaze or point unless the other person and the target object are visible simultaneously. In scenarios where they are not visible simultaneously, an infant must learn, with the mother's help, to turn his head in order to find the object in question.[17]

Vocal Marking of Perceptual Behavior

Bruner claims that, as well as the mother following the child's gaze, "at four months the child (given undistracting conditions) also follows the mother's line of regard, and soon after does so more readily when the mother's phonation is of the pattern of such demonstratives as *Oh look!* "[18] Because it is so hugely varied, perceptual behavior, more than any other form of activity, needs to have its varieties, strategies, phases and termini signposted by distinctive vocals—if it is to be standardized for easy concerting.

One way in which speech, as marker, can be integrated into the proceedings is via the variant of educative concerting observed by Papousek and Papousek.[19] The mother begins by disinterestedly imitating the infant—following the infant's gaze and point, and attending where he is attending—but goes on to construe the denouement of this perceptual adventure according to her own agenda. She adds her own "desired outcome," namely, the appropriate speech for that perceptual behavior. She turns the imitation into a demonstration of something she wants the infant to copy.

Ideally, the mother's use of vocals during educative sessions of concerted perceptual behavior should be strictly germane, and be consistent from session to session. R. G. Collingwood doubts whether this is always the case: "When the fact comes out that when a mother points to the fire she probably says 'pretty,' when giving it milk, 'nice,' and when touching its toe, 'this little pig went to market,' the conclusion can only be expressed in the words of a (possibly mythical) schoolmaster: 'parents are the last people in the world who should be allowed to have children.'"[20] No doubt piggy does go to market quite often, but research also shows that mothers do a lot of straightforward and consistent labeling for their infants' benefit. Collis found that, during joint perceiving, much more often than could be due to chance, the mother's vocal was the name of the object the child is (they are both) attending to.[21]

Probably most early sessions of concerted perceptual behavior are a mix of work and play, education and recreation. Bruner reports the following episode, which includes some deliberate attention-directing and naming (of toes) and some associated irrelevant silliness. "During nappy change, child holds toes up in air expecting game. M ostentatiously mouths and nibbles at C's toes. C laughs."[22] Two months later, educative progress—"Toes game has gone on at home. M asks, while drying C after bath, *Where are your toes?* C vocalizes and laughs and holds legs high. M nibbles C's toes as in previous episode."

It is worth reiterating that talk of names and labels is strictly premature in this early context. The case of vocals used to mark perceptual behavior or aspects thereof is no different from the case of vocals or non-vocal gestures used to mark or ostentate any other kind of action or action aspect. That distinctive vocal is still only a ritual element: "something that is done in the course of" this behavior. When mother (and then infant) make the sound *dolly*, say, the concerted behavior in which this particular vocal belongs happens to be "perceptual behavior of the looking-at-the-doll kind." It is this behavior—and also doll-feeding and doll-throwing—that *dolly* is part and parcel of.

How the Relevant Perceptual Behavior Is Identified

When perceptual behavior is being concerted, it is more difficult than when other behavior is being concerted for the parties to observe each other's behavior. Such observation is required if sharing is to be confirmed—with a success signal such as a nod or a smile. There is no problem with the various large and medium-scale behaviors—being in the right place, looking in the right direction, palpating an object to feel its surface, stopping and listening, etc. These are all evident and confirmable. But the small-scale behaviors—eye movements and focusings, ear-cockings, etc.—are usually so subtle as to be unobservable. How can perceptual behavior be concerted in the required mutually aware way?

For the concerting of perceptual behavior there are two essentials. The first is an efficient marking technique (and speech is best). The second is a learning program consisting of the educative concerting of a series of different activities, in all of which the relevant perceptual behavior occurs. How is it, when the caretaker points at a rabbit and says *rabbit* (or *gavagai* perhaps), that the child knows to look at the rabbit per se and not at, say, some part of the rabbit, the chewing motion of the rabbit's jaws or its suitability as game? The answer lies in the combined use of a marker and a series of different activity contexts that have this family of perceptual behaviors (and as little else as possible) in common. Savage-Rumbaugh and her colleagues have extensively researched language learning—of the kind I call "educative concerting with verbal marking"—in apes and children. One kind of routine activity they studied involved the blowing of bubbles:

Given that the ape (or child) is attending to the routine, how does it learn that the caretaker is using the word *bubbles* to refer to the jar and/or the bubbles themselves rather than to the act of puffing air, the taste of the soapy liquid, the opening of the bottle, the many other indeterminate referents in the situation, or even to the whole routine itself? Indeed, how does the child or ape come to acquire the idea that a word such as *bubbles* should refer to anything at all rather than just occurring as a piece of the routine?

Part of the answer to this question is hidden in what happens as segments of the routine are negotiated and marked. For example, after the bubble bottle has been grasped, the caretaker may say "You open the bubbles," thus engaging him in the subroutine of opening, within the larger routine of blowing bubbles. The marker will continue to be repeated in various forms, along with increasingly explicit action guides and aid, until the next event in the routine is performed. By linking the word *bubbles* to the activity of selecting the bottle from other objects *and* to the activity of acting on the bottle to open it, the word *bubbles* comes to be associated with the one element common to both these different action forms.

[In addition, the word *bubbles*] may also be used in other routines such as "hide the bubbles" or "put the bubbles in the bathwater." In all these instances, the single commonality is the word *bubbles* and the bottle of bubbles. Thus, knowledge of specific referents comes, not from a single routine, but from a group of intermeshed routines that have overlapping markers.[23]

What the different routines and subroutines have in common is a certain family of perceptual behaviors. This family is what fractionates out, and is selectively marked by, the persistent *bubbles* vocal across all the relevant routines.

The child is being taught a perceptual-*cum*-verbal ability. As Davidson explains in the following passage, the perceptual component is inextricable from the verbal component. We learn to perceive "in accord with" specific bits of speech.

You are entertaining a visitor from Saturn by trying to teach him to use the word *floor*. You go through the familiar dodges, leading him from floor to floor, pointing and stamping and repeating the word. You prompt him to make experiments, tapping objects tentatively with his tentacle while rewarding his right and wrong tries. You want him to come out knowing that these particular objects or surfaces are floors but also how to tell a floor when one is in sight or touch. The skit you are putting on doesn't *tell* him what he needs to know, but with luck it helps him to learn it.

Should we call this process learning something about the world or learning something about language?[24]

Without verbal markers to identify the common perceptual elements in the different situations we find ourselves in, we would never be able to concert our perceptual activity. We would never know *which* perceptual behavior is to be concerted. The epigraph from Davidson that starts this chapter is worth re-reading here.

Given verbal markers and a varied and rigorous program of educative concertings, our perceptual behaviors become as easily, effectively, and patently concertable as any of our larger, more overt performances. Standardization of perceptual behavior is achieved by the same means as standardization of any behavior—by repetitions and consistent marking. This applies to all the different perceptual recipes required for the various categories of thing—objects, life-forms, substances, qualities, natural processes, actions, etc. Repetition and consistency are also what standardize the speech that distinctively marks each recipe.

Things in the World

When we think about perception, we think of it in terms of perceiving "things," and we think of things as being already there, in reality or in the world, on the model of objects arrayed in a place. We assume that shared perceiving is a matter of one of us pointing out, and our both then looking at, something that is already there awaiting our scrutiny. When we look at something, we assume that it exists independent of our, or anyone's, perceptions of it. Our act of perceiving is quite separate from the thing that is perceived. Perception is the achievement that occurs when, and only when, our perceptual efforts and the thing perceived come into a certain kind of relation. We speak of perceptions being "of" things in reality.

We define what a perception is "of" by pointing, by ostensive definition of the thing in question. However, ostensive definition of a thing is neither more nor less than the successful concerting, by teacher and pupil, of a given bit of perceptual behavior. When we teach someone the name of something, we undertake repeated and varied demonstration-and-imitation sessions, as discussed above. We demonstrate a certain perceptual behavior, and we mark it verbally.

Certainly, perceiving is more than the effortful large-scale and small-scale perceptual behavior of individuals. Over and above the various perceptual task activities, there is a perceptual achievement thereby accomplished. However, the achievement factor in perception is not determined by something (the thing in reality) that exists independent of the perceptual activity and which the perceptual activity is "directed to" or "of." Nor does the perceptual achievement consist in any internal physiological (nor phenomenological) event. Rather, the perceptual achievement is just the successful *concerting*—confirmed by the correct verbal marking—of given perceptual behavior.

The perceptual achievement occurs when, and only when, perceptual behavior is shared or shareable, and an appropriate verbal act is performed or performable as a success signal to register this sharing or shareability. I mean verbal acts such as *There's a dog on the lawn, The anterior dorsal peduncle bifurcates here,* and *It's a Maserati.* The verbal is appropriate and correct if the perceiving is being or could be concerted and that verbal is by convention,"what one says" to mark the concerting of this perceptual behavior. The perceptual achievement is not a relation between a person and a thing in reality, but a relation—of similarity—between perceptual and verbal behavior of one person and (actual or potential) perceptual and verbal behavior of other people.

One reason for doubting that perception is a relation between our perceivings and a thing in reality is the following. Before there can be a relation, there must be (at least) two things for there to be a relation between. Furthermore, the two things must be different. They must be specifiable independent of each other. Thus, if perception is a relation between our perceivings and things in reality, then our perceivings must be specifiable independent of the things they are perceivings of. However, this is not the case. If we are asked to specify what a "peduncle" is, for example, we must fall back ultimately on ostensive definition. That is, we must go through the same, carefully concerted, perceptual behavior we were taken through when we first learned how to use the word *peduncle.* There is no other way of acquainting a person with a thing in the world. All one can do is elicit from the other person the right perceptual behavior and quickly slap verbals on it. To explain the other end of the putative relation, to explain what "perceiving" a peduncle consists of, one must go through the very same demonstration. The question of what thing X is has the same answer as the question of what perceiving X is. In neither case can we, or need we, go beyond demonstrating the concerting of certain perceptual behavior. Perception and thing perceived are not independently specifiable. Hence they are not two different things and cannot be "related."

Another natural inference from the things-out-there-in-reality assumption, with its implied separation of perceivings and things perceived, is that we can know things only via our perceivings of them and hence can never know them immediately or directly. That is, we can never know things in themselves, as they really are, but only as they appear to us. To this extent, the knowledge we receive via our senses, our empirical knowledge, may seem unfounded and/or suspect. However, this impression—of an irremediable dubiety in our perceivings—is an illusion. The skeptic cannot specify what it is that we cannot know about things in the world. On the other hand, the concerting and marking procedure teaches us, for all practical purposes, all there is to know. As Anthony Quinton says, "Our empirical knowledge already has a basis and as good a one as we can obtain. It is to be found, as we should expect, in those situations in which the use of our language is taught and learnt."[25]

Our word *thing* derives from the Old English *þing*, meaning a conclave or assembly convened to discuss something. Essentially, a "þing" is an occasion of concerted attending. My account of perception suggests that the essence of our notion of a "thing" is also the concerting of attention. I am saying that this particular social interaction, the concerting of perceptual behavior, if it is confirmed by the right speech, is all there is to it. A "thing" is just where we both see the same, where our perceiving is concerted. One indication that objective existence is nothing more than concertability of perceivings is our everyday certainty that, if no one else can or could see it, then it isn't really there. As Jean-Paul Sartre puts it, "The other is the veritable guarantee of the object's objectivity."[26]

How Do Things Acquire Their Apparent Independence of Us?

Why is it that we cannot help but think of things as existing independent of our joint perceivings and referrings? Where do we get the idea that things are "out there"? How did we go from þing, the social transaction of concerted perceiving, to "thing," the putative focus or topic of that concerted perceiving? Related questions have been taxing philosophers' wits for millennia and one can but throw up one's hands despondently. It may be relevant, however, that, as children, we participate in vast numbers of perception-sharing sessions and, in these sessions, certain elements stay constant—the ostensive gestures, the pattern of glancing from the thing to the other person and back, the concerting of the perceptual behavior and the speech, and so on. Once this basic recurrent procedural matrix is mastered, we tend to take it for granted and forget about it. We concentrate only on what varies in the different sessions, namely, the nature of the particular perceptual behavior and what its accompanying verbal marker is. What is important in each session, the salient variable, is the new perceptual-verbal juxtaposition to be tried out. That's the thing.

Concentrating on just the perceptual-verbal element, at the expense of the interpersonal procedure that supports it, might be what gives us the impression that the perceptual-verbal element has an existence independent of our actions and activities. This impression might later be cemented in by our habit of taking objects as the paradigm of things. Certainly, objects are a convenient model: they are easy to perceive, several different perceptual tactics are fruitful with respect to them, they are visually circumscribed, they sit still, they persist unchanged, and they are what we cut our perceptual teeth on. We think of objects as constituting the stuff of reality. We fail to see that thinghood, reality or objectivity is contributed not by the special nature of the perception recipes for objects but by the abiding viability of the procedures we have for concerting our perceivings generally.

Thus, perhaps, we concentrate on the content of the variable (the perceptual-verbal element) and forget about the form of the abiding (the concerting context). It does not occur to us that the latter is necessary to the former, that the concerting is the sine qua non of the perception and the words—and of that perception going with those words.

One of the many philosophical positions with respect to "the nature of reality" is *social constructivism*. Roughly, the idea here is that things do exist all right, out there in the world, but only because people put them there. Reality is "socially constructed" by cultures—presumably by people using techniques such as educative concerting. Those things are socially constructed or instated that will best facilitate prevailing practices in the culture. As an alternative to views that make reality God-given or confine it in the mind, social constructivism is valuable. However, the discussion is still couched in terms of "reality" creation, alternative "realities," etc. More desirable, in my view, would be a formulation that concentrated on the social and educative aspects of perception and ignored the unanswerable metaphysical questions about what in general is perceived.

Well, on my account those questions are unanswerable. My account makes things the product (if there is a product) of concerted perceiving. Our techniques for the concerting of perceptions are essentially techniques for isolating and confirming certain perceptions at the expense of others. To refer to something is to single it out, in particular. If reality is the sum of things, or in some sense contains all things, it cannot itself be singled out. What is reality, then, over and above the social practice of concerting perceptions?

Summary

Corresponding to each thing T that we make the acquaintance of, there is a certain menu of perceptual and verbal skills to be acquired. To acquire and exercise these skills requires an interpersonal transaction involving the demonstration and the concerted performance of the relevant perceptual and verbal behavior. The relevant perceptual and verbal skills constitute our knowledge of T. No other kind of knowledge of T is practically or logically possible.

Referring

Within the primordial sharing situation there arises *reference* in its initial nonrepresentational form: child and mother are now beginning to contemplate objects together. . . . Thus, the act of reference emerges not as an individual act, but as a social one.

—Heinz Werner and Bernard Kaplan, *Symbol Formation*[27]

In early childhood our perceptual skills are conformed to a shared standard, and they are disciplined and invigorated, by innumerable sessions of concerted-perceiving-with-vocal-accompaniment—better known as "learning the names of things." As children our desire for such sessions is obsessive. The enthusiasm never really leaves us. We are always engaged in, or readying ourselves for, perception sharing.

After mastering the respondent role in perception sharing, children soon learn the active, initiating role. One important means of tokening concerted perceiving is pointing. Earlier in the chapter we looked at the infant's mastering the passive role in pointing, learning to follow another's point to an object. Now we look at his mastering the active role—pointing things out to others. Vygotsky explains pointing as an abbreviated (commenced and aborted) version of one common way of facilitating joint perceiving—namely, passing an object to, or being passed an object by, another person. This is an important way of sharing visual and tactile perceivings. Pointing betokens the initial action of reaching for the object, which is a necessary preparation for either the act of grasping something in order to hand it on to someone or the act of being handed something and manipulating it.

Passing and being passed objects are both important in the kind of concerted perceptual behavior the infant is familiar with early on. Later, however, actual manipulation of objects is often forgone. Yet pointing is still useful. The person responding to pointing (in its role as a commencement of grasping) has learned to anticipate grasping by attending in the direction of the point. This effect the pointing acquires—getting the other person to attend in a certain direction—comes to be accepted as a satisfying form of shared perceiving in its own right. One can share at least visual perception of something without having to touch it. Vygotsky describes the development as follows:

Initially this gesture is nothing more than an unsuccessful attempt to grasp something, a movement aimed at a certain object which designates forthcoming activity. The child attempts to grasp an object placed beyond his reach; his hands, stretched towards the object, remain poised in the air. His fingers make grasping movements. . . . When the mother comes to the child's aid and realizes his movement indicates something, the situation changes fundamentally. Pointing becomes a gesture for others. The child's unsuccessful attempt engenders a reaction not from the object he seeks but from another person. . . . The grasping movement changes to the act of pointing. As a result of this change, the movement itself is then physically simplified, and what results is the form of pointing that we may call a true gesture.[28]

The infant's learning to attend in the direction of others' pointings is closely followed by or even contemporaneous with his learning to direct others' attention by pointing. According to Stern, "infants begin to point at about nine months of age, though they do so less frequently than mothers do. When they do, their gaze alternates between the target and the mother's face, as when she is pointing, to see if she has joined in to share the attentional focus."[29] Malinda Carpenter and her colleagues confirm this period as the formative one: "Gaze alternation between the object and the adult during pointing is considered an indication that infants are checking to see whether adults are paying attention to their communicative signal. The first instances of points at objects that are accompanied by such gaze alternation occur between 9 and 10½ months of age."[30]

The literature assumes a distinction between "imperative" pointing, where the infant wants to have the object handed to him, and "declarative" pointing, where the infant merely wants the adult to attend to the object.[31] In my view, concerted attending with the infant involves the adult in doing something just as much as handing the thing to the infant would. The distinction between declarative and imperative pointing is really only a distinction between two imperatives: "look at that with me" and "give me that." In Vygotsky's story, "give me that" may anyway be for purposes of joint investigation of the object. In that case, both contexts for pointing would be both imperative and declarative.

As with the vocal marking of other kinds of behavior, the use of an accompanying vocal to ostentate specific perceptual behavior makes possible another practice. This is invitatory tokening—the use of the same vocal to incite the hearer to join in performing the perceptual behavior in question. The bubble-blowing routines Savage-Rumbaugh et al. use in their research on apes and children can be regarded as consisting primarily of concerted perceptual activity. After the preliminary verbal marking of routines and subroutines by the caretaker, the caretaker can proceed to use a marker to initiate sessions of a routine. The ape or child may then also use the marker for this purpose. For the ape, the verbal act consists of its pointing to a *bubbles* lexigram. The learning process is gradual. In the report I quote in chapter 4, the child or ape's preferred means of invitatory tokening progresses from picking up the bubbles bottle and looking at the caretaker, to pointing to the bottle and looking at the caretaker to, finally, saying the word *bubbles* (or pointing at the lexigram) and looking first at the bottle, then at the caretaker.

The invitatory tokening of concerted perceptual behavior, particularly where it is accomplished by speech, can be called *referring*. The verbal involvement is not essential though. Cases where the tokening takes the form of a gesture such as pointing, or mere swiveling of the eyes, can also be described as referring. In my account, referring is the social transaction whereby a speaker, by speaking and/or gesture, draws a hearer's attention to something—so that they may jointly contemplate it. Put another way, referring is invitatory tokening, by speech and/or gesture, done to initiate a concerted performance of certain perceptual behavior. In colloquial terms, verbal referring consists of "saying the name of the thing being referred to." The name is the speech used to mark this perceptual behavior when it is first learned, in educative concerting sessions, and the name is specific to the concerting of this particular perceptual behavior.

Referring reflects all the recreational, practical, and educative functions of concerting mentioned in chapter 3. As I say, children have a mania for having things pointed out to them and for pointing things out to others, for being shown and showing things, and for learning and using names of things. It is a form of recreation for them, and to some extent remains so for us adults. And referring has a practical function. One directs another person's attention to something in the present situation for a variety of practical reasons—to help the other ensure his safety, to assist him to carry out his part in a joint project, etc., etc. There is clearly an important educative role for referring. It initiates the concerted perceivings that teach people the perceptual-*cum*-verbal skills they will or might need in the future.

It could be said that referring's role is primarily educative. Concerted perceiving that is initially recreational will often generate perceptual skills that prove practically useful, sooner or later. That is, recreational referring—*look Mum, there's a crocodile in our swimming pool*—is plausibly educative and practical too.

Absent-Referent Referring

The form of referring that infants first master involves a present and obvious referent thing—that is, something literally at hand and/or immediately visually accessible. Clearly, this basic "present-referent" referring will work only if it is possible to implement the concerted perceiving right away.

However, we can also speak of referring to something when the referent happens to be absent, and unavailable for present scrutiny. In this "absent-referent" version of referring, following utterance of the referring expression, the parties may undertake travel (or other practical heuristic steps) to implement the joint perceivings being tokened. Alternatively, they content themselves with merely covertly tokening, imagining, the appropriate joint perceiving. They rehearse concerted performance of that perceptual behavior "mentally." We can go over this again. In absent-referent referring, the speaker tokens the concerting of given perceptual behavior by saying a thing's name—perhaps with a facial expression and tone of voice that would be appropriate if that thing were present. Since the referent is absent, the perceptual behavior being tokened cannot be performed. The hearer could nevertheless token the relevant perceptual behavior along with the speaker. However, unless there is any doubt about what perceptual behavior the speaker is tokening, the hearer's reciprocal tokening may as well be covert. So the hearer merely "visualizes" or "imagines" what is being referred to. He covertly tokens the perceptual behavior that would have been performable had the thing being referred to actually been present.

The development of absent-referent referring from present-referent referring is a good example of make-do concerting. The participants make do in the absence of some accessory that is necessary for a full concerted performance of the activity. Recall the "tennis" played without the ball. The participants attempt to compensate for the lack of a ball by imagining seeing one flying through the air, imagining what it would do when hit, etc., and playing on as convincingly as possible. In the case of absent-referent referring, the missing accessory is the referent and the participants compensate for its absence by covertly tokening the (currently unperformable) perceptual behavior that would have been performable had the referent been present.

For the child to grasp absent-referent referring, he must have had considerable and varied experience of the prototype present-referent version—just as one would have to be an experienced tennis player to make any kind of fist of tennis without the ball. To be able to engage in absent-referent referring, the child must have mastered both leader and responder roles in the present-referent version. And, of course, not only the game, the þing, must be familiar but also the focus of the specific þing being verbally tokened— the specific perceptual behavior with which that referring expression is associated. With reservations, a child who has previously done no actual perceiving in connection with *family, Darwin, crocodile,* and *swimming pool* will be unable to respond appropriately to *Darwin family find crocodile in swimming pool.*

Absent-referent referring is still a form of concerting. Once they have achieved their purposes of getting the hearer to covertly token the relevant perceptual behavior, the speaker's invitatory tokenings give way to covert tokenings. Absent-referent referring naturally culminates in concerted covert tokening of the relevant perceptual behavior by speaker and hearer. The subtle exchange that verifies and marks successful concerting here is not very different from the mutual success display when the referent is present. When the referent is present, one glances from the referent to the other person in order to confirm the other's direction of gaze and his facial expression. When the referent is absent, there are analogous concerting checks. But the checks are now to confirm whether the other person is doing the right covert tokening. Although there is no referent to ogle ostentatiously or point to, one might gaze into space perhaps, or shut one's eyes, to display one's covert tokening. There is a distinctive eye-on-the-object look and a distinctive tone of voice that it is also customary to affect when the object is in absentia. And you still catch the other person's gaze from time to time and nod or make confirmatory noises. And you concert your facial expressions.

The Usefulness of Absent-Referent Referring

Children and adults willingly subject themselves to extensive and intensive referring sessions. These sessions—in the form of school lessons, stories, descriptions and explanations, gossip, showing of pictures, television viewing, etc.—rely heavily on absent-referent referrings. In these sessions and by other means the child acquires his eventually vast knowledge of things in the world. As I say, such knowledge consists in abilities to perform innumerable different perceptual behaviors and to perform, in conjunction with them, the customary verbal markers-*cum*-inviters.

But what are these abilities useful for? Neither the ability to imagine things on cue nor the ability to direct other people's attention to things that are not there seems on the face of it to be particularly useful. They seem to have little relevance to practical action.

All actions have a perceptual component. Perceptual behavior may be performed relatively "pure"—in educative (heuristic, investigative) activity the main aim of which is the overt or covert rehearsing of given perceptions—or it may be performed in the course of activity that has practical aims. In practical activity, perceiving plays an essential instrumental role, only the perceiving is not the be-all and end-all as it is in educative activity. Though the boundaries are sometimes vague and shifting, a distinction between educative and practical activity, and between the two kinds of context for perceptual behavior they represent, is worth having.

Roughly speaking, the innumerable absent-referent referrings, and the ostensibly idle perceptual rehearsings they involve, are useful because they provide people with the perceptual abilities, and some of the verbal abilities, they will need in the course of future practical actions. The advantage of having a big repertoire of easily biddable perceptual skills—a knowledge of things in the world—is that it makes it easier to perform new or unfamiliar practical actions when these are required. Perceptual behavior learned in educative contexts will often be similar or identical to perceptual behavior required in new practical actions. Because the person has gained, in educative sessions, the ability to covertly token relevant perceptual behavior, he is able, in a situation that calls for the new action, to covertly token, and thus ready himself for, at least the perceptual component of that action. He is well on the way to being able to perform the action. That is, if we already recognize and know our way around certain things, it will be much easier for us to perform new actions involving those things.

The verbal skills acquired in the course of acquiring knowledge of the world have practical relevance too. The referring expressions (names of things, nouns) learned in educative contexts are utilized later in hortations of practical actions, including new practical actions. Because they are already familiar from the educative context, the perceptual components (at least) of the new action can be successfully exhorted. The person who is familiar from the educative context with the things that play parts in the new action, and familiar with their names, is better placed both to exhort others to perform new actions in which these things are accessories.

Theoretically, it would be possible to have a language that consisted entirely of different single vocal sounds (or any other kind of readily producible token), each capable of tokening, and good for exhorting, a different action. The variety of cooperations that could be implemented and expedited by such a language would be limited by the number—presumably some tens of thousands—of different action-token pairs that the would-be cooperators could remember. Hortation of new, unforeseen, and unnamed actions would presumably be impossible.

However, if actions can be separated into perceptual and executive components, and the two kinds of components can be taught and verbally marked separately, the mathematics of combination will greatly reduce the mnemonic burden. By learning thousands of perceptual cues (nouns) along with, say, hundreds of executive or motor cues (verbs), and learning how to combine them to make composite action cues, a player becomes able, with no extra mnemonic effort, to cue many millions of possible actions, including actions never witnessed or imagined before. The only requirement is that the individual perceptual and motor components have been witnessed or imagined before. Perhaps the earliest languages employed "whole action" cues, with undifferentiated perceptual and motor components cued as one. Perhaps preparatory training in the performance and the cueing of perceptual behavior by itself was a later development. Perhaps, in order to enhance our abilities to exhort actions and thus cooperate with one another, we invented the world.

Presenting and Viewing Pictures

Apart from referring, another familiar kind of invitatory tokening of concerted perceiving, with covert tokening of concerted visual perceptual behavior as the customary response, is the activity of showing and being shown pictures. Presenting a picture is a way of invitingly tokening or demonstrating-a-distinctive-sample-of given perceptual behavior. Viewing the picture is in certain respects similar to viewing the picture's subject matter. Certain features of the perceptual behavior are the same. A picture of a man chopping down a tree thus cues the perceptual behavior viewing-a-man-chopping-down-a-tree. But the picture at the same time inhibits that perceptual behavior: a picture constitutes an inadequate cue situation. The viewing of the picture's subject matter cannot be sustained, because the picture is only a piece of paper. Presenting that picture is thus a way of commencing and aborting, or abortively commencing, the perceptual behavior man-chopping-down-a-tree. We might call picture-presenting "graphic tokening."

As viewers, we see the picture and recognize the presentation of it as a way of tokening the perceptual behavior in question. We see the picture and set about performing the man-chopping-down-a-tree perceptual behavior. However, because it is only a picture, we have to immediately abort that perceptual behavior. We end up actually viewing the picture while covertly tokening the viewing of the picture's subject matter. We visualize the man chopping down the tree, and we do the visualizing "through" the picture. Sartre calls a picture the "analogue" of its subject matter and describes what the viewer does as "animating" the analogue.[32]

We learn to respond to this graphic kind of invitatory tokening by tokening the relevant perceptual behavior merely covertly. If the viewer is familiar with pictures of things generally, and with the subject matter of this picture, and it is a good picture, there is no point in the viewer's overtly duplicating the tokening, with speech or another depiction. It can be done covertly.

We say the picture "represents" the thing T that is its subject matter. We could equally say that what is re-presented, or re-enacted, or demonstrated is the act of perceiving (and drawing attention to) T. This representing is being done not by the picture but by the depicter/presenter. It is the depicter/presenter who is drawing attention to T, inviting and initiating joint contemplation of T, demonstrating (for the viewer to imitate) one way of perceiving T, and so on.

For the viewer, a picture of T is a kind of relic of the depicter's act of drawing attention to T by depicting T. The depicter is absent, and the behavior that would be due were he present is perforce covertly tokened. For the depicter, if he is alone, the concerted perceiving scenario is deficient in a different way. He must covertly token, imagine, a specific or generic viewer.

In a fully realized depicting and viewing scenario, a depicter-*cum*-presenter depicts and presents, and perhaps simultaneously comments, while a viewer watches and listens. Of course, such fully realized depicting and viewing is not the same as actual concerted perceiving of the original subject. Perception of the subject is still being tokened only. However, looking at a picture while someone is making it and pointing to parts of it and explaining what they "are"—as with, say, receiving street directions with the aid of a diagram—is less abstract than someone's viewing or making a picture while alone. In the solitary case there is more that is absent. The scenario is further from (notional) fully realized concerted perceiving. Thus, more must be tokened. When one is making or looking at a picture alone, both the original perceivings and the participation of another person (viewer or depicter, as appropriate) must be imagined. To covertly token both perceptual and social components is more sophisticated and more difficult.

The figure of speech called *synecdoche* involves "the mention of a part when the whole is to be understood."[33] Our saying colloquially that the *picture* does the representing is just synecdoche, convenient shorthand, for a scenario—involving any of several kinds and degrees of defalcation from full-blown concerted perceiving—in which a graphic is used to prompt visualizing.

Referring Is Not Literally a Relation between Word and Thing

I say referring is an interpersonal transaction. One person uses speech (and usually other ostensive gestures) to invite and initiate joint perceiving, or joint perceptual imagining, of some referent thing. As a transaction, referring requires the active participation of both speaker and hearer. It involves actions such as gesturing, attending, visualizing, and mutual acknowledging. Philosophers normally reserve the verb *refer*, however, for a putative "semantic" or "meaning" relation between words and things in reality. This relation is thought to exist independent of any activities, such as attention-directing, that people might engage in.

Besides the picture-representing-thing synecdoche, there is in everyday English another familiar and convenient synecdoche whereby words refer to things—with the tongue-in-cheek implication that they do it on their own. This seems a straightforward part-for-whole synecdoche. We pick out just the verbal referring expression from the total referring transaction not because it is the only effective component but because it (along with the perceptual behavior) is the element that is distinctive to that particular referring transaction. The verbal component, yoked to those perceivings, is the salient variable. Thus, colloquially, it is the word that refers to the thing—and not the speaker who does it, nor the speaker and the hearer together.

In view of this fact of colloquial English usage, the philosophical usage whereby words literally refer to things might have to be attributed to what the *Shorter Oxford Dictionary* calls synecdochism. *Synecdochism* is an anthropologist's term for a certain kind of superstition: a "belief or practice in which a part of an object or person [or activity] is taken as equivalent to the whole, so that anything done to, or by means of, the part is held to take effect upon, or have the effect of, the whole."

Solo Perceiving, Solo Imagining, and Consciousness

Solo Perceiving

At least part of the everyday notion of "thing" is captured in the notion of topic or focus of joint attention. I have mentioned the derivation of *thing* from the Old English *þing*, meaning "conclave." At any rate, there is something in one's solitary perception of things of an ersatz or would-be social occasion. I say solitary perceiving is an incomplete, make-do version of concerted perceiving—with the absent accessories having to be covertly tokened.

The prototype form of concerted perceiving—fully rigged out with participants, speech, ostensive gestures, and actually performed concerted perceptual behavior—is "successful present-referent referring." In absent-referent referring, the speech—the referring expression, along with appropriate tones of voice and token ostensive gestures—is actually performed while the perceptual behavior is merely covertly tokened. There is no perceiving, hence no concerted perceiving, but the other party to the referring is still present and the covert tokening of the relevant perceivings is still done in concert.

During solitary perception the perceptual behavior is performed all right, because the referent thing is actually present; however, it cannot be done in concert with anyone, because the perceiver is alone. Speech and supplementary ostensive gestures are pointless, because there is no one's attention to direct, and so they are forgone too. It takes children a while to stop talking out loud—to themselves as it were—when they are doing things by themselves. They learn to do without this egocentric speech and to refrain from abortively commencing invitatory showing. They learn to substitute mere covert tokening of the speech and the showing. Just as silent reading is a developmental advance on reading out loud, so perceiving alone and silently—while covertly tokening the usual accessories—is more sophisticated than being referred to things by, or referring things to, someone else.

The extensive practice we get in both present-referent and absent-referent referring disciplines our perceptual behavior—conforms it to standard recipes and makes it biddable and physiologically robust. Good grounding in concerted perceiving allows us to "go solo" with confidence. In turn, one's covert tokenings of a referring, attention-sharing context for one's solitary perceivings serve to keep alive one's aptitude and enthusiasm for telling people things. Sometimes, when alone and surprised by something, one turns to share like a child, unmindful that no one else is present. But in the main we do the minimum. The minimum is perfunctory covert tokening of a fellow perceiver and/or an appropriate referring expression and/or ostensive gestures. This token concerting, this conjuring of a companion, of a þing, emboldens our perceiving.

Besides such motivational and maintenance functions, the covert tokening of a social context for our perceivings has other functions. The individual out perceiving by himself is acting as the representative or agent of actual or potential conclaves. Without the possibility of some þing for the individual to represent, any solo perceiving he does will not count, so to speak. With no possibility of sharing and confirming it, it would cease to be *perceiving* at all. The perceptual training we undergo in childhood earns us a license to perceive on our own. But a condition of the license is that we must always be ready to report back to the group. One's solo perceptions are, in essence, incipient "reports back" already. They are readyings of one-self to report back. Our inevitable construal of our perceptions as percep-tions "of things" shows this. Things are by definition public. *There* just means "amenable to concerted scrutiny."

Maybe only people can perceive things. Looking at animal behavior, it is difficult not to believe they perceive things much as we do. But in my story it is only to the extent that a creature can refer its fellows to things, and per-ceive in concert with them—as we do, exchanging glances in the process—and only to the extent that it can, during solo perceivings, covertly token the concerting of them, that it can be said to perceive things.

Solo Imagining

Sartre describes imagining in terms of progressive abstractions from seeing. After describing looking at a picture as "animating an analogue" of the thing represented, he cites as an intermediate example the case of inter-preting a vague splotch on wallpaper as something—a face, say. Visualizing, he says, is doing the same thing on a featureless wall or with one's eyes closed.[34] The idea of a continuum of cases, with progressively extensive compensation for increasing defalcations, accords with my account. But whereas Sartre explains imagining as a vestige of graphic representing, I explain it in terms of abstractions from concerted perceiving generally—whatever the tokening medium happens to be.

We have looked at absent-referent referring, in which speaker and refer-ring expression are present but the referent and actual perceptual behav-ior are done without. And we have looked at solo perceiving, where perceiving is done in the absence of a fellow perceiver/interlocutor. Solo imagining is what results when "concerted perceiving" is persisted with in the absence of just about every element of it—the other party, the osten-sive gestures and speech, and the perceptual behavior. Well, it is no longer a matter of persisting with or making do. In solo imagining, concerted perceiving is in no sense being actually performed. Visualizing is not a kind of seeing, let alone concerted seeing, any more than tennis without the ball is tennis. Solo imagining is the solo, covert commencing and aborting, or "tokening," of concerted perceptual behavior. Rather than being a kind or version of concerted perceiving, it is a substitute for it. Imagining, like solo perceiving, is merely a way of readying oneself for concerted perceiving.

Consciousness

The individual's solo perceivings and imaginings of things in the world are, for philosophers at least, the stuff of consciousness. Alone, one is nevertheless "conscious" of things around one. George Butterworth tells us the following about the word *consciousness*:

Originally the word derives from the Latin *con*, meaning "together with" and *scire* meaning "to know." In the original Latin the verb *conscire* (from which came the adjective *conscius*) meant literally to share knowledge with other people. In time the circle with whom the knowledge was shared became tighter and tighter until it included just a single person, the subject who was conscious. That is, consciousness shifted from being a matter of public knowledge to being one of private knowledge.[35]

If we substitute *perception* for *knowledge*, we can see that Butterworth's notion of a gradually tightening ring of confidants has connections to my story—and to Sartre's and the abbreviationists'. Perhaps the original application of the verb *conscire* was to shared attending and, subsequently, the verb was also applied to the "abbreviated"—that is, covertly tokened—shared attending that is all the solitary individual can essay.

The prevailing philosophical opinion is that consciousness is (a) an endowment of evolution and our genes and (b) a direct function or product of brain processes. In contrast, I claim that consciousness is not a biological but a cultural product. Consciousness can plausibly be equated with perceptual, cognitive and linguistic ability on the individual's part. In my account, the matrix from which consciousness develops is concerted activity. Like solo practical action, empathy, and communication by speech, solo consciousness develops, over a period of several years, as the infant and then the child masters various techniques for making do in the absence of (and/or readying himself for) occasions of actual concerting. Ability to imitate may be biologically given. However, it takes, apparently, six or eight weeks, and lots of encouragement on the caregiver's part, before true, mutual concerting appears. Consciousness is not biologically given but learned.

Granted, if imitation is innate, we are biologically endowed with ability to learn concerting. It is hard to know whether the caregiver's obsessive counter-imitatings and burblings, which are crucial in the very early stages, are biologically prescribed themselves, or whether they constitute a cultural intervention. At any rate, there is no doubt that deliberately brought about concerted perceiving and speech, both of which are necessary for the development of solo consciousness, are cultural interventions.

If concerting is the matrix from which consciousness emerges, it is in this sense the original form of consciousness. We customarily think of solo consciousness as something autonomous and sui generis. But I am saying that solo consciousness is in reality an incomplete, solo-ized, diminished version of shared consciousness. Shared consciousness is always *concerted doing* of some kind.

Consciousness is only allowed out on its own—it can only be exercised in isolation from concerted performance—on a conditional basis. If it doesn't get home in time (if one does not sooner or later realize one's solo consciousness in a shared performance), then one's "consciousness" evaporates. When, by catching the café owner's eye and raising a finger in a certain way, P gets the cost of the lunch put on her account, she has in one sense avoided paying for lunch—although in another sense she has not. It is only in the sense that P has lunched without paying that consciousness can occur without concerted activity. Essentially, as raising the finger *is* paying, so consciousness *is* concert.

Apart from one or two unusual features, thinking is an ordinary learned and voluntary action of the person. One unusual feature is the frequency, or constancy, with which we think. We engage in thinking of one kind or another practically all our waking hours and even intermittently while we sleep. Another unusual feature of thinking is its physical subtlety. The movements this activity involves are often (although not always) so attenuated and inconspicuous as to be difficult or impossible to observe. Along with the adjective *subtle* I use *covert*, but the latter should not be taken to imply there is anything literally hidden about thinking. The idea of thinking going on in a sequestered location is only a metaphor. It's just that the movements the person is making are often too small to be observable. Certainly, there can be an element of secretiveness about thinking—but only in the sense that, in certain circumstances, a person might choose to just think something rather than say it out loud. A thinker deliberately refrains from—he merely *readies*—speech and/or other behavior.

Paradigmatic Self-Educative Thinking

A useful preliminary description of thinking of the classic Penseur type might be "the covert commencing and aborting of the speech-mediated educative concerting of some activity." In this reflective, problem-solving thinking, what the thinker is covertly tokening (or attempting to token) is the educative concerting of some activity with which he is having difficulty. In an attempt to ready himself for action, the thinker is imaginatively re-convening an educative scenario like those in which he has learned similar actions in the past. The scenario will involve demonstration and imitation of the action, and verbal and other marking of important phases and junctures in it. In order to ready himself for X-ing, the thinker is imagining giving and/or receiving a lesson in X-ing. Or he is imagining participating in a discussion about X-ing. And so on.

In thinking, one does not normally covertly token—imagine, conjure up—all the elements in an educative concerting session. One might imagine the speech, say, or the presence of an interlocutor, or certain relevant bodily movements, or the perceivings the activity would involve—or some combination of these. The fragmentary nature of our covert tokenings of educative activity is due to the fact that, when we think, we naturally spend more effort on (covertly) tokening some aspects of the lesson than we spend on tokening other aspects. The aim of thinking, and of covert tokening generally, is to ready oneself for action. If a very perfunctory effort will achieve the required readiness, then a very perfunctory effort is all that will be expended. Depending on what aspects of the activity we most need priming on, some parts of the imagined lesson will be concentrated on at the expense of others. The background tokenings are normally, and properly, so cursory as to be unconscious. For reasons I will discuss shortly, most of the effort in thinking goes into the covert tokening of the speech component.

I said in chapter 5 that most of our adult experience of concerted activity—educative, recreational, or practical—is of compromised versions in which solo performances (with or without an audience) stand in for concerted performances and/or in which much of the activity is merely overtly and/or covertly tokened rather than fully performed. An alternative explanation of the fragmentary nature of the thinker's imaginings of educative contexts is that the contexts the thinker imagines in his solitary thinkings are more like the ones he might experience in everyday situations than they are like ideal, full-blown prototype educative concerting. The educative scenarios we imagine in our thinking are like life: compromised by absences and other defalcations and makings-do.

The educative context the reflective thinker covertly tokens might approximate any of a number of kinds. It could be a lesson, an investigation, an experiment, a demonstration of action, a shared perceiving, a depicting or other representing of something, a description, a debate, or an interrogation. Perhaps most often, the educative transaction we covertly token in our thinking is a conversation or a discussion. Piaget thinks it is always some kind of public truth-finding procedure, involving presentation of evidence and persuasion:

The adult, even in his most personal and private occupation, . . . thinks socially, has continually in his mind's eye his collaborators or opponents, actual or eventual, at any rate members of his own profession to whom sooner or later he will announce the results of his labors. This mental picture pursues him throughout his task. The task itself is henceforth socialized at almost every stage of its development. . . . The need for checking and demonstrating calls into being an inner speech addressed throughout to a hypothetical opponent whom the imagination often pictures as one of flesh and blood. When, therefore the adult is brought face to face with his fellow beings, what he announces to them is something already socially elaborated and therefore roughly adapted to his audience.[1]

In the same vein, Hampshire envisages argument and debate in the minds of legal and diplomatic professionals:

Discussions in the inner forum of an individual mind naturally duplicate in form and structure the public adversarial discussions. "Naturally," because advocates, judges, and diplomats rehearse what they are to say before they step on to the public stage. Anyone who participates in a cabinet discussion, in a law court, in a diplomatic negotiation, acquires the habit of preparing for rebuttal by opponents. He acquires the habit of balanced adversary thinking. The public situations that I have mentioned give rise to corresponding mental processes which are modeled on the public procedures, as a shadowy movement on a ceiling is modeled on an original physical movement on the floor.[2]

In thinking that isn't so difficult and isn't bent to problem-solving—if it's more like musing, say—the educative aspect fades. But it is still a social interaction that is being tokened. Plato's description, "the soul conversing with herself," economically points up the fact that (usually) in thinking there is no one else actually present and there is no actual talking, yet there is still in some sense a "conversation" going on. However, Plato's expression *with herself* falsely implies that conversation may be a solo undertaking. One cannot literally address oneself. The imagined interlocutor is necessarily someone else—which is not to say that the someone else is anyone in particular. Where the job of internal instructor or interlocutor cannot be assigned to a known individual (say, a friend or a parent), or to "colleagues" (as in the Piaget and Hampshire examples), we might press Stern's "evoked companion" or Mead's "generalized other" into service.

Second-Order Tokening

The higher mental activities—conception and purpose, memory and imagination, belief and thought—so far as these are distinctively human, are found to be closely dependent on speech. They are fundamentally social in origin, being due indirectly to the development of *conversation*, which . . . has the primitive function of preparing for concerted group action. . . .

—Grace de Laguna, *Speech: Its Function and Development*[3]

Language is, in a sense, . . . "meta-action." In this sense, language is behavior about behavior. It is used to determine what "we" are going to do next, in a constantly changing stream of events that are only partly predictable. Without language, any single individual can determine autonomously what he will do next, and if the behavior of individuals do not need to be coordinated, the decisions of single individuals are sufficient. However, when behaviors must be coordinated—and they must when any two individuals are going to interact by exchanging patterns of action— communication about this coordination must take place before the intertwined actions themselves occur. . . .

—E. Sue Savage-Rumbaugh, Stuart Shanker, and Talbot Taylor, *Apes, Language and the Human Mind*[4]

Many cognitive scientists believe that the brain creates neural and/or mental representations of external reality and that these representations are primarily linguistic—that their medium is a "language of thought" or "mentalese." Variants of Vygotsky's "inner speech" or Skinner's "covert verbal behavior" have provided the basis for many accounts of thinking by philosophers and psychologists. The layperson has the notion also that, although we sometimes think "in pictures," we mostly think "in words." Is there any chance that we can get past these various metaphors and move toward a literal explanation of how speech is involved in thinking?

I have insisted that speech is a bound radical in certain interpersonal communicative transactions. Speech is originally the verbal invitatory tokening of concerted activity. Later it also serves to initiate the concerted covert tokening of concerted activity. In either role, speech in isolation from its transactional context is nothing. Speech is an essentially interpersonal and cooperative ploy. The problem with explaining thinking in terms of "inner speech" or "linguistic representations in the brain" is a problem that theories of thinking as internalized social activity leave conspicuously unsolved. How it is possible for the lone individual to "perform in abbreviated form" or "internalize" an activity that requires the participation of other people? How can you solo-ize, let alone covertize, speech? How can any kind of social interaction be rehearsed by an individual?

Human beings have opted for a survival strategy based on concerting and cooperation, and in a big way. It is mostly true that any action by an individual will involve others in some way. Even if the active cooperation of others is not required for the success of personal action, their informed consent, their passive cooperation, probably is required. The individual must take others with him, abide by the law, not tread on toes, make use of public institutions, do the customary thing, and so on.

Animals engaged in solitary activity—a lion stalking a zebra, a hyena waiting—are able to ready their own behavior by covert tokening. They can take advantage of the self-readying trick. But it looks as if humans cannot. By opting for the advantages of concerted and cooperative action, humans seem to have denied themselves access to the equal boon of action-readying by covert tokening. Cooperation is something only groups can do, and covert self-readying is something only individuals can do. Without telepathy, or without something like Sheldrake's "morphic resonance" to coordinate, ready, and trigger joint action, it seems we are stymied. Well, to some extent we are stymied. But we have found a compromise solution.

As Savage-Rumbaugh et al. explain in the passage that appears as the second epigraph to this section, joint action—in fact any, even individual, action in a social context—requires preparatory communication, preparatory "educative sessions." The primary function of educative sessions is to ready would-be participants in a goal activity for their participation. They may involve perceptual and verbal education, skills practice, persuasion, hortation, rule setting, role allocation, empirical research, and debate as to method. The prime means of readying the participants are demonstration and overt tokening. The overt tokening is by speech and/or graphic and/or gestures and body language, but primarily speech.

Educative sessions work. By overtly tokening an activity to an audience of would-be participants, leaders can get the would-be participants to covertly token, and thus ready themselves for, their parts in the activity. The readying is done beforehand and in concert. Overt tokening is socially effective. Unlike covert tokening, it does influence other people—and is thus capable of readying concerted and cooperative activity. However, it is not quite as good as morphic resonance. Educative sessions are cumbersome. They require people to assemble. And overt tokening lacks the speed, the versatility, and the creativity of private, covert tokening.

An individual can enable and ready some cooperative goal activity—and thus enable and ready his own actions in contribution to that activity—by convening and leading an educative session. For individuals content to play a follower role in educative sessions, the problem is solved. Their covert tokenings and action-readyings are enabled (and hence their goal activity is enabled) by the educative sessions. However, their readying problem is solved only by giving it to others, namely the conveners and leaders of educative sessions.

People have a great proclivity for assembling and talking, and we can grant that the logistics of educative sessions are manageable. The problem is still loitering somewhere, but not there. Now the specifics of the educative session—the specific teaching, planning, and negotiating—make up the hard part. How is the educative activity itself readied? Not by another, meta-educative session. At this point, the power of covert tokening is required. The specific content of the public session has to be privately readied. Someone has to "think things out" beforehand.

Thinking is the covert tokening, hence readying, by individuals of the overt tokenings that will feature in educative sessions. This notion is captured in a slightly extended version of the de Laguna passage I quoted in chapter 2:

The form of conversation from which thought springs is the discussion, which has for its end agreement among the participants regarding some specific conditions of common action. . . .

Thinking is the internalization of this form of conversation and its independent practicing by the individual. This is originally and primarily a rehearsal in direct preparation for his active participation in the social enterprise of discussion. It serves also, though more indirectly . . . as a preparation for his own individual primary action.[5]

However, educative sessions and the overt tokening (the speech) they involve are interpersonal affairs too. How can an individual ready them any more than he can ready the joint activity that was the original goal? The answer gets us close to seeing why and how speech plays the integral role in thinking it does play.

The movable feast of educative sessions in our lives, the constant invitatory and hortative verbal tokening, has two crucial effects. It standardizes, and it greatly intensifies, the action-readying power of the verbal tokening repertoire, the language. The effect of the original marking function of speech is to standardize—to concert the substance and the detail of—our perceptual and other behavior. The language travels to every part of our community and to every part of our repertoire and is a constant insisting force to which we adjust. Our lives are regulated and regimented by speech. One's repertoire is organized under verbal headings. Speech tracks our every move, captures it, and puts a handle on it so our fellows and betters can drag or push us as they think fit. And we adjust to language, we use and respond to it, with pleasure, since it is a certain and abundant source of concerting.

Actions flagged and cued by speech are standardized across the community. Speech reliably elicits from its hearers the covert tokening, and thus readying, of specific perceptual and other activity. Verbal tokening becomes an extremely easy and efficient method of inducing precise action-readinesses in people. Speech is also very easy to covertly token. The muscular activity required to produce speech is already quite subtle and complex. Subtlety and complexity lend themselves to covert commencing and aborting.

The cumulative effect of all this is to make it possible for the individual to think—to covertly token the hard part of an educative session—with some chance of success. If language is thoroughly entrenched in the community repertoire, if the thinker is fully familiar with the language, and if educative sessions are easy to convene, all the thinker need do to ready a useful contribution to an educative session is covertly rehearse the appropriate speech. The tokening power the community has granted to speech ensures that that speech will efficiently bring about corresponding action-readiness in the hearers.

Although the thinker still cannot ready the others for the goal activity directly, he can efficiently and reliably ready himself to ready the others. Language enables him to do this part of educative-session-readying by himself. And he can exploit all the speed and versatility of covert tokening in doing so. Thus the human strategy turns out to be viable after all. Second-order tokening—the covert tokening of overt tokenings—enables the huge benefits of concert and cooperation and covert tokening to be combined. Language and thinking exploit each other. The benefits of both tokening techniques are optimized.

In the above sketch I have, for convenience, imagined a clear difference between people who conceive and actively contribute to educative sessions and those who merely benefit from them (or get bossed around in them). However, in any reasonably healthy group, educative sessions will be characterized by a democratic alternation of leader and follower roles. Educative sessions should exploit the covert tokenings of a variety of individuals. I also imply that nearly all thinking is done before the educative session. This is also exaggeration or plain falsehood. Many people think best in the thick of actual speech. There is often, and there should be, a productive interplay of covert and overt tokening in educative sessions, each prompting the other to new vantage points. Finally, most of my discussion earlier in the book has concerned the thinker who is readying himself for some goal activity. In this section I have concentrated on thinking that is designed to ready the thinker to ready others. However, as I have also indicated in this section, readying oneself and readying others are largely interdependent too.

Other Varieties of Thinking

By selecting solitary, silent, and motionless thinking as the paradigm of thinking, I am conceding that the label *thinking* sticks best on performances that involve nothing but covert tokening. This is thinking one does lying in the dark alone, or when with others but paying no mind to them. One is in another world, absorbed in one's thinking, as Le Penseur is. It is not just some accessory to or portion of a social transaction, not just some fraction of the action, that is missing and is being covertly tokened; it is the whole show.

Potential Contributions to an Existing Social Situation

We also use the word *thinking*, albeit perhaps in a derivative sense, to cater for covert tokenings that are less than comprehensive—that compensate for defalcations of personnel, setting, and/or behavior that are merely partial. That is, *thinking* is sometimes used to refer to covert tokenings done to compensate for the lacks and omissions in the make-do concertings described in chapter 5. During a conversation, one "thinks about" the thing one's interlocutor is talking about or one "thinks of saying" such-and-such. When reading, one "thinks about" what one is reading. On the telephone, one "imagines" the smile of the person on the other end. Seeing the empty shoes "reminds" one of the person who usually wears them. At the politician's dinner party you catch yourself "thinking" *If my daddy could see me now*. . . . In these cases, some social transaction short of concerting is under way, and we use the term *thinking* to describe our covert tokening of potential contributions to it.

Perhaps most commonly, one is a participant or an interested spectator in a conversation or some other speech-dominated transaction and one's "thoughts" are covert tokenings of potential speech acts. They are bits of speech one keeps to oneself. Almost any reasonably brief speech act may be covertly tokened in such contexts, and it may merit being called a thought: *Uncommon civil, I'm sure. Oh, yes please!, Someone will give him a ride home, surely. One more comment like that and I'll.* . . . Incipient non-verbal contributions to prevailing transactions can also qualify as thoughts. One might "think of" blowing someone a kiss, or going over to talk.

Thinking What One Is Doing
Thinking what one is doing is also, plausibly, a variety of thinking. Here too the thinking consists of one's covert tokenings of activity components that are missing from the present situation but which would be present in a full concerted session of the activity. As was mentioned in chapter 5, if one is doing something on one's own, one often covertly tokens, during and ancillary to one's actual performance, the giving or receiving of admonitions, commentary, or explanation concerning that performance. Where one is acting on explicit instructions, the thinking accompaniment may well consist of an imaginative reprise of conferrings and instructings that have actually been performed. One may even recollect tones of voice. On the other hand, if one is acting on one's own initiative, the thinking may consist of the covert tokening of instructions of one's own devising, and thus be more demanding.

Thinking what one is doing in this sense—that is, covertly tokening some form of educative context for one's present solitary performance—is equivalent to being "self-aware" in action. Being self-aware in the performance of some action is nothing more or less than doing this—this overlaying or enriching of one's performance with a covertly tokened self-educative commentary. As Ryle might put it, one affects a certain more attentive and "thinking" style of action-performance. This aware mode of action-performance, this covert self-educative tokening while you work, is one variety of consciousness. It is "self-awareness." It is our doing something, and/or our manner of doing something, that is being talked about here: the terms *consciousness* and *self-awareness* too easily prompt fancies of lights going on in the brain.

Thinking Out Loud

Another thing we do is "think out loud." This kind of tokening, which both Vygotsky and Piaget call egocentric speech, is often done in the same context as, and is then arguably an example of, thinking what one is doing. However, it is also often done by a person apropos of no current overt undertaking. It is perhaps not so much a special kind or variety of thinking as an immature or clumsy way of doing ordinary thinking. At any rate, thinking out loud is another example of thinking that is characterized by overt doings. Vygotsky places egocentric speech—which is usually fragmentary, elisive, garbled and gabbled, or whispered—well down the developmental road toward the "silent" speech that is, for Vygotsky, bona fide thinking. During play and problem-solving, the child learns to rely less and less on instructions from others and on audible self-instruction, and learns to instead covertly token the relevant instructions.

Daydreaming

Another category of deviants from Rodin's paradigm are thinkings in which the covertly tokened concerting is not so much self-educative as recreational or simply idle. Ryle's adverbial theory emphasizes the self-educative, intent, investigative nature of Le Penseur's thinking, but Ryle concedes that idle reverie is thinking too:

> The title "thinking" is not reserved for the labors of trying to decide things. I am thinking if I am going over, in my head, the fortunes of the heroine of a novel that I have been reading; or if I am re-savoring a well turned argument, though I have long since accepted its conclusion. Or if I am drifting in idle reverie from one topic to another. Only some thinking is excogitation; only some thinking is work. . . .[6]

In the reverie cases, the conversation being covertly tokened is no kind of practical, purposeful discussing; it is more like passing the time of day, gossiping, boasting, or showing someone something just for fun. The ulterior communicative transaction is neither instructive nor hortative, and the covert tokening of it is not done self-readyingly, in preparation for an actual performance. Rather, it is done in lieu of actual communicating, actual sharing, as a substitute pleasure. What is covertly tokened is what the thinker would like to say or hear were a suitable interlocutor present.

Imagining, Remembering, Intending, Hoping, Believing, Desiring, . . .

From the beginning I have contemplated a considerable range of actions and activities as representative of thinking—not only the variations mentioned above, but also the various things Le Penseur might be doing (cogitating, pondering, musing, reflecting, meditating, ruminating, anticipating, doing mental arithmetic, making decisions or imagining, visualizing, remembering, intending, conceiving) and such closely related actions and actional states as perceiving, believing, knowing, hoping, feeling emotion, being conscious of something, empathizing, observing what someone else is doing, and following what someone is saying. My claim is that underlying all the above named varieties is one species of activity: the covert token performance of the speech-assisted educative concerting of some activity.

What distinguishes the individual varieties of thinking is, essentially, the nature of the activity the thinker is covertly tokening an educative session of. What is distinctive about remembering or visualizing, for example, is the kind of action the thinker is covertly readying himself to perform.

In "remembering," what is being covertly tokened is a description (and possibly a demonstration or other re-enactment) of an action done in the past. To "intend" to X is to covertly token (a) promising that one is going to X at some future time and to covertly token (b) X-ing at that future time. With intending, the future X-ing is necessarily imagined as witnessed and public.

To "feel emotion" is to token the performance of some demonstrative and speech-accompanied, possibly stylized and/or abbreviated, public display of grief (aggression, love, solicitude, admiration) or some other expressive behavior. And one would normally also covertly token appropriately sympathetic responses on an audience's part.

To "visualize" thing T is to covertly token certain visual perceptual behavior. Typically, one imagines the visual behavior as being performed with someone, to whom one imagines showing, pointing out, referring to, or describing features of T. Or visualizing is the covert tokening of the act of depicting T for someone, or viewing a depiction of T with someone.

Thus the different forms of thinking all involve the agent covertly tokening some speech-mediated educative activity. And the varieties differ chiefly with respect to the nature of the activity an educative performance of which is being covertly tokened.

So-called mental actions such as doing mental arithmetic are simply covert tokenings of actions. In the case of mental arithmetic, the actions are calculations done on paper or blackboard, or spoken out loud. Other, seemingly non-actional categories of mental phenomena—putative states or objects such as concepts, beliefs, and desires—can nevertheless be fully explained in terms of actual overt and covert tokenings of actions and/or dispositions and abilities to perform and/or to overtly and/or covertly token actions. For example, a state of rage is covert and/or overt token performance of aggressive acts plus a presently active disposition to perform aggressive acts. Beliefs and concepts are dispositions to covertly token and to actually perform both certain descriptions and hortations and actions consistent with those descriptions and hortations. Mental "events," such as sudden realizations, are termini, junctures, and phases in covert token performances of actions. And so on.

It is illuminating to contrast my account of thinking with the dispositional account Ryle offers in *The Concept of Mind*. Ryle defines thinking in terms of dispositions, readinesses, and abilities to act in certain thinking ways—for example, to improve techniques, to be careful and circumspect, and to teach or explain things to others. Thinking is identified not with the behavior itself (e.g., the teaching) but with the disposition (or readiness or ability) to perform the behavior. And the disposition, readiness, or ability is a purely formal or logical entity. Thus, for Ryle, thinking is nothing actual. Ryle ignores the possibility of categorical bases (underlying causes) for the relevant dispositions, readinesses, and abilities. I agree with Ryle that the overt (educative, etc.) behaviors are important. I say they are important insofar as they are what thinking is a covert token-performance of. I agree also that the thinking is not to be identified with the behaviors. In my account, however, thinking has an actual and not merely a notional or logical existence. It is an action of the person. In my account, acts of thinking are the categorical bases for the behavioral dispositions and abilities in question. They are P's covert tokenings of the relevant educative activity. It is these acts of covert tokening, or thinking, that dispose, ready, and enable P to perform both the educative activity and, normally, the infra activity it teaches.

Ways in Which Thinking Is Public

Thinking is popularly, and by philosophers, regarded as the quintessentially private activity. The metaphors of goings-on inside the head make this vivid. However, thinking is in important respects a public enterprise.

The establishment and maintenance of an overt tokening medium, a language, is a public undertaking. A language requires public conventions and public practices to sustain it. It is publicly accepted that, instead of fully convening a session of some concerted activity, it is often useful to merely token it in speech. The whole rigmarole *could* be embarked on if necessary, but by general consent we let this abbreviated performance do instead. So, for example, we can talk about things when they are not here. Apart from this general convention, there are innumerable detailed conventions about what tokening—what speech, say—is the customary substitute for (the forgone concerting of) what behavior. It is by public convention that *There was a Maserati in the car park* can do duty for our ogling the thing. It is not just a matter of convenience that the tokening system is public—that everyone knows about it and everyone participates—but a matter of necessity. The practice of token concerting is designed for initiating shared activities, and, unless the practice is mastered by all the would-be sharers, it is not going to be useful.

The maintenance of widespread knowledge, skill, and debate in relation to important activities is also a public responsibility. This widespread knowledge is necessary if there is to be readily available educative material for P to invoke when he is thinking about these activities. In any culture, there is an ongoing "macro-conversation" about the activities that are important in the culture. Insofar as they are preparations for participation in this macro-conversation, the individual's thinkings can be seen as contributions to it. Private tokenings are contributions to a public enterprise.

It could also be said there is a public understanding, similar to that which sanctions overt tokening, covering our covert tokenings. There is, as it were, a space set aside in our interpersonal dealings for us to do covert tokening in. One has leave to undertake covert readyings of oneself before, and while, participating in everyday business. One may visit the powder room of the mind. How we actually go about the readying is left veiled in euphemisms and in metaphors of ephemera such as thoughts, feelings, mental images. But what is clear and public is the assumption that taking time out to covertly token actions before performing them is something we all do.

Is Thinking Observable?

Overt thinking is observable. When P is thinking out loud, thinking what he is doing, saying something to you, making a face, or gesturing something, you can usually perceive not only that but what P is thinking. However, the observation of any action presupposes certain abilities on the part of the observer. Perceiving overt thinking is not something just anyone can do. For a start, you have to know what to look for. You have to know what thinking is.

For the Cartesian dualist convinced that thinking is internal and non-physical, nothing could count as directly observing P's thinking. No observable behavior could be constitutive of thinking; it could at best be the external effect of which thinking is the inner cause. Nor could any internal, physiological phenomenon observable with special instruments qualify. At best, that would be the mere physical correlate of the non-physical thinking process. For the dualist, and perhaps in the minds of some lay folk, thinking is by definition unobservable.

The cognitive scientist would also have difficulties recognizing thinking out loud as thinking. For the cognitive scientist, thinking is a function of physiological mechanisms in the brain—an inner functional phantom that combines new information with stored information and computes behavior. Again, no observable overt behavior could count as thinking. There might be no internal physiological phenomenon that would count either. If thinking is a function of a mechanism, then—though one might be able to observe the anatomical mechanism in question and observe the physiological events that constitute the operations of the mechanism—the mechanism's "function" or "causal role," being an abstraction and in this sense non-physical, would surely elude direct scrutiny. There is even an argument that implies that any mechanism underlying thinking, if there is such, must be impossible to identify, owing to chronic difficulties in isolating, in an essentially holistic physiological milieu, just those processes and only those processes that are relevant to the putative thinking function.[7]

For the observer who believes that thinking is the act of token-performing (or commencing and aborting, or "making as if to perform") some educative procedure (e.g., spoken instruction or explanation, graphic depiction, or demonstration) for the purpose of readying oneself and/or others for some action, the chances of identifying P's overt thinking as such are better. Knowing what one is looking at means knowing what to look for and where, and knowing how to look. The audible or visible activity fragments produced by the person thinking out loud, gesturing, etc., will be recognized by the observer as tokens of larger educative performances. Such recognition presupposes that the observer is familiar with thinking (at least, with overt thinking) as a practitioner and is familiar with the kinds of larger performances of which the overt thinker's tokenings are tokenings. If P's fragmentary behaviors are to be seen as representative fragments (tokens), the observer must already know thinking. And if the fragments are to be seen as representative of X-ing, the observer must already know X-ing. Past experience and corresponding present imaginative participation are required of the observer. Thus, from the thinker's muttering, the competent observer should be able to reconstruct an intelligible sentence or two.

An observer's own experience of the kind of action he is witnessing should also equip him with the ability to distinguish movements and other actions that are constitutive of the action from movements and bodily agitations that are mere irrelevant by-products or epiphenomena of it. The latter are not subsidiary skills one acquires when one learns the action. Whereas raising your heels off the ground is a constitutive part of the act of going on tiptoes to look over the fence, the concomitant visible tensing of your calf muscles and your tiny "Oh" of temporary imbalance are mere epiphenomena of this action. They are not things you have to learn when you learn how to go on tiptoes. In the introduction to this book I made this same distinction with respect to the behavioral constituents and by-products of thinking, and in chapter 1 I chided Ryle for not making it. Murmuring *But what if this one goes there?* while drawing in sand is almost certainly constitutive of an act of thinking. However, gripping one's chin between thumb and forefinger and frowning, though a frequent accompaniment, even an index, of some people's thinking, could hardly ever be a part of it. Recognizing constituent tokenings allows an observer to see both that and what P is thinking. Recognizing epiphenomena allows an observer to see only that P is thinking.

Is Covert Thinking Observable?

The covertness of thinking is often a matter of degree, as Ryle's varied examples and the smile for the professor (see chapter 4 above) illustrate. However, it is often completely covert, and by definition the covert is unobservable. Well, it is unobservable to the naked and/or untrained eye. Covert thinking remains observable in principle. If we had suitable observational prostheses, enabling us to clearly see the very subtle eye, lip, larynx, and other muscle movements—and perhaps other, even subtler and deeply internal body and brain events—that tokenings covertize down to, we could still observe the thinking.

Employing sophisticated scanners to better see someone thinking is no different in principle from peering over the fence to better see if the neighbors' boy Jonas is still teasing the dog. With the scanners, we can see more and in more detail. However, this makes the ancillary interpretive tasks not easier but harder. Because there is now so little of the tokenings to go on, and so much of so little, it is far harder to sort out what is the tokening, and thus constitutive of the thinking, from what is merely epiphenomenal. As the tokenings become increasingly vestigial, given just them to look at and no fuller version for comparison, the task of determining what action the tokenings are tokenings of becomes unrealistically difficult. As Watson concludes,

Even if we could roll out the implicit processes [covert tokenings] and record them on a sensitive plate or phonograph cylinder . . . they would be so abbreviated, short-circuited and economized that they would be unrecognizable unless their formation had been watched from the transition point where they are complete and social in character, to their final stage where they will serve for individual but not for social adjustments.[8]

What this "Watson caveat" suggests is that covert thinking may be in principle observable but, because of the amount of ancillary research necessary to recognize them, the subtler tokenings—which may reduce to small brain events—will remain in practice unobservable no matter how sophisticated our observational technology becomes.

Is Thinking Scientifically Observable?

Thinking is not amenable to scientific scrutiny, even in principle. The reason is that scientists must be objective, and thinking is an action. Thinking is not scientifically observable for the same reason that playing hopscotch, whistling the Hoagy Carmichael classic *Skylark*, signing a check, and scratching one's nose are not scientifically observable. As I will argue in detail in chapter 11, in order to observe actions the observer must empathize with the person performing the action. And, although empathy is universal in everyday interpersonal contexts, it is out of bounds to objective scientists.

The bodily movement that thinking involves might typically include subtle eye-muscle activation from commenced-and-aborted visual scanning, slight activation of face muscles from commenced-and-aborted facial expressions, slight activation of larynx muscles from commenced-and-aborted speech, other slight muscle and/or gland activation, and often a marked overall stillness. Viewed objectively, as bodily events, these movements are in themselves meaningless and inexplicable. They have no biological significance. They serve no biological purpose, nor do they signify any physiological malfunction. Their only potential significance to an observer is as actions or bodily epiphenomena of actions. However, they can acquire significance as components or epiphenomena of an act of thinking only if the observer empathizes—that is, reconvenes his own firsthand experience of thinking and recognizes the other as a fellow thinker. Only then can the other's stillness be seen as indicative of heed and his various movements and agitations as would-be, truncated, token actions or bodily corollaries of these. In chapter 3, I quoted Stern describing how a solitary infant will "evoke a companion." A solitary infant's excitement when it sees a rattle remains inexplicable unless we see this excitement in the context of the infant's regular rattle play with its mother. To understand the excitement, we must imagine the infant as a participant in the rattle game, and to do that we must, like the infant, imagine participating. We cannot do this unless we have a player's or would-be-player's knowledge of the game. This knowledge cannot be obtained from the infant's present bodily agitations alone. (For one thing, we have to recognize the rattle.)

Similarly, we could not determine, without a player's knowledge of what thinking is and solely by observing (supposing we could) the various vestigial and inhibited movements which P's covert commencing and aborting of action X amounts to, either that or what P is thinking. As thinkers ourselves, however, knowing what thinking is, we can and often do read, in these subtle actions P is producing, the fact and the nature of P's thinking. If we had observational aids, we could see actions subtler than those we customarily observe. This might help us to more confidently judge whether and what other people are thinking. However, no matter how sophisticated is the observational technology and how extensive is the training required to use it, these observations would still not be scientific observations, nor would our interpretive judgments be scientific judgments.

I am suggesting that, in order to identify action X as such, any observer of X must have previous experience of X-ing and must bring this experience to bear in the present situation as an empathy informing his perception of the other's X-ing. Only by doing this can an observer identify what he sees as action X. A scientist is also a functioning layperson, and he will have first-hand experience of many actions irrelevant to science. However, because objective scientists are professionally barred from empathizing their subject matter, no would-be scientist of actions could bring this firsthand experience to bear in observing actions brought into the laboratory for investigation. For the scientist qua scientist, other people's actions are unobservable.

An Interpretation of Abbreviation Research

As I described it in chapter 1, abbreviation research involves recording selected physiological indices of given overt actions and comparing these with the same indices recorded during the imagining of the actions in question. The term *abbreviation* is appropriate insofar as the physiological events recorded during imagining are generally found to be reduced or abbreviated versions of those accompanying the respective overt actions. A variety of scanners and other recording devices and techniques are employed. The objective experimental methods and the rigor of research reports in the literature clearly demonstrate that modern abbreviation research cannot be faulted in terms of reliability as far as documenting the physiological facts goes. However, if we are to take seriously the idea that thinking is neither a supernatural process nor the functioning of physiological mechanisms but an action of the person, then perhaps there is room for a new interpretation of the findings abbreviation research has come up with.

In my story, the "physiological" phenomena abbreviationists record during imagining must be either epiphenomena of the act of imagining or constituents of it. This opens up the possibility of the abbreviationists' observational hardware and methods allowing us to directly observe acts of thinking being performed by the person. In this new scenario, the possibility of locating "physiological mechanisms responsible for thinking" has gone, but in its place is the possibility of directly observing thinking. The Rizzolatti findings, for example, would still look very interesting, or more so. The mirror neuron activity during action observation by the subject would no longer be evidence of an underlying physiological mechanism for empathy. But it could be reliable epiphenomenal evidence that empathizing is going on. Or the mirror neuron firing could be the empathizing itself.

The fee for viewing actions of this subtlety would have to cover more than just the cost of the hardware. Extensive analysis would also be required to distinguish actions (and action constituents) from epiphenomena. And the Watson caveat must be granted. Presumably it would require a considerable expansion of the abbreviationists' experimental procedures to track actions from their original "complete and social" manifestation right down to the ultra-subtle, "abbreviated, short-circuited and economized" tokenings of those actions that thinking consists of.

The training in experiment design and hardware use required for abbreviation research of this new "actional" type might be similar in many respects to the training a physiologist receives. And the conduct of experiments and use of hardware could justifiably be called scientific. However, the interpretation of findings, and the drawing of conclusions—since they are findings and conclusions about actions—would require empathy on the analyst's part and therefore could not be called scientific. This is not to say that these findings and conclusions would be any less precise, reliable, verifiable, informative, or useful than physiologist's findings are. It is only to concede that watching P think cannot in principle be any more scientific than watching Jonas tease the dog.

8 Where Our Notion of the Mind Comes From (1)

Since before Plato it has been believed that thinking goes on in people's heads. Either the person does it, in a special place in there, or thinking is the operations—in that special place—of a special impersonal agent. In English, the supposed special intracranial place and/or agent has for hundreds of years been called "the mind."

The modern idea that the brain is responsible for thinking is descended from the idea that the mind is responsible for it. Early in the twentieth century, psychologists and philosophers of mind decided that the traditional notion of mind, although still popular with the masses and still convenient for everyday purposes, is too vague and confused, and carries too many suggestions of the supernatural (or at least non-physical) to be useful for scientific purposes. They turned to behaviorism, which has no room for the mind. However, after several decades in the cold, the idea of an inner agency responsible for thinking arrived back in theorists' calculations. It was decided that there must, after all, be some such thing as the mind. And the computer looked like a useful model of what kind of thing the mind must be.

A consensus developed that a serious scientific study of thinking, a "cognitive science," should redefine mind in terms of what actually is inside people's heads, namely, the body's own computer, the physical brain. Cognitive science undertakes to explain thinking—or "mental phenomena"—as functions of neural mechanisms in the brain. From its founding in the 1970s, optimism about the possibility of progress in cognitive science has been encouraged by reports of significant advances in brain and neurophysiological science.

My theory is that thinking is something the person does. To establish this, I must show that, contrary to the widespread present-day assumption, the brain is not the agent and/or venue of thinking. I must show that the brain does not itself think, nor is it "responsible for" thinking. One way to discredit the notion that the brain is the agent and/or venue of thinking is to discredit its parent notion: that there is any inner, impersonal agent and/or venue of thinking in the first place. I can try to show that both the notion of thinking being carried out by an agency other than the person and the notion of its being carried out inside the person are fanciful. If the original role of "impersonal agent and/or inner venue for thinking" is unfillable, it is immaterial whether the mind (if there is such a thing) or the brain is nominated to fill it.

Certainly, the traditional idea of mind is dubious on the grounds of vagueness, confusion, and supernatural overtones. And certainly, substituting "brain" for "mind" dispatches these dubieties. However, attention to those difficulties with the mind notion distracts us from the most significant difficulty with it: that it is redundant. Thinking does not need a special venue, and it already has an agent. This redundancy problem is not solved by giving the job of venue and/or agent to the brain.

I hope my account of thinking as the covert commencing and aborting of lessons, conversations, etc. has established some initial plausibility for the idea that thinking is an action of the person. The aim of chapters 8–10 is to remove the appearance of plausibility from the contrary notion that thinking is accomplished by an agent other than the person and that it goes on inside the person's head. I argue in these three chapters that the notion of an inner agent and/or venue of thinking rests on nothing more substantial than figures of speech. The notion arises because we employ metaphors to highlight some aspects of thinking and, for various reasons, we take these metaphors too literally. The misconception is further entrenched when we give the putative venue and/or agent a name, "mind." Our main, initial mistake, however, is to allow ourselves to be misled by the metaphors.

Theory Theory

The received wisdom as to the origin of the mind notion is that it is part of a theory—an objective, proto-scientific theory that lay people have come up with during their attempts to understand and predict other people's behavior. We infer the existence inside people's heads of unobservable entities, agents, states, and forces, causing them to act in the ways they do. And the governing agent in there we call "the mind."

According to the lay theory, the mind takes in information about external reality via the sense organs, and forms beliefs on the basis of this information. The beliefs then interact with already existing beliefs and with current desires to produce a decision as to how the person should act in the present situation to best satisfy the desires. There are laws governing these interactions of perceptions, beliefs, and desires (and other mental phenomena) and resulting actions. An example of such a law is the following: "If a person sitting at a bar wants to order a beer, and if she has no stronger desire to do something that is incompatible with ordering a beer, then typically she will order a beer."[1] And Paul Churchland cites the following examples: "if P fears that x, then P desires that not-x," "if P hopes that x and subsequently perceives that x, then P is pleased," "if P desires that x, and believes that if y, then x, and is able to bring it about that y, then P will, other things being equal, bring it about that y."[2] After reaching decisions based on calculations like these, the mind instructs the body to act.

As Churchland tells us, the whole theory, including the postulated internal entities and the informal laws governing them, has been given a name. "Each of us understands others, as well as we do, because we share a tacit command of an integrated body of lore concerning the law-like relations holding among external circumstances, internal states and overt behavior. Given its nature and functions, this body of lore may quite aptly be called 'folk psychology'."[3] Daniel Dennett puts it thus: "Very roughly, folk psychology has it that *beliefs* are information-bearing states of people that arise from perceptions and that, together with appropriately related *desires*, lead to intelligent *action*."[4] Andrew Meltzoff and Alison Gopnik concur: "Normal adults share a network of ideas about human psychology that are often described as "common-sense" psychology. Although we directly observe other people's behavior, we think of them as having internal mental states that are analogous to our own. We think that human beings want, think and feel, and that these states lead to their actions."[5]

And folk psychology is an empirical theory. The analogy with science is thought to be very real. In Churchland's opinion, "Not only is folk psychology a theory, it is so *obviously* a theory that it must be held a major mystery why it has taken until the last half of the twentieth century for philosophers to realize it. The structural features of folk psychology parallel perfectly those of mathematical physics; the only difference lies in the respective domain of abstract entities they exploit. . . ."[6] Like scientific theories generally, our folk theory of mind tends to internal consistency and it remains sensitive to empirical corroboration. In Janet Astington's words, "The concepts are coherent and interdependent, and the theory can interpret a wide range of evidence using a few concepts and laws. The theory is not static, but is open to defeat by new evidence, that is, it is subject to replacement by a new theory. . . . Or the theory is not replaced but extended, as scientific theories sometimes are, in order to cope with the new evidence. . . ."[7]

We plain folk all subscribe to the theory, it is claimed, and we rely on it to predict and explain one another's behavior. We take note of what the other person's circumstances and behavior are and, using the theory, compute from this data what beliefs and desires are likely to be operating in him and, consequently, what he is likely to do next. This enables us to plan our own behavior accordingly. "We use folk psychology all the time, to explain and predict each other's behavior; we attribute beliefs and desires to each other with confidence,"[8] Dennett says. Meltzoff and Gopnik agree: "Our ideas about these mental states play a crucial role in our interactions with others and in the regulation of our own behavior."[9] According to theory theory, our scientific-type observations of others' behavior and our application of folk theory together constitute our basic heuristic strategy as far as other people are concerned. Without the theory, it is believed, we would be completely in the dark about others' actions and intentions.

Theory theorists hold various opinions as to the overall veracity and usefulness of folk theory of mind. Obviously, the layperson is not au fait with the advances of modern cognitive science in the way the philosopher and cognitive scientist are. It is assumed that such recent intellectual achievements as the mind-as-brain concept, the computational model of brain function, and the insight that the brain and the neurophysiological mechanisms it comprises have been designed by evolutionary forces are well beyond the scope of folk theory. However, despite this assumed ignorance on the folk theorist's part and his alleged vagueness, confusion, and naiveté elsewhere, many cognitive scientists believe that the folk postulates are basically correct. They believe that there are in fact internal information-bearing (reality-representing) states—although they are neural rather than mental—that have pretty much the causal roles vis à vis our perceptions and our behavior that folk theory says they have.

Others believe that folk theory is more like myth or superstition than like potential science. These "eliminativist" philosophers believe that it is not worth trying to improve the folk story. It is not worth trying to tidy it up so it can be reconciled with the scientific model. It is too full of fancy and superstition to ever be laid, as a candidate for empirical investigation, at neuroscience's door. Eliminativists believe that it should be abandoned entirely, that progress will only come with improved brain science, and that there is no reason to expect that the future findings of brain science will be in any way anticipated or aided by folk theory.

Theory Theorists' Views on the Origin of Our Concept of Mind

The most interesting aspect of theory theory for our purposes is its diverse claims about how the folk concept of mind originates. Theory theory is not merely a theory about the nature of our concept of mind; it is also a theory about how we acquire it. The central assumption is that children infer the existence of mind and mental phenomena for and by themselves by theorizing from their own observations of others' behavior. Findings in developmental psychology are relevant. Meltzoff and Gopnik report that "recent research has shown that by the age of five years, children operate with many of the elements of a common-sense psychology. By five years old, children seem to know that people have internal mental states such as beliefs desires, intentions and emotions"[10] Astington concludes that "children's concepts of mental states are abstract and unobservable theoretical postulates used to explain and predict observable human behavior"[11] Children are pictured as small amateur scientists, hypothesizing on the basis of accumulating empirical evidence.

The idea of the child as a theoretician, appealing to abstract entities for theoretical purposes and "generalizing over unobservable bearers of causal powers,"[12] is not obviously plausible. However, no one claims that each child invents the theory anew. Most theory theorists concede some cultural influence on the child's developing concepts. Plausibly, children acquire the basic notions of mind and mental phenomena from their elders, via their developing grasp of the colloquial mentalist vocabulary in which these concepts are already registered. That is, the everyday language that children learn already has names—*belief, desire, intention, feeling, mind,* etc.—for the entities folk psychology posits. This makes the theory much easier to grasp.

This theme of theory acquisition in the course of acculturation is prominent in the writings of many theory theorists. Paul Churchland describes folk psychology as "quotidian commerce of explanation and anticipation," "familiar homilies," "commonsense laws," and "a shared body of lore."[13] Elsewhere in the same paper he compares folk psychology to "popular myths" such as underlie astrology and alchemy. Dennett also is explicit about folk psychology's being an item of popular culture: ". . . it exists as a phenomenon, like a religion or a language or a dress code, to be studied with the techniques and attitudes of anthropology. It may be a myth, but it is a myth we live in."[14]

The appeal to cultural influences is clearly realistic, and makes it easier to explain the child's early grasp of folk theory. As well as learning from their own theorizing, children rely on lessons from their elders and take a lead from the colloquial vocabulary. However, mention of cultural factors merely postpones the question of how folk theory originated in the first place. How and by whom was the mind notion first mooted? Was it devised, after long scrutiny of people's behavior, by some great genius of the past?

Jerry Fodor, for one, thinks not. He points out that cooperation is essential for human survival and reasons that, to enable the coordination of one's actions with others' actions that cooperation requires, a reliable theory of mind is necessary.[15] Fodor's point is that, if the discovery of a reliable theory of mind had had to await the cogitations of a genius, we all would have perished in the meantime through inability to cooperate. In fact, any delay in an individual's acquisition of the mind concept counts against his survival. Not knowing about the hidden mental causes of behavior would expose individuals to too much danger and insecurity in their relations with others. Fodor concludes that, if he had been faced with this problem in designing *Homo sapiens*, he "would have made knowledge of commonsense *Homo sapiens* psychology *innate*; that way nobody would have to spend time learning it."[16]

Patricia Churchland had already speculated that "for all we can tell now, the mind-brain may have an innate disposition to favor and 'grow' the rudiments of certain folk theories, including folk psychology."[17] The idea that at least the basic concepts of folk psychology are innate, and that some in-built "module" corresponding to our folk theory has evolved in the human brain, is now widely accepted in both developmental psychology and philosophy of mind. In the considered opinion of Meltzoff and Gopnik, for example,

Infants are, apparently, never strict behaviorists: one fundamental assumption of mentalism—that external, visible behaviors are mapped on to phenomenologically mental states—is apparently given innately. Clearly infants have much to learn about the nature of mind, but apparently they need not learn that it, or something like it, exists, and perhaps not even that it is shared by themselves and others.[18]

Apart from "theorizing from observed behavior" and "an innate theory-of-mind module," there is a third possibility as to the original source of folk theory. This is that people, including children, are directly aware, via introspection, of their own minds and the states of them and the goings-on in them. Seemingly, given such firsthand acquaintance with mental phenomena, the child's theorizing burden would be greatly diminished. To explain the behavior of others in mentalist terms, all the child need do is apply laws about behavior and mental states learned from his own case to the cases of others. The fact that mental states in others are unobservable would make this analogizing process more speculative, but at least the child would already know what kind of phenomenon he was positing. A high degree of inventiveness and intellectual sophistication would no longer be required of the child. However, introspection may not supply as much assistance as it promises. It may not be able to provide the child's knowledge of mind with the initial leg up. As Richard Gregory notes,

. . . concepts of mind must be invented or discovered, much as in physics, for we cannot see at all clearly into our own minds by introspection. . . . If we could see "directly" into our own minds by introspection, perhaps we would not need explanatory concepts for understanding at least our own psychologies. But as it is, introspection tells us virtually nothing about how our minds work or what they or we are. So we need . . . concepts for psychological understanding. In this way concepts of mind are not so different from concepts of physics . . . for both underlie appearances and are more-or-less helpful tools for thinking and understanding.[19]

Even if introspection is a genuine form of observation, one cannot introspect a mental state *as such* without prior knowledge of what a mental state is. To task the child with acquiring the necessary preliminary knowledge of mental states, to ask him to "invent or discover" the basic concept of mind, as Gregory puts it, is still unrealistic. The intellectual tasks being allocated to the child are still too onerous.

An Alternative View

In my opinion, the core claim of theory theory—that mind is the central concept of a theory—is wrong. I explain why in the rest of this chapter. Theory theory is also mistaken, in my view, as to what it is we find out when we find out what others are thinking and feeling. Theory theory says that what we find out is what is going on in the other person's head. I say that what is found out is what the other person is *doing*—namely, what activity he is covertly tokening. I also think theory theory's various suggestions as to how we pick up folk psychology—the infant scientist, the genetically programmed-in theory module, and inferrings from introspection—are unconvincing. They would be unconvincing even if it were true that there is a "theory of mind" or "folk psychology" to be picked up.

The only above-mentioned suggestion as to the origin of the mind notion that I do (wholeheartedly) endorse is one that is somewhat peripheral to theory theory. It is the suggestion that the child's notion of mind derives in large part from his learning to use the colloquial vocabulary we have for talking about thinking. I claim that we come to entertain the fancy that people have minds inside their heads as a result of our uncritical indulgence of the metaphors that we customarily employ to describe thinking. I argue for this explanation of our notion of mind in the remainder of this chapter and in chapter 9.

The Colloquial Vocabulary for Talking about Thinking

At the beginning of the introduction and elsewhere, I list under the heading *thinking* some varieties of thinking, some aspects of it, and some dispositions and abilities relating to it. The verbs we use to name these varieties, aspects, dispositions, and abilities include *think, remember, intend, imagine, believe,* and *desire.* Such are the core referring expressions in the colloquial vocabulary we have for talking about thinking. These terms specify the vocabulary's subject matter as thinking-type actions and activities, and logical constructions out of these actions and activities.

It may seem obvious that thinking is the subject matter of our "colloquial thinking vocabulary," as I shall call it. However, it is commonly believed (by theory theorists in particular) that the subject matter of the colloquial vocabulary is not actions and activities at all, but special category of unobservable entities and states called "mental phenomena." These are minds, beliefs, desires, consciousness, mental images, concepts, and so on. The nouns that name these putative entities are roughly as numerous and as commonly employed in the vocabulary as the thinking verbs. If these nouns were the names of things in the way nouns normally are, then it would be reasonable to believe that there really are such things as mental phenomena (in people's heads) and that these nouns are the vocabulary's core referring expressions. It would be reasonable to believe that these mental phenomena are what the vocabulary is primarily about. However, in my view, which I unpack later, the nouns in the colloquial thinking vocabulary—nouns such as *mind, belief, desire, consciousness, image,* and *concept*— are by no means ordinary names. I say they are, rather, special noun forms or "nominalizations" of the corresponding thinking verbs.

Apart from the distinctive verbs and nouns in the colloquial thinking vocabulary (and some adverbs and adjectives), there are a great many figurative expressions. In fact, there are more stock figurative expressions in the vocabulary than there are basic verbs and nouns. Many of them are straightforward metaphors: *it dawned on me that, it hasn't sunk in yet, use your head, couldn't follow what he was saying, a change of heart, I gradually pieced it all together, give it some thought, not thinking straight, grounds for believing, her attitude hardened, it conjures up images of, express it in words.*

However, the dominant type of figurative expression in the colloquial thinking vocabulary is metaphor used in association with a nominalized verb. Look at the following expressions: *filled with admiration, to nurse a grudge, harbor a suspicion, satisfy her desires, food for thought, form a concept of, grasp the meaning of, reach an understanding, hold a belief, express your feelings, slipped in and out of consciousness, don't get your hopes up, refresh your memory, acquire knowledge, a piece of reasoning, store the information away, seeds of doubt.* There are scores of other examples. The metaphor component is clear enough in each case. And I am claiming that the nouns in the examples above are all nominalized verbs. The verbs of which the nouns are nominalizations are respectively *admire, begrudge, suspect, desire, think, conceive, mean, understand, believe, feel, be conscious of, hope, remember, know, reason, inform,* and *doubt.* I discuss the metaphor component in this chapter and the nominalization component in the next.

There are many philosophically interesting things to be said about metaphors used in combination with nominalized verbs—including those involving the nominalizations *belief, desire, concept, meaning,* and *consciousness.* However, in these two chapters I will concentrate on the most interesting ones: those metaphors that involve the noun *mind.*

All our everyday uses of the noun *mind* are couched in familiar metaphors. Here are some examples: *going over it in my mind, she withdrew into her own mind, it crossed my mind, my mind was in a turmoil, keep it in mind, his mind was playing tricks on him, her mind seized on the idea that, his mind's grasp on reality, my mind wandered, the mysterious workings of her mind, you could see his mind ticking over, my mind was racing, her mind is still sharp, get my mind around it, set my mind to work, his mind turned to thoughts of, his mind snapped under the strain, it focuses the mind wonderfully, keep one's mind on the job,* and so on. There are about 200 such "mind metaphors" in common use. Most are listed in the appendix.

My argument in these chapters is that we come to believe that there is such a thing as the mind by becoming too blasé and credulous in our response to the familiar mind metaphors. It appears as if the subject matter of these expressions, what they are about, is a special entity called the mind. Because the expressions are used so frequently, and in such a variety of forms, we tend to take this appearance at face value. We come to believe after a while there really is something (the mind) being referred to by these expressions. However, what I claim the mind metaphors actually refer to, albeit in a roundabout and picturesque way, is nothing other than what the basic thinking verbs refer to—that is, varieties and aspects of, and logical constructions out of, acts of thinking. The mind metaphors are just figurative periphrases of thinking verbs, and they have the same subject matter. To appreciate this, we should be clear about how metaphors work.

Using Metaphor to Refer to Features of Things

Metaphor is a special referring technique. It works roughly as follows. You are talking to P about X, and there is a feature F of X which you want to draw P's attention to but for which our language does not have a word. You think of something else, Y, which has feature F and has it in an obvious way, but is otherwise quite unlike X. You then speak of X as if it *is* Y. In trying to work out how X could possibly be Y, P comes across feature F. Feature F is the only thing X and Y have in common, the only respect in which X could "be" Y. So P twigs that F must be what you are referring to. Since it is X and not Y that you are primarily talking about, Y is recognized as a red herring and it is to F *as a feature of X* that P's attention is directed.

Because it is a referring technique, metaphor is an interpersonal transaction. However, we also use the word *metaphor* to name the verbal expression, the form of words, that prompts a particular metaphor transaction. It is important not to confuse the form of words and the transaction. And it is important to see that the metaphor (form of words) does not literally by itself achieve the metaphor (referring transaction). There is another synecdoche at work here. Like ordinary referrings, metaphors are interpersonal transactions that include the use of words. They are not words alone.

Metaphor is more complicated than ordinary absent-referent referring. There are three distinct stages in metaphor, and sometimes four. The special usefulness of metaphor is that it allows us to refer to features of things, usually unnamed and often subtle, that would be difficult or impossible to refer to otherwise. Mostly, there would be no point in coining a name for the feature in question, because reference to it is so seldom necessary. In other cases, where reference to feature F is going to be often necessary (and there is a corresponding gap in our existing vocabulary) the metaphor becomes the stock way of referring to F. In both cases the metaphor technique is a kind of extender kit that makes our ordinary stock of words go further.

Whereas simple referrals have one referent, metaphors have two: a general referent and a specific referent. The *general referent* is what the speaker and the hearer are primarily talking about: the general subject matter, the X which the special feature F is a feature of. The *specific referent* is F itself. John Wisdom asks us to "suppose now that someone is trying on a hat. She is studying it in a mirror. There's a pause and then a friend says, *My dear, the Taj Mahal*. Instantly the look of indecision leaves the face in the mirror."[20] Here the general referent X is the hat, and the specific referent F is its grand, elaborate, excessive look (which *Taj Mahal* refers us to so efficiently). In the metaphor *The hills moved in a vast herd across the horizon*, the general referent is some hills, and feature F is the way the hills are disposed, massed in the distance. In the more prosaic metaphors *river mouth* and *our team got thrashed*, the general referents are respectively a river and the result of a sporting contest. The specific referents are a certain part of the river and a certain quality of defeat. My "general referent" is called other things by other writers. Ivor Richards[21] calls it the *tenor* of the metaphor. Max Black[22] calls it the *principal subject*. George Lakoff and Mark Johnson[23] call it the *target domain*.

Stage One: Establishing the General Referent X

The first stage of a metaphor is the general referral. The speaker must indicate what the general referent is and ensure the hearer is rehearsing appropriate perceptual behavior. In the cases of the hat and the sporting defeat, the general referent is established before the metaphor. The parties to the metaphor are already covertly tokening (or, in the case of the hat, actually performing) appropriate perceivings. Metaphors that presuppose an earlier general referral are quite common. For example, *Swine!* does instead of *You swine!* when it is obvious who the speaker is looking at. In the other examples above, the general referral is effected in the course of the metaphor. This is done by including the referring expressions, *the hills* and *river*, respectively, in the metaphors (forms of words). Thus, in the metaphors *The hills moved in a vast herd across the horizon* and *river mouth*, the general referral is explicit rather than merely tacit. The expressions *the hills* and *river* refer in the ordinary way, and ensure the hearer is covertly tokening the same perceivings the speaker is.

Stage Two: The Mock Referral to Y

At the second stage in the metaphor transaction, the speaker makes what can be called a *mock referral*. The expression used for the mock referral is usually called "the word used metaphorically," and I follow this convention. In our metaphor examples, the words used metaphorically are, respectively, *Taj Mahal, moved* and *herd, mouth, thrashed,* and *swine*. With the mock referral, the speaker appears to have suddenly changed the subject and be now referring to something else, Y, quite irrelevant to the general referent. Despite this appearance, however, the speaker is not attempting to refer to any new thing Y at all: the speaker has not unilaterally and unaccountably started talking about the Taj Mahal, or a herd of bison, or someone's mouth, or a particular caning, or a pig.

Implicit in all bona fide absent-referent referring is what can be called a *location guarantee*. The speaker tacitly guarantees that, although the relevant perceptual behavior cannot be performed here and now and must perforce be merely covertly tokened, there are other circumstances—granted travel and/or time travel and possibly special heuristic procedures and/or tech-

nology—in which the relevant perceivings could be done. The location procedure is a guarantee of the perceivability of the referent at some (perhaps
unspecified) time and place. The covert commencing and aborting of
perceptual behavior is done on this basis. It is a readying of oneself for a
theoretically possible bit of perceiving.

In metaphor, as far as the ostensible referral to Y is concerned, the location guarantee is withdrawn. The expression Y is being used for another
purpose here. It is not being used to refer to anything. Y is being used "in
vain," if you like. It is being used for a mock referral rather than a bona fide
one. What is normally a referring expression is now being used merely to
get the hearer to imaginatively rehearse Y-type perceptual behavior—that is,
perceptual behavior such as would be appropriate to rehearse if Y (the Taj
Mahal, bison, or whatever) *were* being referred to.

Up until just before the mock referral, the hearer is attempting perceptual
imaginings appropriate to the general referent X. The grammar of the
metaphor (form of words) suggests that the speaker is going to say something about the general referent. The hearer expects some new verbal
prompt to assist in further refining his imaginings of X. The speaker in fact
cues imaginings appropriate to the very different Y. However, because it can
be assumed that the speaker is not dramatically changing the subject to Y,
and that the original referent X is still the main topic, the hearer is not
going to abruptly abandon his X-imaginings. The result is that the hearer is
obliged to undertake two very different imagining tasks simultaneously.
The diverse and apparently incompatible imaginings can be reconciled or
synthesized only if the new Y-type visualizings are somehow relevant to X.

Stage Three: Picking Out F in X

Prompted by the speaker's apparent identification of X with Y—implied
in the grammar of the metaphor—the hearer attempts to simultaneously
covertly token two different perception recipes in respect of the one referent X. This attempt marks the third stage of the metaphor transaction.

When any two actions are attempted, or covertly tokened, simultaneously, they will tend to synthesize—that is, integrate into one action—as far
as is possible. Elements that the two performances have in common will be
performed as one and, being "doubly performed," will tend to be performed
more enthusiastically than elements that are incompatible. The two
perception recipes (cued respectively by the expressions X and Y) our hearer

is trying to token simultaneously are for the most part incompatible. The portion that can be performed relatively enthusiastically, as one action, is correspondingly small. The upshot is that only the Y-compatible features of X will be attended to. The hearer ends up covertly tokening, quite vividly, certain very specific perceptual behavior in the X recipe. Roughly speaking, what X has in common with Y, the F feature, is highlighted, while the other, irrelevant characteristics of X (and Y) are effectively screened off.

The overall effect of the metaphor is now achieved. The speaker has referred the hearer to some specific (and possibly subtle) feature of the general referent X. The mock reference to Y has functioned solely to emphasize one aspect of the X-perception recipe at the expense of the remainder. The Taj Mahal metaphor draws the hearer's attention to just the Taj-Mahal-like feature of the hat. The others draw attention, respectively, to just the distant-bison-like appearance of the hills, to the being-physically-chastised-like pain and humiliation of the sporting defeat, to the anterior-orifice-like part of the river, and to the hearer's porcine qualities. The metaphor puts characteristic F of X in a false light, by making F out to be part of Y. But it puts it in the light.

The Y has to be carefully chosen—to suit that X and that F. The metaphor won't work if X and Y are too similar overall. If the X and Y perception recipes are too similar, it will be unclear which feature of X is being singled out for special attention.

My three-stage description might imply that metaphors are laborious and time-consuming. In fact, a metaphor usually does its work immediately and effortlessly—the whole referral to F being transacted in the time taken to utter the words. Our imaginative responses to referring expressions are normally so practiced as to be automatic. The grammar of the metaphor has us conflating the general referral and the mock referral—imaginatively assimilating X and Y, imagining X *as* Y—before we realize what's going on. The subsequent synthesis of the X and Y perception recipes and the highlighting of what is common to the recipes, seems to happen automatically too. The hearer is, as it were, tricked into attending to F.

Theorists of metaphor committed to the idea that referring words are in a permanent referring relationship with something in the world generally claim that the word used metaphorically, the *Y* word, actually does refer to something. The Y referred to is then, supposedly, compared with X, and the common characteristics noted, or Y is "used as a model for" X, or it is "used as a lens through which to view" X. However, I stick by my view that the word used metaphorically is merely a mock-referring expression in this context. I say no Y is being referred to. At no point in the metaphor does the speaker draw the hearer's attention to the Taj Mahal, to any bison, to anyone's mouth or to any thrashing. We don't need a Y in the picture—only Y-type perceptual behavior.

Dead Metaphors

When a metaphor is often employed for a particular referring job, it tends to get "idiomatized." The metaphor form of words becomes a stock, idiomatic expression and when we hear it we are referred immediately and effortlessly to the specific referent F—in much the same way as we would be referred by an ordinary literal referring expression. This idiomatization process has happened, obviously, to *getting thrashed* in sport, and to *river mouth, you swine, glaring error,* and about fifty thousand other metaphors in English. Among them are the stock metaphors in the colloquial thinking vocabulary, including all the familiar expressions containing the noun *mind*—*it slipped my mind, she poisoned his mind against them, keep it in mind, in two minds,* and so on.

Metaphors entrenched in the vernacular by frequent usage in this way are known as "dead" metaphors. *Dead metaphor* is itself a dead metaphor. The expression refers us to the fact that a given idiomatic expression—*glaring error,* say, or *weigh the evidence*—was once a metaphor. It was once the verbal instrument of a full-blown metaphor transaction. It also refers us to the fact that the expression no longer functions as a metaphor. We no longer need to go through the three stages to find what the expression is referring us to. We have been through them so often in response to this form of words—with the distinctively metaphorical part of our imaginative response becoming more cursory each time—that eventually, on hearing the expression, we go straight to F, without needing to covertly token any Y-perceivings at all. The metaphor transaction has died, although its empty husk, the form of words, refers on. This is not to say that the dead metaphor thus becomes an ordinary referring expression or name. To appreciate how a dead metaphor refers, its historical role as the script or text of a metaphor transaction must be appreciated.

As well as being sharp-eyed, long-beaked pickers-out of subtleties in their general referents, metaphors may also serve to misrepresent. A metaphor may persuade the hearer to see its general referent in a misleading way. A metaphor may encourage the hearer to see an F in X when it is not actually there.

For example, the expression *dead metaphor* is more misleading than enlightening, I would say. The fact about old and much-used metaphors it aims to bring into prominence is that, although they once required to be responded to as metaphors (requiring hearers to "see X as Y," etc.) in order to do their referring jobs, this is no longer required. Yet an old metaphor is still a metaphor in the sense that that distinctive, metaphor-generating form of words remains. Thus, *weighing the evidence* both is and is no longer a metaphor, much as a dead parrot both is and is no longer a parrot. However, unlike the parrot, the metaphor is readily resuscitated. We can easily re-read hackneyed metaphors anew. And, as I argue below, in many cases our imagining-X-as-Y performance is not forgone but is merely so habitual and cursory as to be subconscious. That is, in many cases *dead metaphor* is misleading. The metaphors in question are just asleep.

The consensus in the metaphor literature is that dead metaphors are not metaphors at all. They were metaphors once, but they are no longer, to any extent. The view is almost universal among the pundits that dead metaphors are in fact literal expressions. They have become literal from overuse. Donald Davidson says "Once upon a time, I suppose, rivers and bottles did not, as they do now, literally have mouths."[24] Richard Rorty concurs: ". . . the very same string of words which once formed a metaphorical utterance may, if the metaphor dies into literalness, come to convey such a [literal] truth."[25] This approach was adopted early on by Paul Henle, who talked about "an idiom or a 'dead metaphor' which, properly, is no metaphor at all"[26] and who went on to explain that "metaphors of this type tend to vanish, not in the sense that they are no longer used, but in the sense that they become literal, so that no one would think of saying that *plastron of a turtle* or *hood of a car* were metaphors."[27]

This received view is often called the "polysemy" (multiple meaning) theory. The idea is that words such as *mouth* and *hood*, by virtue of having a metaphorical usage that becomes customary, acquire new (literal) meanings and end up as polysemes like *bank* and *cleave*. Thus *mouth* comes to straightforwardly refer to that part of a river as well as to the familiar facial orifice, and *hood* comes to straightforwardly refer to either the millinery item or a part of a car. A thrashing is either a beating or a sporting defeat.

To my mind, the polysemy theory is unconvincing. I would argue that it is not the expression *mouth* that refers to the river part, nor *hood* that refers to the car part, but rather the whole expressions *river mouth* and *car hood* respectively. Of course, in a live context, where the general referent (river or car) is already obvious, then we would normally leave off *river* or *car*. In that case though, *mouth* and *hood* are abbreviations of *river mouth* and *car hood*. Thus, it is not that *mouth* by itself now refers to two different things. By itself, it still refers solely to the facial orifice. It is *mouth* and *river mouth* (or the abbreviation of *river mouth* to *mouth*) that refer to the two different things. In any event, to get the "second meaning" going—and justify the claim of polysemy—you have to add in the rest of the metaphor. And this means that the two referring expressions are no longer the same, and that the question of polysemy does not arise.

Alternatively, in cases where the general referent is not specified in the metaphor, as it is not in *we got a thrashing*, either the general referent (here a sporting defeat) must be already clear from the context or it must be specified independently before the second meaning can become apparent. To make the general referent of the expression *we got a thrashing* explicit is effectively to re-run the metaphor transaction. It is the same as when you have to restore *mouth* to *river mouth* in order to specify the "other" meaning of *mouth*. To exhibit the "second literal meaning" of *thrashing*, one is obliged to resuscitate the original metaphor. One is still left with two quite different referring expressions: an original literal one and a very tired metaphor.

Galvanic Stirrings

The important question for us is whether our usual imaginative response to dead metaphors—and especially to the dead metaphors in the colloquial vocabulary for talking about thinking—retains anything of the original metaphor procedure, the imagining of X as Y. For instance, in our everyday responses to *vivid mental image, strongly held belief, my mind wandered,* or *you could see his mind working,* is there any Y-visualizing being done in connection with the respective Xs, or do we go straight to the Fs? That is, when we hear these expressions are there any (superfluous but) persistent Y-connotations?

Do we still indulge imaginings of, respectively, a bright picture, an object grasped, an ambler, and an inner mechanism? The orthodox answer is clear: "A cursory glance shows just how much of the language of mind is metaphorical in origin. These metaphors die, of course, and lose their metaphorical force though their origins may still be visible."[28] That is, the received wisdom is that our metaphorical response to the erstwhile metaphors in the colloquial vocabulary has been fully extinguished, and that these expressions now refer us to things in the same way ordinary names do.

We can put the mind metaphors aside for a moment and look at dead metaphors in general. There are good reasons to think that, contrary to the received wisdom, dead metaphors generally do still prompt at least a vestigial version of the three-stage imagining procedure I described earlier.

Infelicities of Style

Among the infelicities of verbal style are mixed metaphors. A mixed metaphor may juxtapose a dead metaphor with an expression that prescribes imaginings either notably compatible or notably incompatible with the imagining the metaphor would prescribe if it were being responded to as a live metaphor. If there is any felt disruption in the hearer's response to the juxtaposed expressions, this is evidence that, at some level, imaginings are being attempted for both. That is, the dead metaphor is eliciting an imaginative response just as surely as the other expression is. The lexicographer H. W. Fowler reports that

the line of distinction between the live and the dead is a shifting one, the dead being sometimes liable, under the stimulus of an affinity or a repulsion, to galvanic stirrings indistinguishable from life. Thus in *The men were sifting meal* we have a literal use of *sift*; in *Satan hath desired to have you, that he may sift you as wheat*, *sift* is a live metaphor; in *the sifting of evidence*, the metaphor is so familiar that it is about equal chances whether *sifting* or *examination* will be used, and that a sieve is not present to the thought—unless indeed someone conjures it up by saying *All the evidence must first be sifted with acid tests*, or *with the microscope*. Under such stimulus our metaphor turns out to have been not dead but dormant.[29]

Consider the sentences *The idea of chewing gum stuck in my mind* and *The decision to dam the stream caused a torrent of criticism*. Consider also this monstrosity devised by George Orwell: "*The fascist octopus has sung its swan song, the jackboot is thrown into the melting pot*."[30] That such travesties are universally deplored is evidence that we still go through the motions of these very hackneyed metaphors (and metonymies, such as *jackboot*). We still at least perfunctorily rehearse the Y-imaginings the metaphors prescribe. We still attempt the relevant seeings-as.

Theme Metaphors

In their influential book *Metaphors We Live By*, Lakoff and Johnson argue that the metaphors that are customary in a culture for talking about a given general referent (or "target domain") will all tend to have a consistent theme.[31] That is, nearly always, the same kind of Y is invoked for seeing X as. Argument is referred to as "combat," emotions are pictured in terms of "temperature" and "pressure," interpersonal communication is construed as "transmission" via a "medium," and so on. David Cooper, who sensibly calls dead metaphors "established" metaphors, claims that where the metaphors established around a concept are true to a theme or "systematic" in this way, any new metaphors coined to bring out new aspects of that concept will tend to conform to, or be easy extensions of, the existing theme.[32] For this begetting of like from like to occur, he suggests, both the theme and the metaphors that promulgate it must have life in them.

In addition, Lakoff and Johnson claim that "certain concepts are structured almost entirely metaphorically . . . and therefore must be comprehended indirectly, via metaphor."[33] Lakoff asserts that, in general, we are obliged to construe abstractions as if they were physical things. Thus "Metaphor is the main mechanism through which we comprehend abstract concepts and perform abstract reasoning. . . . Metaphor allows us to understand a relatively abstract or inherently unstructured subject matter in terms of a more concrete, or at least more highly structured subject matter."[34] That is, access to an abstract concept is often strictly via metaphors.

A family of metaphors that can not only reproduce itself but also control access to a conceptual territory is still in some good sense alive. Cooper concludes that

it is natural, if not inevitable, to regard systematic established metaphor as partially structuring our thought about one kind of thing in terms of another. If so, it is actually achieving, in its quiet way, what many fresh metaphors more stridently invite us to begin doing. We are blinded to this if we focus on an isolated example, like "waste time," and are impressed by its failure to conjure up, any longer, images of rubbish dumps or squandered cash. Taken in isolation, that expression may be of little moment, but taken alongside a battery of related impressions—"invest time," "giving time," "save time," etc.—it is hard to resist the impression that something of importance in our thinking about, and attitude towards, time is marked.[35]

The stylistic infelicities mentioned earlier and the metaphorical themes Lakoff and Johnson and Cooper highlight constitute evidence that our imaginative response to established metaphors persists, if only at the backs of our minds. There is at least one good reason why this should be so. The concepts we use metaphors to express—including those Lakoff and Johnson talk about, such as emotion and communication—are often those we feel are "abstract" and difficult. The standard way of reassuring oneself that one has grasped a difficult concept is to covertly token perceptual behavior relating to that concept. Even when we do not need to, we often do some reassurative visualizing anyway. This is particularly so in regard to the abstract concepts that Lakoff and Johnson and Cooper report as being permanently attended by metaphors having a certain theme. Because these metaphors are in many cases our primary or only means of understanding this concept, rehearsing them is often the only way we can reassure ourselves of our grasp of the concept.

Pictures Holding Us Captive

It is likely we do a lot of this reassurative imagining in connection with the metaphors surrounding concepts philosophers are interested in— including *mind* and such other "abstract concepts" as *time, meaning, truth,* and *reality.* It could even be that philosophers, because they are on one level more skeptical than others of concepts accessible only via figures of speech, are also, paradoxically, more dependent on the metaphors and more credulous about them. Strawson remarks that "philosophers are prone to be influenced in their theorizing by models or pictures or figures of which they are not fully, or at all, conscious as such; to think they are advancing a literally correct account of some phenomenon when they are actually engaged in elaborating, or being puzzled by, features of the figurative mode in which they are thinking about that phenomenon."[36]

When Wittgenstein describes philosophy as "a battle against the bewitchment of our intelligence by means of language"[37] and complains "A *picture* held us captive. And we could not get outside it, for it lay in our language and language seemed to repeat it to us inexorably,"[38] he can be taken as saying that the philosopher often gets enmeshed in confusions because of a too literal, or too earnest and uncritical, reading of certain metaphors in colloquial speech.

Strawson suggests that philosophers can be misled into constructing theories that accommodate metaphors as if they were literally true. Another kind of mistake is to misconstrue colloquial use of metaphors as indicative of folk theorizing. In explanation of certain passages[39] in Wittgenstein that suggest that use of figurative expressions need not signify corresponding beliefs, Hacker says:

Presumably [Wittgenstein] is alluding to such psychological turns of phrase as "A thought flashed through his head," "He said in his heart . . . ," "In my mind I saw. . . ." In such cases we use expressions into which a certain picture (not a theory) is built. . . . These are the pictures we use and their validity is not in question. But when doing philosophy it is important that the application of these pictures be clarified, lest we be misled by the pictures into constructing philosophical theories or, worse, into criticizing our ordinary ways of expressing ourselves as embodying false theories.[40]

Perhaps theory theory is a philosopher's mistake of this "worse" kind. In general, the metaphors that are useful and familiar in an area of inquiry will, if they are not critically examined, grow scions, harden into false assumptions, and may eventually obfuscate the area. The philosopher's job then becomes one of weeding, pruning, and patiently unpicking tangles. At any rate, perhaps the need for philosophy constitutes evidence of a third kind that dead metaphors are not defunct. Dead metaphors still make intellectual trouble.

One reason for our relative ignorance about metaphor-bound subject matters such as mind and meaning is very likely our over-indulgence in and our over-reliance on the metaphors themselves. However, it is possible to set the metaphors aside. Understanding how metaphors work and understanding that dead metaphors are by no means defunct are important early steps. To fully understand the mind metaphors, though—as we must if we are to free ourselves of their influence—we need also to understand the special relationship these metaphors have with the noun *mind*. Lakoff and Johnson's talk of metaphors "helping us to grasp" or "controlling access to" abstract things or abstract concepts is unsatisfactory as an explanation because it is itself too reliant on metaphor.

9 Where Our Notion of the Mind Comes From (2)

The Conventional Wisdom about Metaphors and Mind

Several philosophers have noticed that the noun *mind*, when used in everyday discourse, is almost invariably accompanied by a metaphor. The metaphors in question are those I introduced in chapter 8 as the mind metaphors: *going over it in my mind, she withdrew into her own mind, it crossed my mind, my mind was in a turmoil, keep it in mind, his mind was playing tricks on him, her mind seized on the idea that, his mind's grasp on reality, my mind wandered*, and so on. The tendency nowadays is to wave these metaphors away as having "died and lost their metaphorical force," as Robert Sharpe says. In the past, however, it was suspected by some that metaphors play an important role in our thinking about the mind. There were some attempts to explain this role.

It is nearly universally assumed—both by philosophers who think that the mind metaphors are important and by those who don't—that *mind* is the name of something abstract, which we are initially acquainted with, and form a concept of, without the metaphors. Those who think the metaphors might be important tend to stress the "abstract" nature of the mind and the vagueness and inadequacy of our concept of it. They tend to conclude that the mind metaphors have a heuristic function. The metaphors help us single out certain features of mind and help us visualize, and thus more clearly understand, the mind generally. For example, Bishop Berkeley reports that "all talk concerning the soul is altogether, or for the most part, metaphorical"[1] and talks about "most part of the mental operations being signified by words borrowed from sensible things; as is plain from the terms *comprehend, reflect, discourse*, etc., which being applied to the mind, must not be taken in their gross original sense."[2] He goes on to explain: "We illustrate spiritual things by corporeal. . . . Hence we speak of spirits in a figurative style, expressing the operations of the mind by allusions and terms borrowed from sensible things.[3] And in his philosophical notebook the bishop writes:

Speech metaphorical more than we imagine insensible things & their modes circumstances &c being exprest for yᵉ most part by words borrow'd from things sensible. the reason's plain. Hence Manyfold Mistakes.

The grand Mistake is that we think we have Ideas of the Operations of our Minds. certainly this Metaphorical dress is an argument we have not.[4]

Cooper attributes a similar view to Hegel:

Hegel thought that metaphors were originally required by people to represent "mental" (*geistig*) phenomena in terms of the "sensory" (*sinnlich*) phenomena which, necessarily, their understanding had first encompassed.[5]

Hampshire believes the view is widespread:

It is characteristically a philosopher's complaint (e.g., Bradley, Bergson and many others) that we normally describe mental processes and conditions in terms which have been transferred from an original use in application to physical objects. As transferred terms are, by definition and etymology, metaphors, most commonplace psychological descriptions may therefore be said to be ultimately metaphorical.[6]

Berkeley, Hegel, and Hampshire all seem to be assuming that *mind* and *the mental* are the names of an abstract something which the metaphors are figurative characterizations of. The idea is that the metaphors do for the mind concept what Lakoff and Johnson claim metaphors do for abstract concepts generally. The metaphors suggest a convenient way of picturing the mind "in concrete terms." We know the mind somehow "through" or "via" the metaphors. None of these writers express doubt that there is such a thing as the mind. The picture is consistently one of the mind as existing "underneath" the metaphors—even if we cannot know it except via the metaphors—and of the mind as the subject matter (the "general referent," in my terms) of the metaphors. The mind is in some sense there first.

This assumption is consistent with theory theory's notion of the mind as a theoretical construct, an unobservable internal agency posited to explain certain aspects of people's behavior. Even though our concept of the posited entity is abstract or unstructured, the reality of the entity is not questioned. There has to be *something* there, there has to be some intracranial agent at work, to explain those aspects of our behavior. It is this unobservable something, which we call the mind, that we then characterize with metaphors.

The Metaphorical-Origin Theory

I claim that the traditional view outlined above is misguided and that we do not have, independent of the metaphors, any concept of the mind at all. I say there is no sense in which the mind is "there first." Our notion of mind is entirely a product of the metaphors. The metaphors accompanying the word *mind* in everyday speech *constitute*, rather than just supplement, any understanding we have of mind. Furthermore, they do not furnish us with a concept, let alone a theory, of mind. They provide only numerous diverse and mostly incommensurable images, collectively undeserving even of the term *notion*. Collating a concept from such ill-assorted imaginings would be impossible.

To clarify the relations between theory theory and my theory, which I will call the *metaphorical-origin theory*, I will list the respective answers the two theories provide to four questions.

What kind of notion is the lay notion of mind? Theory theory answers that the lay notion of mind is a theoretical construct, a proto-scientific postulate as to unobservable intracranial causes of behavior. The metaphorical-origin theory claims that there is no folk-psychological theory or lay concept of mind, and that all we have is various habits of imagining associated with the noun *mind*—imaginings determined by the metaphors to which the noun *mind* cleaves.

What is the real subject matter of our colloquial thinking vocabulary? Theory theory assumes that various kinds of mental phenomena really exist inside people's heads (probably in the form of neural representations), that the core referring expressions in the colloquial thinking vocabulary are the nouns (*mind, belief, desire, concept*, etc.), and that these nouns straightforwardly refer to the mental phenomena. The metaphorical-origin theory suggests that, despite appearances, the subject matter of the colloquial thinking vocabulary is nothing mental, nor is it internal processes of any other kind; it is, rather, a class of subtle actions of the person (explicable as covert "tokenings" of communicative interactions) and dispositions, abilities, states, etc., related to those subtle actions. The metaphorical-origin theory says the core referring expressions in the colloquial thinking vocabulary are the verbs of thinking.

How do we acquire our notion of mind? Theory theorists claim we acquire a theory or concept of mind by some mix of personal observation, theory-construction, innate endowment, enculturation, and introspection.

The metaphorical-origin theory claims that we learn to associate certain imaginings with the noun *mind* by becoming accustomed from early childhood to using certain metaphors (in which the noun *mind* is incorporated) to refer to certain varieties and features of thinking.

What use is the lay notion of mind? For theory theorists, our concept of mind and the logic of mentalist terms together constitute a psychological theory that we employ to compute, from our observations of others' behavior and circumstances, hypotheses about their mental states and future behavior. Such hypotheses help guide our interactions with others. The metaphorical-origin theory suggests that we are largely ignorant as to what kind of activity thinking is, and that the imaginings we indulge in connection with the figures of speech in the colloquial thinking vocabulary allow us the impression that we do know roughly what thinking is. It is also suggested by the metaphorical-origin theory that the imaginings encouraged by the mind metaphors—especially, the persistent notion of an impersonal intracranial agent—may influence, in socially convenient ways, how we perceive other people.

There are four main planks to the metaphorical-origin theory. The *exclusive-use* claim is that, in everyday speech, the noun *mind* is only ever used as part of a metaphor. The *precedent* claim is that, corresponding to any property that philosophers customarily attribute to the lay concept of mind, there are familiar mind metaphors in which mind is pictured as having that property. The *no-concept* claim is that we have no concept or theory of mind—only stock metaphors and the various imaginings they prescribe. The *nominalization* claim is that the present-day noun *mind* is a "metaphorical accessory nominalization" of the archaic verb *mind*—that is, the noun *mind* is not a referring expression in its own right but merely a figurative noun form of the verb *mind*.

The exclusive-use claim and the precedent claim are both consistent with a Lakoff-Johnson-type approach to the metaphor-*mind* association. The no-concept and nominalization claims are not. As far as I know, they are unique to the metaphorical-origin theory.

Exclusive Use

My exclusive-use claim is that all everyday, non-philosophical uses of the noun *mind* are as parts of metaphors—almost always familiar or "dead" metaphors. That the exclusive-use claim is substantially true is evident from the list of expressions in the appendix. The list includes nearly all the everyday vehicles of the noun *mind*, and all or nearly all of them are clearly metaphors. The question is whether there is any significant class of exceptions.

Certainly, *mind* is often used as part of newly coined ad hoc metaphors, and a small proportion of these—those that are clever and/or useful enough—will in time supplement or replace metaphors now in fashion. Many of the new metaphors will be extensions of, or otherwise consistent with, themes established in the existing stock. However, the fact that our repertoire of mind metaphors changes (albeit slowly) hardly affects the metaphorical-origin claim. Perhaps our notion of mind changes too.

There are some stock similes involving *mind*—e.g., *a mind like a steel trap* and *a mind like a sewer*), and similes are not metaphors. However, I agree with Aristotle that metaphor and simile are basically the same.[7] The purpose of the device (to refer to a specific unnamed feature of a subject matter) and the imaginative "seeing X as Y" that is required to achieve this are the same in simile and metaphor. The spirit of the exclusive-use claim can breathe again.

There is a third kind of possible exception. It may be questioned whether some of the many expressions of the form *P has a such-and-such mind* are metaphorical. *P has a sharp (clear, brilliant, piercing, dull, twisted, dirty) mind* are clearly metaphors, but *P has a good (ruthless, generous, logical, scientific, eager young, powerful) mind* may not be. I tend to think they are metaphors— not so much by virtue of the adjective, but by virtue of the verb *has* (or sometimes, *possesses*). The *has* here is modeled on the *has* and *possesses* used in reference to people's body parts—*P has big feet, a barrel chest*, etc.—and its use in connection with *mind* must be metaphorical. One cannot have a mind in the same sense in which one has body parts. Whatever it is, if it is anything, the mind is not literally a part of a person's body.

Finally, there are expressions in the main appendix list (and in the appendix list of obsolete usages of the noun *mind*) that do not seem to be metaphors. Or, if they are, I can't understand them. Try *time out of mind, the mind boggles, put me in mind of,* and *fall to mind*. However, even if these expressions are not (or are not now) intelligible as metaphors, they are still idioms and hence idiosyncratic. These expressions do not imply anything about what the noun *mind* used on its own might refer to. Again, the spirit of the exclusive-use claim is safe.

Precedents in Metaphors

My *precedent* claim is that, if we plain folk do have a concept of mind, then the colloquial metaphors are where we got it from. For each property that lay people attribute to the mind, there is a precedent in some familiar mind metaphor, or some family of them. That is, there is at least one mind metaphor portraying mind as having just that property. I say "portrays as" because the metaphors do not state that mind has such and such a property. Rather, each invites the listener to imagine—albeit disingenuously, and just for ad hoc referring purposes—that mind has the property in question.

The *Oxford English Dictionary* gives as meaning III, 17 of the noun *mind* the following:

Mental or psychical being or faculty. The seat of a person's consciousness, thoughts, volitions and feelings: the system of cognitive and emotional phenomena and powers that constitutes the subjective being of a person; also the incorporeal subject of the psychical faculties, the spiritual part of a human being; the soul as distinguished from the body.

Despite the dictionary's authoritative definition, the properties by which lay folk characterize the mind are by no means easy to elucidate. Even when you have isolated some plausible ones, you can't press them too hard. You can't say whether folk really *believe* this or that about the mind or whether it's just their way of talking. This is to be expected if, as I claim, there is really no lay concept of mind, only a way of talking.

Most philosophers believe there is a lay concept of mind, though, and most of them would cite as integral to the lay concept the following four properties (or clusters of properties). First, a cluster: mind is a *place* that is *internal* in the person, and hence *private*, to which the person has *privileged access*. Second, the mind is an *agent*. Third, minds and their contents have *intentionality*. Fourth, minds are *non-physical*. I will briefly explain each property—as a philosopher might explain it—and then identify metaphors in the vernacular that portray mind as having the property.

(1) The mind is conceived as a *place* inside people's heads. (Some expressions substitute *head* or *brains* for *mind*—e.g., *What is going on in your head?* and *He doesn't have two brains to rub together*.) There are three or four different kinds of "place" the mind can be. It can be an internal organ where mental processes occur—as implied in *all the things going on in his mind*, *couldn't get it out of my mind*, *it lodged in my mind*, and *in my mind's eye*. The

notion of the mind as an internal organ is also implicit in metaphors that ascribe various kinds of mind, such as *she has a brilliant (dirty, sick, trained, logical, twisted, one-track) mind, broad-minded, open-minded,* and *small-minded,* and it is implicit in expressions such as *mental condition (illness, defect, qualities).*

Or the mind can be an internal venue where the person performs special mental actions. Thus we have expressions like *she went over the proposal in her mind, in my mind I could see him there, he returned to the scene in his mind, she mentally calculated,* and *in my mind I'm going to Carolina.*

Or the mind may be a third kind of place, a receptacle or repository, as in metaphors like *keep it in mind, kept it at the back of his mind, mind filled with notions of, thoughts crowded into her mind, couldn't get her out of my mind,* and *empty your mind of all thoughts of.* . . .

The internality of the mind is logically inextricable from its privacy. Mind is private just because it is inside the person (inside the head) and mind's intracraniality explains why thinking, which by definition goes on in the mind, is private to the person doing it. The thinker has privileged access to the contents and/or workings of his own mind. A person P may directly experience (or "introspect") the contents of his own mind, but the acquaintance anyone else has with the contents of P's mind can only be second-hand—and via P.

The "inside the person," "privacy," and "privileged access" themes are traceable to metaphors like *revealed what she had in mind, tell me what you have in mind, tell me what's on your mind, I could see into her mind, you never know what's going on in her mind, he withdrew into his own mind, in her mind she was privately thinking that, she mentally undressed him, in her mind she was counting the minutes, I knew in my (own) mind that,* and *I'm no mind reader.* The source of the introspection idea is metaphors like *I looked into my mind, I searched my mind, know my own mind, see in my mind's eye, see a picture of it in my mind,* and *aware of something at the back of my mind.*

(2) In addition to being a place, the mind is imagined to be an *agent*—a power operating from inside the person. It interprets information gathered by the sense organs, and it motivates, monitors, and controls the person's behavior—usually in rational ways. Sometimes the mind controls the person, and sometimes it is used by the person (e.g., for solving problems). The "mind as agent" theme is established by metaphors such as *his mind was playing tricks on him, her mind wandered, my mind ran on ahead,*

her mind seized on the idea that, her mind turned to thoughts of, his mind couldn't cope, his mind couldn't grasp it, and *my mind couldn't take in what I was seeing.*

The more specific idea of the mind as a controller of actions and demeanor is expressed in *mental control, mental attitude (fortitude, stamina, weakness), mind over matter, bloody-minded, keep your mind on the job, her mind was elsewhere, presence of mind,* and *strength of mind.*

There are metaphors that construe the mind as an agent of the mechanism variety: *that's how her mind works, you could see his mind ticking over, put my mind to work, the mysterious workings of his mind, his mind raced, mental block, it blew my mind.*

Mind is also cast as an instrument used by the person—for example, in *apply my mind to, mental work, put your mind to work on the problem,* and *I kept my mind focused on the goal.* Lastly, to the extent that an internal organ can be an agent that does things, then the mind-as-internal-organ metaphors (cited above in connection with mind as place) also carry implications of mind as an agent.

(3) The layperson is also said to believe in the *intentionality* of the mind and of mental phenomena. That is, the layperson believes that the mind is linked in a special cognizing or meaning way to things in the outside world. According to theory theorists, the layperson's conception is that, from information gathered via perceptions, the mind forms images, concepts, and memories that are quite accurate mental representations of how things are in the world. Mental phenomena thus inherently represent, "relate to," or are "about" things beyond themselves.

The general idea of intentionality can be sourced in expressions like *her mind's hold (grasp) on reality* and *his mind had lost touch with reality.* Particular intentionality relations—between mental phenomena and things in the outside world—are implied in the many expressions that picture something "in" the person's mind: *I had Africa in mind, a white wedding in mind, it never entered my head,* and so on. There is a link here to the receptacle and repository versions of mind as a place. Intentionality relationships are also pictured in ways other than containment—for example, in: *one thing on her mind, a one-track mind, Georgia on my mind, my mind was focused on it, see a mental image of it, it crossed my mind, it rose up before my mind, call it to mind, it was impressed on his mind that, gave me the mental impression that, what springs to mind is.*

(4) The mind is (thought to be) popularly conceived as *non-physical*. It is regarded as a "part" of a person that is separate from the physical body. It is real but "abstract." Thus, in the *Oxford English Dictionary* definition quoted above we find "the incorporeal subject of the psychic faculties, the spiritual part of a human being; the soul as distinguished from the body." Unfortunately for my precedent-in-metaphor claim, there does not seem to be a single colloquial metaphor that casts mind as abstract or non-physical.

What is to be said here? My suggestion is that *the mind is non-physical* and *the mind is abstract* are themselves metaphors. However, the general referent of these metaphors, what they are about, is in my opinion neither mind nor thinking but mind *talk*. And the special feature of talk "about the mind" these metaphors are intended to bring out is its figurative character. Most people are intuitively, albeit dimly, aware that mind talk is figurative, and aware that, although thinking is very real, talk about an inner venue, repository, agent, or mechanism in connection with thinking is merely metaphorical. However, even a person who is aware that mind is a rhetorical figment will likely be unable to explain just what kind of rhetorical figment it is.[8] All the same, if my impression is correct and the intelligent layperson does believe that mind is something like "a fictional product of figures of speech which describe something real," then the metaphor of something real but incorporeal is very apt.

No Concept

The third plank of my metaphorical-origin theory is the no-concept claim—that the layperson's notion of mind does not amount to a concept or theory as most philosophers, and especially theory theorists, assume it does. The no-concept claim follows from the exclusive-use and precedent claims. If "everything we know about the mind" is derived from metaphors, and if metaphors do much as I say they do in chapter 8 (that is, if they prescribe fanciful seeings-as for attention-directing purposes), then we know nothing about the mind except a whole lot of *as-ifs* and *so-to-speaks*. Metaphors are no arguments.

If the mind metaphors all had a single theme, as Lakoff and Johnson's consistency thesis suggests they should have, there would be a case for saying that the mind notion fits into their special (and to my mind dubious) category of "concept constituted entirely by metaphors" or "conceptual metaphor." However, in the mind case there is no single theme. There are several themes, and the main ones are those I have mentioned in connection with the precedent claim—the mind as internal, a venue, a repository, an agent, a mechanism, an instrument, and so on. These themes are for the most part incompatible with one another. Something cannot be both a place where things are done and the agent that does those things, nor can it be an agent and an instrument, nor both repository and mechanism, and so on. Thus, even if we restricted ourselves to just those mind metaphors representing the above themes, there would still be no possibility of forming a coherent concept from them. Moreover, if we look at the whole range of mind metaphors (starting with the list in my appendix, say), we see that those representing themes are in the minority. The majority of mind metaphors are quite idiosyncratic—*his mind was unhinged, she was playing with his mind, mind-numbing, mind-expanding, out of his tiny mind, she poisoned his mind against them, warped mind, dirty mind.* There is no hope of synthesizing anything even remotely concept-like, let alone theory-like, from this raggle-taggle lot.

Nominalization

When the mind was conceptualized as an organ located within the person, it was assigned the job formerly given to its more active predecessor *minding*, which included imagining along with thinking and remembering.

—Theodore Sarbin, "Imagining as muted role-taking"[9]

Unfortunately the word mind has been almost universally employed to signify both that which thinks and the phenomena of thinking.

—*Oxford English Dictionary*[10]

It might be objected that, at best, the exclusive-use, precedent, and no-concept claims discredit only the detail of our mind concept. It might be claimed that I have shown only that, to fill in the details of what mind is, we must resort to metaphor. This is not dissimilar to what Berkeley, Hegel, Hampshire, and Lakoff and Johnson are saying. It might be said that I have left unchallenged the basic assumption—that there is something in people's heads, something abstract, non-physical, incorporeal, and unperceivable, existing over and above the various acts of thinking (and dispositions and states relating to them). It might be said that I have not queried this ulterior entity, which *mind* is the name of and which the mind metaphors are metaphorical descriptions of.

To counter this suggestion, I must show, in effect, that *mind* is a noun in grammatical terms only and that, considered in isolation from any metaphor, it does not refer to anything. I must show that *mind* is not the name of something. What I actually attempt to show in this section is that *mind* is a special, figurative noun form—a "metaphorical accessory nominalization"—of the verb *to mind*.

Ordinary Act and Accessory Nominalizations

Suppose that we already have a verb for referring to action X, but we have no noun to refer to the practice of X-ing in general or to particular instances of X-ing. In this circumstance, we can adapt the original verb (or simply re-use it unchanged) for the new referring jobs. For example, from *laugh* we can form *laughing* and/or *laughter* to refer to laughing in general. And we might convert *laugh* unchanged for naming an instance of laughing: *we had a good laugh. Laughing, laughter,* and *laugh* (the noun) are *nominalizations* of the original verb. They are essentially "honorary nouns." They are verbs granted a noun role in a sentence because we want to talk about the original action (which the verb names) in a certain formal way. It is still the action that is being referred to, only we are putting a certain logical construction on it. We are viewing that action generally, or we are picking out a particular case of it, as a topic or "thing." And if we are going to look at an action in one of these quasi-objective ways, convention requires that the verb become a noun. This kind of nominalization, where it is just the act of X-ing being talked about in a certain objective way, is *act nominalization.*

Where the verb is re-used unchanged for the noun job, we call the new noun a *conversion.* Here are some act nominalizations that also happen to be conversions, and which also happen to be able to refer either to X-ing in general or to a particular instance of X-ing: *work, worry, touch, dance, command, sleep.* And here are some act nominalizations, also conversions, that refer just to an instance of X-ing: *fall, cry, guess, fight, repair, kiss, sneeze, stop.* In fact, most act nominalizations are formed by adding suffixes (especially *-ation* and *-ing*) to the verb. My reason for preferring simple conversions as examples will be apparent soon.

Act nominalization must be distinguished from *accessory nominalization,* in which case the original verb is again made into a noun—and is again either modified or left unchanged in the process—but for a very different kind of referring job. Accessory nominalizations are used not to name the action or activity itself but to name things that are involved in, or are "accessories" of, that action or activity. Thus, by adapting the verb *receive,* we can identify respective accessories of receiving—*recipient, receiver, receipt, receptacle,* and *reception* (area). In the main, the accessories of an action that most need naming are the agent, the patient, the product, the instruments used in the course of the action, and/or the distinctive venue where the action takes place. This is assuming that the action in question has a patient, a product, an instrument, or a distinctive venue.

At any rate, when we are finding a new name for an accessory of some action it is often easier to nominalize the action verb—especially if we simply convert it—than to come up with an entirely new word. Here are some examples of accessory nominalizations—again, all conversions of the respective verbs:

Agent: *nurse, judge, rebel, fly, cheat, tease, guide,*

Patient: *convert, roast, drink, display, chant, smell, plant.*

Instrument: *paint, drill, probe, rake, brace, whistle, drain, cover.*

Product: *deposit, sweat, bruise, spill, coil, cut, produce, work.*

Venue: *dump, sleep-out, lounge, retreat, forge, hide, store.*

Clearly, the important difference between act and accessory nominalization is that, whereas act nominalizations are only "honorary nouns"—verbs in disguise, referring to nothing other than the action or activity the original verb refers to—accessory nominalizations are nouns in the full sense. They name objects, persons, places, etc. that clearly exist apart from the action or activity after which they are named.

The Noun *Mind* as a Nominalization of the Verb

Three or four centuries ago, the rubric term that covered most varieties of thinking was *minding.* According to the *Oxford English Dictionary,* the verb *to mind* used to mean "remind, remember, think of, bear in mind, be aware of, perceive, intend, plan and wish." It had these meanings in addition to its modern meanings: care, care for (look after), be careful about, and heed. My suggestion is that the modern noun *mind* might well be a nominalization (and a conversion) of the archaic verb *to mind.*

Which kind of nominalization could it be? Is there a viable English usage of the noun *mind* as an act nominalization? That is, can the noun *mind* mean the practice of minding (i.e., thinking) in general, or a particular instance or occasion of minding? Is *mind* like *talk*, *love*, or *work* in this respect? The *OED* seems to think *mind* is sometimes used this way. However, if there is such a usage—and it would qualify as an exception to my exclusive-use claim—it is old-fashioned and rare. The important point is that using *mind* like this would be, as with any act nominalization, just a special, formal way of referring to the action or activity to which the verb refers. This is not how *mind* is used in the colloquial mind metaphors, and it is not how philosophers use it. In both colloquial and philosophical talk, the impression is given that some independently existing entity is being referred to.

Is the noun *mind* an accessory nominalization of the old verb? Well, no, it is not that either. Minding (in the archaic sense of "thinking") has no accessories needing to be named. It has an agent, but the agent already has a name. It is the person, Le Penseur, doing the minding. Minding might be said to have a patient, i.e., that which is minded or thought about. But even if what is minded (winning the lottery) is a genuine patient of the minding, we do not use *mind* to name this patient. And minding has no product; it is not a producing kind of activity. Nor does it employ instruments or have a characteristic venue. If minding has no accessories, then the noun *mind* cannot be an accessory nominalization of the verb.

On the other hand, as it features in the mind metaphors, the noun *mind* does seem to name accessories of thinking. After all, I have just argued the precedent claim—that there are metaphors that portray mind as the impersonal agent, venue, and/or instrument of thinking. The truth is that, although minding/thinking *literally* has no accessories of the relevant kinds, the metaphors give us the idea that it has such accessories. The various accessories—inner agent, venue, and/or instrument—are creatures of the metaphors.

A Conspiracy of Metaphors

For several reasons—including thinking's frequent inconspicuousness, the very early age at which we learn how to do it, the frequency (or constancy) with which we do it, and the clouds of metaphor surrounding it—we are not very good at thinking about thinking. When we need for some everyday purpose to refer to some variety or feature of thinking, we have to rely on the available metaphors. As I have suggested, in a metaphor, the speaker, by strategically inserting an apparently irrelevant referring expression into a description of some general referent X, effects a "mock referral" to something Y and thus pushes the hearer into momentarily imagining X as if it were Y. Because X and Y have just feature F in common, the hearer's attention is drawn to F in X. In the case of the mind metaphors (and most other metaphors in the colloquial thinking vocabulary), the general referent X is some act of thinking and the specific referent F is some feature of (or construction on) that act of thinking. In each case, the metaphor gets us to imagine a given act of thinking as something else (some action, process, event, state, etc.), which it is only a bit like—so that our attention can be drawn to the like bit.

A metaphor is more likely to succeed if the Y being invoked for imagining-as purposes is some familiar, easily imagined thing. Thus, the Ys employed in the mind metaphors are generally familiar, easily imagined processes, actions, events, etc. Our knowledge of actions (and processes and events) consists in large part of our knowledge of their accessories—the things, people, and states of affairs involved in them. Action specifications are laced with nouns. When we think about the actions, the accessories are our reference points. We imagine perceiving the accessories, and this sets us on the way to empathizing the action itself. At any rate, familiar actions—such as the Y actions invoked by the mind metaphors for imagining-as purposes—will tend to have familiar, easily imagined accessories.

Mention of the familiar action "storing" immediately puts us in mind of a storage place or receptacle. The familiar metaphor that characterizes remembering as storing exploits this. Remembering has a feature in common with storing—a subtle, somewhat abstract and difficult-to-define feature, say "leaving something but being able to return to it at will." By speaking of remembering as if it were a matter of storing something away, the speaker directs our attention to this feature. However, storing requires an accessory, a storage place, which remembering does not have. The aptness of the metaphor in the salient respect—absenting oneself while retaining ability to access—suggests to the hearer that remembering may also be like storing in having something corresponding to a storage place. When the speaker then adds a new noun (*mind*) to the metaphor, this noun is taken for the name of the accessory that is going begging. The hearer takes *mind* as naming a putative accessory in remembering that has the same role in remembering that storage places do in storing. The common metaphor for "remember" is not just *keep it*—which might have sufficed by itself—but *keep it in mind*. To carry out the metaphor plus the add-on, the hearer has to imagine a storage place called *mind*.

Other mind metaphors work in the same way. Imagining is in some respect akin to privately viewing a picture, and the aptness of this metaphor persuades us to extend it. Since picture viewing is customarily (or at least notably) done in a place such as a gallery, the aptness of the metaphor persuades us to also fancy, in the case of imagining, an accessory akin to a private picture gallery, that is, a notional "venue" for imagining, a fancied place where imagining qua "picture-viewing" is customarily done. By the same token, feeling an emotion can feel a bit like having a physical disturbance inside one's body, and several colloquial metaphors for emotion-feeling are variations on this theme. Their aptness leads us to posit a disturbing agent inside—if not inside the body then inside the mind—of a person who is described as feeling an emotion. Cogitating is somehow like holding a discussion inside one's head, and, since discussions often have venues, an intracranial venue for cogitating is posited. Solving a problem is in some respects reminiscent of successfully plying an instrument or a tool, so there must be an instrument being brought to bear in problem-solving. And so on.

In each case, the positing of an accessory to the thinking in question is a result of a metaphor's inviting the hearer to imagine the thinking as some process, activity, or event that notably does have that sort of accessory. Without the metaphors, it would never occur to anyone that thinking might involve an inner storage place, or a picture gallery, or a discussion venue, or inner agitations. Mind is a figment of the metaphors.

To go so far as *naming* the fancifully inferred accessory of thinking is to lock in the extension to the metaphor. Presumably, the name *mind* is chosen on the basis of the same kind of eponymy that justifies legitimate accessory nominalizations. *Mind* not only christens the fictitious accessory; because it is the noun form of *minding*, it also reminds the hearer that what is being talked about is a variety of minding. That is, *mind* both embellishes the metaphor and serves, in lieu of an explicit literal referral, to establish the metaphor's general referent. Evidently, the noun *mind*, as it appears in the mind metaphors, is neither an act nominalization nor a genuine accessory nominalization. How should its rhetorical status be characterized? I call it a *metaphorical accessory* nominalization.

The above story explains why the lay "concept" of mind is such a mess. The nature of this "mind" thing is at the mercy of the metaphor we happen to choose to highlight the feature of thinking we are interested in. *He put it to the back of his mind* casts mind as a keep or a repository. *I had to make up my mind* needs mind as the patient of an act of composition. *She gave him a piece of her mind* has mind as an object or a substance. *He went over it again in his mind* and *thoughts crowded into her mind* prescribe a venue. *They poisoned her mind against him* casts mind as a living creature, perhaps. And there are innumerable other idiosyncratic suggestions as to what kind of accessory to thinking this "mind" might be. At the thought of a "concept" of mind, the mind boggles. *Mind* is just a kind of dummy noun that helps augment the metaphors we use to talk about thinking.

What the Dictionary Says

In English, in the great majority of cases of a cognate noun and verb, the verb is derived from the noun. However, the verbs of thinking buck this trend. The *Oxford English Dictionary* allows that the following nouns all are derived from the corresponding verbs: *thought, belief, desire, concept, intention, emotion, feeling, fear, admiration, doubt, memory, heed, hope, attention, recognition, cognition, decision, opinion, anticipation, grief, regret, purpose*. And I presume there are others. In everyday talk, these nouns seem to function mostly as act nominalizations, although sometimes, when accompanied by metaphor, they can look a bit like metaphorical accessory nominalizations. For instance, see the list of metaphor-plus-nominalized-verb combinations in my introduction to the colloquial thinking vocabulary in chapter 8. What is most interesting, however, is what the dictionary says about the origin of the noun *mind*.

Unfortunately, the *Oxford English Dictionary* does not bear out my speculations about the relation of the noun *mind* to the verb. The dictionary is specific and unequivocal. It says of the verb "[f. MIND *sb*.]." This means that the verb derives from the noun. Rather than being a noun form of the verb, the noun is the original, and the verb is a verb form of it. However, three things should be said before the forehead-smiting commences.

First, in adjudging that the verb derives from the noun, the dictionary is contemplating the same scenario that traditional philosophy contemplates, with mind identifiable separately from any actions or processes in which it might be an accessory. Mind is assumed to exist, and to have been named before any minding or thinking of which it is the agent, venue, or instrument. Mind has been discovered "in its own right," and has been dubbed by the noun, before its roles in thinking have been ascertained. Only after this initial discovering and naming of the mind can the verb *to mind* have been coined as a name for the activity in which the mind is involved. Certainly, this kind of derivation scenario is plausible in cases where we are talking about an action or a process that has *actual* accessories—as with, say, the actions named by the verbs *drink, probe, hammer, nail, bruise, farm,* and *store.* Here it is a simple question of etymological fact whether the noun or the verb came first. Either possibility is feasible. However, when the activity the verb names is such as minding or thinking and has no accessories of the required kinds, this scenario is impossible. Entirely fictional accessories of an activity cannot be encountered and named, by a given noun, *before* the (very real) activity is itself encountered and named.

Second, in all or nearly all of its colloquial uses, *mind* fits neither "act" nor "accessory"—the two officially recognized types of verb nominalization. The *OED* authorities may have seen this and, without a concept of verb-nominalization of the third, "metaphorical accessory" kind, concluded that the noun *mind* cannot be a nominalization of the verb and that therefore the verb must have derived from the noun. By default, the noun would have been categorized as an "abstract" noun naming an "abstract thing."

Third, the Indo-European root from which *mind* is descended is *men-, mon-,* or *mn-,* which meant the action of thinking, remembering and/or intending. This root gave rise (in languages that contributed to English) to verbs meaning love, remind, exhort, advise, remember, deny, despise, think, believe, and desire.[11] Although in English the verb *mind* may come from the noun, the English noun itself derives from a foreign verb. It is the same with *imagine* and *image.* Although *imagine* comes from *image,* the English noun *image* comes from the Latin verb *imitari,* to imitate. And the situation is similar with the English word *consciousness,* which derived from the Latin verb (*con-*) *scire*—albeit via the English adjective *conscious.* At any rate, nominalization of a foreign verb is still nominalization of a verb.

The traditional explanation of why *mind* so attracts metaphors, the explanation Lakoff and Johnson embellish, still posits a concept of mind—or the form or bare bones of a concept of mind—which we flesh out with metaphors. The metaphors are still seen as metaphors for or about something called mind. The metaphorical-origin theory's nominalization claim goes much further. It suggests that the reason for *mind* and the metaphors being in cahoots, and never being seen apart in public, is not that mind needs them for public-relations purposes. Rather, it is that the mind notion is a mere add-on to—an epiphenomenon of, or an excrescence on—the metaphors. The apparent references to mind that the metaphors effect carry no more ontological commitment than does the mock reference effected by the Y term. Mind is no more real than the bison on the horizon, the famous Oriental palace now being returned to the hatbox, or the big cane with which our team got thrashed.

Precursors of My Metaphorical Accessory Nominalization Story
As far as I know, my explanation of the logic and provenance of the noun *mind*—in terms of metaphor and the special figurative kind of verb-nominalization—is original. However, Thomas Reid (in particular), R. G. Collingwood, Richard Taylor, and Theodore Sarbin all contribute raw materials for an explanation like mine.[12] Taylor concludes as follows:

> . . . if having a mind just means, among other things, being able to do such things as lay plans, deliberate, select appropriate means to ends, pursue goals, make certain things happen in oneself and one's environment in order that certain other things may happen, and so on, then it is no real *explanation* of how men are able to do such things, to say that they have minds. It is only a strange way of saying the same thing again.[13]

A Last Detail
Because acts of thinking have no accessories, apart from their agents and their objects, there is no call for (genuine) accessory nominalizations in the everyday thinking vocabulary. The primary role of the everyday non-*mind* nouns of thinking—e.g., *thought, belief, desire, memory, concept, intention,* and *emotion*—is as act nominalizations. They are used to refer to particular instances of thinking or believing, etc., or to thinking or believing, etc., as phenomena. With these usages, there is only the noun form and the grammar of the sentence to distract from the fact that it is someone's act (or actional disposition or whatever) that is being referred to. There is no real sense of a thought as other than an actual or potential piece of thinking by someone, and there is no real sense of thought in general as being other than the thinking that people do—no suggestion that intracranial entities are being referred to.

Yet the non-*mind* thinking nouns also attract metaphors from time to time—e.g., *struck by a thought* or *hold a belief*. And the influence of the metaphor changes things. What was a formal reference to the action (of thinking, believing, etc.) becomes a fanciful reference to a fancied accessory of the action. The sense that something intracranial is being referred to is stronger, but, again, in everyday conversation, this sense is fleeting and neither here nor there. The assumption that it is people's active thinkings being mentioned is not seriously challenged. Incidentally, the metaphors seem to have a stronger influence on the nouns of thinking when they are bandied by philosophers. As Hornsby remarks, "Reading contemporary philosophy of mind, one is often distracted from personal-level explanation."[14] Philosophers talk about belief, for example, as if it were really and primarily some kind of object inside people's heads, "as if a person's believing something were an impersonal state, something brutely there."[15]

The above raises the possibility that the noun *mind* may have once been a simple act nominalization of the verb *mind*, occasionally attracting a metaphor or two in the way the other nouns of thinking do now. However, perhaps, in the case of the act nominalization *mind*, the metaphors kept coming and eventually overpowered the original formal reference to the act of minding. In the process, the metaphors installed mind in the popular imagination as the all-purpose intracranial accessory of thinking. This scenario seems more likely than one in which the mind metaphors originally seduced the verb. Something that was already (in grammar, anyway) a noun would be easier for the metaphors to lead astray.

10 Literal Paraphrases of the Mind Metaphors

The argument of chapters 8 and 9 can be reprised as follows: In order to draw attention to and/or provide fanciful explanations of certain features of thinking, English speakers have used metaphors and nominalized verbs to disingenuously posit an entity called "mind." The metaphors portray mind as having the four properties of (1) internality, privacy, and introspectibility, (2) agency, (3) intentionality, and (4) non-physicality. I introduced these "properties of mind" in connection with the precedent claim in chapter 9. On the assumption that thinking is a process in or an operation of the mind, these putative properties of mind are taken as explaining the features of thinking we are interested in.

Although explanations of thinking in terms of mind and its properties are figurative and fanciful, many people—including philosophers—regard them as literally true. The credibility accorded to mind talk gives rise to several intractable philosophical problems about mind, and hence about thinking. Discussion of the philosophical problems tends, in turn, to further entrench naiveté about the relevant figures of speech. The result is that these figures of speech no longer clarify the features of thinking they were initially devised to clarify—not even in a preliminary, picturesque way—and instead serve to chronically obfuscate them.

In this chapter, using the four "properties of mind" as headings, I discuss in turn four features of thinking. With respect to each property, I attempt, without relying on the noun *mind* or the standard mind metaphors, to identify what underlying feature of thinking this property of mind (or set of metaphors) is meant to gloss. I then suggest an alternative literal explanation of the feature in terms of token concerting. In each case, I mention philosophical problems that result when the metaphorical characterization is taken literally.

Internality, Privacy, and Introspectability

This family of properties could also be labeled "intracraniality." The central idea is that the mind is and/or inhabits a place inside people's heads. Thinking is taken to be a mental process carried on by or in the mind. Thoughts, the products of the thinking process, are among the various mental phenomena that occur in the mind. Thinking occurs and thoughts are, almost by definition, inside the head.

The feature of thinking that mind's (and hence thinking's) being inside the person is meant to explain is the fact that a person's thinking is often difficult or impossible to observe. What the mind-as-intracranial metaphors suggest is that thinking is unobservable because of where it goes on. It goes on inside the thinker's head, where only the thinker can see it.

One philosophical problem that results from taking this idea too literally is the problem of other minds: if people's minds are internal to them, and we have no direct access to others' minds, we can never know for sure what other people are thinking.

The metaphor of thinking's going on in a private place inside the person is a little beauty. It neatly captures the hint of secrecy—so compelling for both thinker and spectator—that characterizes some thinking. However, it is just a metaphor. Thinking is an action, and actions cannot be performed by people inside themselves. Moreover, applied to many kinds of thinking, the internality metaphor is quite misleading. As I argued in the introduction, in chapter 1 (in connection with Ryle's adverbial theory), and at length in chapter 7, much of our thinking *is* observable. You can often observe the performance: mutterings, hand gestures, pregnant pauses, sudden frowns or grins. Covert token-doing is often fully covert but often only partially covert. Full covertizing may be necessary for speed, or when one is simultaneously tokening diverse actions. Or it may be necessary for withholding, concealing, or dissembling. Most often, though, when others are present, the extra subtlety and inconspicuousness is unwelcome or unnecessary and we speak our minds.

If P is doing such things as muttering sotto voce, making a series of "intent" facial expressions, holding the top of his head down, and pacing in circles, stopping occasionally to say things out loud, apparently to no one, there is no doubt that he is thinking. We can see him thinking, and we can hear what he is thinking. We can see Le Penseur thinking too, even if we don't know what he is thinking. Often, we see thoughts cross people's minds. We catch a "darkening" of the eyes, the flicker of a smile or a smirk, or a bruised look scampering across. We say *you could see his mind ticking over*; we mean that you could see him thinking, or that you could see him thinking such and such.

There are four main ways we learn what P is thinking. (1) P tells us; (2) we see what ordinary overt action P is performing; (3) we see P's demeanor, including any deliberate expressive displays and/or involuntary bodily agitations in it; and/or (4) we ascertain P's present social and physical circumstances. We empathize on the basis of all four kinds of cue. Arguably, the first and third kinds afford us direct acquaintance with P's thinking.

Basically, it is up to P. If P does not wish us to know what, or even that, he is thinking, then, even if he is right in front of us, he can easily make his thinking undetectable. Admittedly, reticence or inscrutability requires skill. Children, whose thinking is usually laborious and obvious at first, take a while to properly covertize it—just as they take a while to acquire the complementary ability to feign other thinking as a red herring.

As I have suggested, the availability of reticence is sometimes an important factor in our dealings with others and a sensitive issue. We depend a lot on our interlocutors' telling and/or showing us what they are thinking. The metaphor of internality—the notion that thinking takes place intracranially, in the mind of the person—focuses on the reticence option and dramatizes it. Like all good metaphors, it grossly misconstrues the real situation in order to make a point. It goes much too far. Locking thinking away permanently inside people's heads is like a neurotic response to anxiety about others' frankness. It is to say "We can *never* know what is in the mind of another." However, the truth is that we *often* don't know what others are thinking.

Generally speaking, why do we covertize our thinking (when we do)? In my "covert tokening" story, acts of thinking are inconspicuous (when they are inconspicuous) simply because, for normal adults, thinking can be very subtle and quick. Impressed by the social importance of inscrutability and feigning, Skinner,[1] Hampshire[2] (perhaps following Freud), and Dennett[3] all believe that, as the privacy-through-internality metaphor implies, defensive concealment, coyness, and dissembling are the main reasons for covertizing tokening. But I side with Ryle,[4] who says that "celerity and facility" are the main reasons. Much of the time we are with others, we want to *share* what we are covertly tokening.

When you are alone, there is no point in your tokening actions overtly, unless to practice the delivery. Your tokenings can be as streamlined, perfunctory, and fast as you can make them, so long as they still achieve the readiness you want. But someone looking at you through the keyhole might still be able to see that you are thinking—that is, see you thinking. And this is *see you thinking* on exactly the model of, for example, *see you knitting*. If thinking literally took place inside people's heads, no one would ever see anyone thinking, and Rodin could not have sculpted Le Penseur.

Introspection

Introspectability is a kind of auto-observability feature popularly attributed to the mind. It is assumed that, although they are directly and immediately knowable by no one else, the mind and its contents are directly and immediately knowable by the person whose mind it is. People have a natural quasi-perceptual ability to directly "introspect" the contents of their minds. This gives them unique and privileged access to things others can never directly know.

Giving mind this property is an attempt to account for the fact that people generally know what they themselves are thinking even if no one else does. Those who talk about introspection know well enough that we are generally aware of our own thinkings, but this knowledge is distorted by the misapprehension that the thinkings in question are not our own actions but are impersonal processes, states, and entities occurring in a mysterious arena inside our heads. Now, if thinking is an impersonal intracranial process, our self-awareness in the act of thinking becomes difficult to explain. Prima facie, people have no way of knowing what is going on inside their own heads. However, if a faculty of introspection is part and parcel of minds, self-awareness of one's own mind and its contents is easily explained. One can simply look inside one's own head and see what is in there.

Several philosophical problems accompany the notion of introspection. What kind of faculty is introspection? If it is itself a mental ability, is its exercise also observable by introspection? Does this lead to a regress? If introspection is an ordinary perceptual faculty, why has no relevant sense organ ever been discovered? And how could *mental* phenomena be perceived via it?

Incidentally, the problem of how we know our own thoughts is just as intractable on a physicalist definition of mind. If thinking is a brain process, then, with suitable x-ray scanning equipment and an arrangement of screens and mirrors, it might be possible for a person to witness goings-on inside his own brain. However, even if this kind of observational technique is credible—at least, more credible than introspection—what then becomes incredible is that our everyday awareness of our thinking is achieved by such a technique or by anything remotely like it.

Roughly speaking, to "be aware of what one is doing" is to "be ready and able to give a demonstration and/or explanation of what one is doing, should one be asked." Very often a person will achieve this readiness by covertly tokening explanatory words or ostensive gestures simultaneous with his performance of the infra action. This is "thinking what one is doing." Often also, however, when performing well-mastered actions, one is ready and able to explain what one is doing without any overt or covert tokening of educative measures. One does X without thinking, yet stays well aware what one is doing.

If thinking is an action of the person, we should be able to tell much the same story about one's awareness that and what one is thinking. Well, we can, but with some provisos. Let us assume that, normally, thinking is a well-mastered and familiar activity, and thinkers are well aware of their thinking and would be ready and able to give a demonstration and/or explanation of it if asked. And let us assume that thinkers can usually maintain this readiness without having to actively rehearse this overt demonstrating and/or explaining by covertly tokening it. I have identified thinking as the covert tokening of a demonstration and/or explanation of some infra activity X. Thus, we are asking of the self-aware thinker that he be ready and able to demonstrate and/or explain his act of covertly tokening the demonstrating and/or explaining of some activity X. This task seems complicated, and it seems to lead to a regress of awarenesses—of thinking about thinking about thinking about. . . .

In practice, the regress is short-circuited before it starts. To demonstrate and/or explain one's thinking—which is what we are asking the self-aware thinker to be ready and able to do—is simply to demonstrate and/or explain the original infra action X. If someone asks you what you are thinking, you need not demonstrate and/or explain the covert tokening part. All you need demonstrate and/or explain is the X-ing. You do this by actually performing what it was you were doing a covert token performance of. You demonstrate or explain what you are thinking by *telling* the other person what you were thinking. You do the speech out loud rather than just covertly tokening it.

Alternatively, in the fairly unlikely event that your original covertly tokened demonstrating and/or explaining of X includes no covertly tokened speech, and includes only covertly tokened mute demonstrating or depicting or depicting or gesturing, to "demonstrate and/or explain" one's thinking would be simply to perform the mute demonstration or depiction or gesture in question. One usually makes appropriate faces as one confides one's thoughts. Sometimes the face says it all. Either way, the verbal and/or non-verbal educative performance for which one's original thinking readies oneself is the very same performance one must be ready and able to produce in order to demonstrate one's awareness of one's thinking.

Why do I say that we need not worry about the covert tokening part? "Being aware of one's thinking" would generally be taken to involve being aware *what* one is thinking. Awareness *that* one is thinking—i.e., awareness that one is covertly tokening rather than actually undertaking the relevant educative measures—is different.

Can one demonstrate and/or explain covert tokening per se? At first glance, the task of demonstrating covert tokening looks to be self-defeating. What one can demonstrate, however, and what one can do in concert, is the covertizing by degrees of an overt demonstration. And all the circumstances and consequences of covert tokening can be taught. Such educative achievements are part of the process, described in chapter 4, whereby covert tokening is taught to infants and children. By various means, which come very close to (or achieve) explicit demonstration of covert tokening, the child learns how to think silently. He also comes to be able to recognize covert tokening by others and to be aware of doing it himself.

Being able to explain what covert tokening is is another thing. In one sense we can do this perfectly easily. We can talk about having thoughts in our minds, seeing mental pictures of things, having feelings about such and such, and so on. But someone might want to argue that, because our everyday vocabulary for talking about thinking is so thick with metaphor and other figures of speech—and this is the only vocabulary we have for talking about thinking—we don't really know what we are doing, or at least we cannot explain what we are doing, when we are thinking. However, the important thing about the figurative descriptions is that they work. In the final section of this chapter I suggest that the purpose of everyday descriptions of people's thinking is to enable hearers to empathize—i.e., rehearse for themselves—the thinking being talked about. The figurativeness of the descriptions doesn't seem to diminish their utility for this purpose, at least not seriously. Whether reports of thinking couched in literal terms—of covert tokenings of such-and-such actions—would be any more effective at inducing the relevant empathies I do not know. Perhaps such a mode of description would interest the philosopher less, and that would be a blessing.

Agency

One can, surely, say that men "have minds," but what is this but another way of saying that men sometimes think? And if it is known by everyone that men sometimes think, what but confusion is gained by expressing just this fact in a way that might lead someone to think . . . that it is not men, as we ordinarily think of them, who think, but rather their minds?

—Richard Taylor, *Action and Purpose*[5]

The mind is popularly pictured as an internal organ or mechanism—a quasi-natural or supernatural agent—that does things inside the person that affect the person's outer appearance and behavior. The idea of an inner agent was probably invented to help explain three different features of thinking. First, there is the ease and automatic nature of much thinking. Second, there is the fact that most of our behavior is rational—that we perceive and interpret a situation, think about it, then act on the results of our thinking. Third, there is the fact that some of our behavior is irrational, and is accompanied (sometimes) by bodily agitation. The notion of mind as an agent can put a plausible gloss on all three of these features of thinking.

The "Automatic" Appearance of Thinking

If we have an organ inside us that is responsible for our thinking, then the ease and efficiency of (most of) our thinking is explained. This is just the mind operating normally and efficiently, after the manner of any properly functioning internal organ.

On my account, the usual ease and efficiency of our thinking is explained by the amount of practice we get in doing it. We become so adept at covert tokening, after practicing it constantly from early childhood, that, yes, it does seem to happen automatically, and it does seem as if it is being effected by some internal organ or mechanism. If one is unaware of the clumsy beginnings of overt and covert tokening in infancy, one may never realize that thinking is a learned skill that requires considerable effort and practice to get good at. One might easily surmise that we are born equipped with an internal organ responsible for doing it. However, to infer this would be as misguided to infer that, because most of our speech is effortlessly and efficiently devised and delivered, there is some mechanism in our lips, larynx, and brain that is doing the speaking for us—that we just have to open our mouths, so to speak.

Why Our Behavior Is Usually Rational

If the overall rational nature of people's behavior seems mysterious, then positing an internal organ dedicated to ensuring rationality may give the impression of explaining this too. The popular notion of how the mind produces rational behavior is, as I have said, roughly as follows: The mind perceives, and then forms images or concepts of, things in the external world. The mind compares these images or concepts with previously stored ones (memories) and, before storing them also, weighs up possibilities for action in the light of how current images and concepts compare with tried and true ones. Having decided on a course of action, the mind commands the body to act.

The predominance of rational behavior can be explained in my covert tokening story by the person deliberately and habitually ensuring, by the covert tokening (the self-readying) he does, that his behavior is rational. Ensuring the rationality of our behavior is not something we can ever relax about. It is work, and we don't have a "mind" to do it for us. Even if, as I say, it is work at which we are generally very good and work that (usually) requires little effort, we still have to do it.

Anticipatory and concurrent covert tokening guide action roughly as follows: Between actions, a person is usually performing perceptual behavior. If the current perceivings have been in the past done as part of action X, then it is likely the person is covertly tokening X-ing along with his current perceivings. Alternatively, action X is already being covertly tokened for other reasons, and current perceptual behavior is increasing the enthusiasm of this covert X-tokening.

There is an interesting possibility of theoretical parsimony here. Suppose it is true (and it seems to me that it is) that perceiving is generally done "with some action in mind." That is, suppose there is no such thing as disinterested perception. If so, then, for theory purposes, we might as well include perceiving as part of the normal preliminary covert tokening (now not quite so covert) that takes place in advance of action. That is, perceiving can be included in the commencing phase of normal anticipatory commencing and aborting. To perceive something is to already foretoken some action concerning it.

Covert tokening readies and primes the X-ing response yet holds it in abeyance until conditions are optimal for full performance. However, the covert X-tokening is still amenable to being modified by (by synthesizing) any other compatible behaviors whose covert tokening is also being triggered by current perceivings. Perceptions of the current situation may fine-tune the X-ing, or even change it majorly, while it is still at the covert tokening level of performance.

Eventually, X-ing-conducive perceptual behavior accumulates to the point where the person embarks on a full performance of X. Or else, suitable X-triggering perceptual behavior fails to accumulate. In the latter case, X-ing is abandoned and the person starts covertly tokening some other action.

Overall, covert tokening functions as a buffer or clutch, enabling gradual preparation and well-timed, appropriately modulated delivery of behavior. The "imperative" aspect of thinking—traditionally pictured as the mind's issuing instructions to the body—is captured in my account by covert tokening's readying and priming effect on behavior. But of course covert tokening is done as much to ensure that behavior is not undertaken prematurely as to ready it. The holding back is as important as the priming.

Why Our Behavior Is Sometimes Irrational

The presence of a suitable inner mental (and/or physiological) agent seems to also help explain our occasional irrational behavior and to help explain the bodily agitations (blushing, trembling, a frail voice, etc.) that may accompany irrational behavior. According to several familiar metaphors, the mind may disrupt a person's behavior or appearance from within. In these cases, the mind is not acting normally. It is some "mental disturbance," "emotional upheaval," "inner turmoil," or "unbalance of the mind" that is having the disturbing effect on behavior. A person may be "gripped," "overcome," or even "paralyzed" by the inner aberration. In this picture, the mind is still the effective agent; however, it is not its usual self. The observer's stance here is a quasi-medical one.

The main philosophical problem that results from taking the mind-as-inner-agent metaphor too seriously is called "the problem of psycho-physical causality." How can something non-physical (the mind) have effects on something physical (the body)? How could, say, a feeling (of a certain kind) cause a person to do things (of a certain kind) and to suffer bodily agitations (of a certain kind)?

The various bodily agitations I mention from time to time—blushing, blanching, weeping, shivering, clenching fists, becoming sexually aroused—are not, in my account, the outer manifestations of inner disturbances. Rather, they are, examples of covert tokening that, often because it is over-excited, is being performed in a heedless, clumsy, incompetent way. What we are looking at is simply inefficient and undisciplined covert tokening. The commencing or the aborting has got out of hand, or both have. Covertness has gone by the board. The hypothesis of an ulterior mental (or physiological) cause is as inappropriate here as it would be in respect of normal, well-controlled thinking. A careless, clumsy, and/or incompetent performance of an action has no more to do with interventions from within than a careful, adept and/or polished performance has. *When he heard the news fear gripped his vitals* refers not to an internal event but to a task of covert behavior-tokening that is proving a handful.

Intentionality

Intentionality is a philosopher's notion. The idea that it features in the layperson's "concept of mind" is a philosopher's notion too. The intentionality relation is supposed to hold between mental items and things other than those mental items—usually, things existing in the world. To define the intentionality relation, philosophers use metaphors of aboutness, directedness toward, indicating, meaning, pointing, and aiming. Lay folk employ similar metaphors to characterize the relations between things in the world and the minds that think about them—and between things in the world and the thoughts that are "about" or "of" them. As I said in chapter 9, lay folk use the metaphor of the mind as a container to put anything from a very small grommet to World War II in people's minds. Bishop Berkeley owns up to this: ". . . when I speak of objects as existing in the mind or imprinted on the senses, I would not be understood in the gross literal sense, as when bodies are said to exist in a place, or a seal to make an impression upon wax. My meaning is only that the mind perceives or comprehends them."[6]

The fact that the philosophical notion of intentionality is intended to explain is the fact that the grammar of mentalist terms seems always to imply some relation between the internal mental phenomenon (that is apparently being referred to) and some external entity. Accordingly, one is afraid "of" something, interested "in" something, grateful "for" something, fascinated "by" something, in love "with" someone, or astonished "at" something, and one has beliefs "about" things, attends "to" things, and so on. A similar "aboutness" or "directedness" quality appears to be, and is held by many philosophers to be, a feature of all linguistic items. Thus, words are "about" or "refer to" things.

Intentionality is its own philosophical problem. The notion of intentionality is the problem of intentionality. John Searle asks "What exactly is the relation between Intentional states and the objects and states of affairs that they are in some sense about or directed at? What kind of a relation is named by *Intentionality* anyhow and how can we explain Intentionality without using metaphors like *directed?*"[7] Debate is still alive as to whether mental or linguistic intentionality is primary. Which category possesses basic intentionality, and which possesses derivative, secondhand, or borrowed intentionality? The idea of a "language of thought" or "mentalese" in which our thoughts are couched—or of bits of which our thoughts *consist*—was invented by a philosopher to account for mental phenomena having intentionality, on the assumption that linguistic intentionality is primary.[8]

In my account, the apparent intentionality or thing-relatedness of thinking is a special case of the apparent thing-relatedness of actions generally. We specify actions by reference to the things in the world that are the accessories of, or things relevant to, these actions. Certain actions are by definition or inherently "to do with" certain things. You cannot specify feeding the hens without mentioning the hens.

Thinkings are, in the same way, "inherently about" their topics. Because thinking is the covert tokening of educative sessions of activities, it involves the covert tokening of referring—that is, the speech-mediated concerting of perceptual behavior. Referring sessions have topics, or referents. Even thinking that is the covert tokening of idle conversation is in the same boat. Conversations have topics too, by virtue of their involving referring. If an ultimate source of intentionality is to be nominated, it had better be concerted perceptual activity. The lost font of aboutness is the referring transaction. Thinking "has aboutness" because, and insofar as, it betokens þings. For similar reasons, speech or any other means of tokening joint perceptual behavior "has aboutness."

If there is such a thing as intentionality, then in my story it is a function of *the whole referring transaction*—a transaction comprising two or more agents, perceptual behavior, ostensive gestures, speech, and concerting procedures. The conventional notion of linguistic intentionality is problematic because it is specified as attaching not to whole transactions but to words or other linguistic items—or "semantic materials," as Lawrence and Valsiner might say.

A word is essentially an action (or action-component) and is thus inseparable from its wider transactional context. To imagine that words can somehow exist in their own right, as (linguistic) objects in the world, is to contemplate the bizarre notion that they can by themselves reach out and "mean" other things in the world. However, as I said earlier in connection with the fancy of "words referring to things," it is only by synecdoche that one ingredient in an activity (a vocal utterance, say, or a mark on paper) can accomplish what the whole activity accomplishes. The referring transaction as a whole can perhaps be said to have intentionality. Referring sessions can be about things. Other actions and activities can be about or directed toward things too. But things cannot be about things.

Strictly, acts of thinking, because they involve no actual referring, cannot have intentionality either. Because thinking is only the tokening of referring (etc.), not the actuality, it possesses only "as if" or would-be aboutness. The mental states or mental objects we conjure when we nominalize the verbs of thinking have no better claim to intentionality. The fancy that mental states have intentionality is partly a consequence of not realizing that talk about mental states and their properties is in reality talk about acts of thinking and partly a consequence of not realizing that thinking has no chance of actual aboutness, only a chance of would-be aboutness. Thinking is part actual performance (the meta-action of covertly tokening the lesson or conversation or other referring session) and part make-believe (the putative infra lesson or conversation or referring session itself). The aboutness belongs to the make-believe part.

Non-Physicality

It is difficult to elaborate on the supposed non-physicality of mind. Descartes tried and found himself landed with a whole new invisible and intangible world—a dimension of reality that is real but inaccessible to any of the senses, a world that is inside people's heads and directly experienced by them, but which no anatomist or physiologist has ever seen.

I suggested in chapter 9 that calling the mind non-physical or abstract is a metaphor and hence disingenuous. I said that the metaphor might have been devised to show up the fact, dimly apprehended by at least some lay folk, that mind talk is figurative. So *non-physical* is a metaphor and euphemism for "fictitious" or "notional." Rather than define mind's ontological status precisely (as, say, the illegitimate progeny of bogus accessory nominalization and metaphor), it is easier, if not quite philosophically correct, to posit the entity initially, so one has something to attach one's ontological reservations to.

Thus, the aspect of thinking this "property of mind" is invented to explain is the fact that the language we employ to exhort and otherwise communicate and talk about acts of thinking is figurative and should be taken with a grain of salt.

Another way one could conceivably take *mind is non-physical* is as a way of construing thinking's (supposed) trademark unobservability. In this view, the attribution of non-physicality would be an addition or alternative to the unobservable-because-hidden-inside metaphor. We would now be asked to believe that thinking is unobservable, when it is unobservable, because it occurs in an immaterial medium or dimension. This would make mind and thinking not just contingently but necessarily unobservable. However, I don't think the notion of a "non-physical dimension of reality," or whatever, has much currency outside philosophy. Even within philosophy, dualism is generally recognized as an appeal to the supernatural and, as such, something of a paper tiger. In the vernacular, the ontological status of mind is left unspecified. If, as I suspect, there is lay awareness of the dependence of the mind notion on metaphor, this reticence is just what one would expect.

A third possibility is that non-physicality is attributed to mind in an attempt to specify that particular ambivalence in our attitude toward others that the mind idiom—with its implication of an impersonal agent inside people's heads, controlling their behavior—allows us. The mind is real and is working away in there behind the person's eyes. This justifies an objective, perhaps wary attitude and a suspension of empathy. On the other hand, the mind is not "really" real, it is not "physically" there. It is "nonphysical"; it is "spiritual." And the mind's being spiritual removes—to the extent we want it removed—the obstacle to empathizing with others. Perhaps the mind idiom, and the colloquial thinking vocabulary generally, make it easier for us to hover, in our dealings with others, between empathy and objectivity. Much of the time we like, or need, to hover in that way. Just possibly, the oxymoron of an abstract or non-physical thing, the notion of mind as a thing yet not a thing, was devised to rationalize or obfuscate such hovering. Claude Lévi-Strauss thought myths are made for reconciling the contradictions in cultures. "The purpose of myth," he commented, "is to provide a logical model capable of overcoming a contradiction (an impossible feat if, as it happens, the contradiction is real)."[9]

Other Metaphors in the Colloquial Thinking Vocabulary

In addition to the metaphors with the noun *mind* in them, the colloquial thinking vocabulary has a second tier of metaphors about thinking. We have come across some of them already. An example is the metaphor of "expressing" thoughts and feelings in words or deeds. The expression metaphor, which I mentioned in connection with Hampshire's theory, is an attempt to explain the relation between covert tokening and overt tokening or actual performance. The metaphor pictures the overt behavior or speech as the externalized, released, or pushed-out product—the "expression"—of the inner thought or feeling. The reality underlying the expression metaphor is the ambivalent and often changing relationships—reflecting the dual commencing and aborting aspects of tokening—between covert and overt tokening, and between tokening and actual doing.

Related to the expression metaphor are metaphors of internal pressure, intensity, vividness and violence. These are used to characterize not only emotions but also memories, imaginings, realizings, and insights. The situation these metaphors were devised to describe is the one I mentioned earlier in connection with the notion of the mind (or some mental phenomenon) acting as a disruptive, disturbing agent. In this situation, the person is, for whatever reason, having difficulty keeping covert tokening covert. The muscular effort associated with the contrary commencing and aborting may give the person the impression that there is some disturbing force inside his body. It is often also the case that the behavior being covertly tokened is by nature vigorous, loud, and/or effortful. Keeping the commencing and aborting of it covert may be difficult. We say that the feeling—of joy, dread, grief, relief, lust, triumph, or whatever—is so "intense," so "strong," that it is difficult not to cry out. We mean that we are (nearly) unable to abort the commencing of the emotional display.

In the same vein, a person might have an idea so brilliant that it is difficult for him to "contain" his enthusiasm. It is difficult to do the overt or covert tokening in a properly restrained manner. The person may leap out of his bath, shouting in Greek and sending water everywhere. This is not to say that restraint in tokening is always important in interpersonal situations. It is only to say that such restraint or the lack of it in the covert tokening of inherently vigorous or "expressive" activity is what the intensity metaphors are about.

Another family of metaphors I have already mentioned includes *thinking in words, thinking in pictures, putting my thoughts into words, expressing the idea in words, say what you think,* and *speak one's mind.* The facts about thinking that this metaphor picturesquely construes for us are the facts I explained in chapter 7 under the heading "Second-Order Tokening." That is, the metaphor of doing one's thinking "in the medium of" speech or graphic representation is an attempt to highlight that feature of thinking whereby we do not usually covertly token the infra activity directly—rather, we covertly token the overt tokening (in speech or graphic, etc.) of the infra activity.

The "conduit" metaphor described by Michael Reddy is influential in the colloquial vocabulary we use for talking about communicating.[10] A naively literal acceptance of it is responsible for what Roy Harris calls the "telementation" model of communication.[11] This model has its most absurdly literal formulation in Ferdinand de Saussure's well-known diagram of two women speaking.[12] Arrows of "meaning" emerge from the mouth of each and enter the ears of her interlocutor—an image Michael Toolan calls "the acme of telementational orthography."[13] The general referent or subject matter of the conduit metaphor is those make-do versions of concerting described in chapters 4–7, which involve one party's overtly tokening some joint activity and the other party's reciprocating by covertly tokening, or empathizing, the same activity. That is, the conduit metaphor attempts to gloss what happens during ordinary interpersonal communication, such as conversation.

The image the conduit metaphor proposes is of thoughts' being transported by words from one mind to another. This can be spelled out as follows: Thoughts are first generated and converted into words in the speaker's mind. The words are then broadcast out of the mind/head, via the mouth, as speech. The spoken words then travel through the air and enter the ears, and the head and mind, of the other person, and are decoded back into thought. The thought thus travels from one mind to the other. Quite likely, this spelling out of the conduit metaphor is more detailed and coherent than it ever is in the folk mind. The rule in the vernacular is rough and ready, not rigorous and theoretical.

Philosophers of language and professors of linguistics have extended the conduit metaphor. The noun *meaning* is sometimes an act nominalization of, and sometimes a metaphorical accessory nominalization of, the verb *to mean*. The word *meaning* conjures an entity that seems to fit very well into the conduit picture. If word meanings are thoughts in the mind, and words carry their meanings with them, the transport problem—how thoughts or meanings can actually move through the air—is as good as solved.

I have mentioned the mind metaphor in which remembering is imagined as storing in the mind. As well as this metaphor, which paints mind as a repository, there are other storage metaphors for remembering. In these, old memories "become stale," "fade," or "remain vivid"; new ones are "fresh." Memory can be "refreshed" too. The faded-vivid contrast and the old-fresh contrast are probably both adaptations of the general strong-weak contrast customarily applied to emotions and ideas. When the overt or covert tokening of some perception or other experience is, even after years, difficult to inhibit—if the tokening is difficult to control or do gracefully—we call this a "strong" ("vivid," "well-preserved") memory. Alternatively, if too much time has passed, or if the original perceiving or other doing was not memorable enough at the time, then the problem with the tokening may be on the commencing side. In this case it is not a problem of keeping the performance down to a token level but of coaxing out at any level of performance at all. Here we speak of "weak," "faded," or "dim" memories—memories stored improperly or not refreshed often enough.

In reality, nothing is stored, nothing is preserved, and nothing fades. Remembering is not really like storing and retrieving from storage. Remembering is being able to do again, at least in token form, something one has done—once, a few times or often—in the recent, intermediate, or distant past. Sometimes it is easy (sometimes all too easy) and sometimes it is difficult. In the latter case, work of the self-educative, self-prompting, self-readying kind may be required.

The above is a small sample of the non-*mind* metaphors in the colloquial thinking vocabulary. There are others. All of them function to highlight, and put an easily understood gloss on, certain features of thinking.

Why We Depend on Metaphors for Talking about Thinking

As the number of stock metaphors in the colloquial thinking vocabulary indicates, we rely heavily on figures of speech to pick out features of thinking, and to otherwise talk about it. This is due in part to our ignorance of thinking relative to other everyday activities. Some of the factors that contribute to our ignorance of thinking are the following: As infants and children we were shown rather than instructed how to think. We learned how to do it before we could have understood instructions, or descriptions of what is involved. Now it is second nature, something we do all the time— and it is difficult to be aware of so familiar an action. Furthermore, as I have conceded, thinking is often inconspicuous, involving no overt movement at all. And finally, thinking has no accessory things (apart from what it is about) that we could use to get a handle on it. As a result, our concept of thinking is something of a runt. To say anything about it, we must turn to metaphor. Even the *Oxford English Dictionary* relies, in its definition of thinking, on expressions such as *to conceive in the mind, exercise the mind, form in the mind, have in the mind as a notion, to do in the way of mental action, to form or have an idea of (a thing, etc.) in one's mind, picture in the mind,* and *call to mind.*

Several writers have pointed to the value of metaphors as a preliminary heuristic recourse, especially in science. Apart from their specialized referring function, metaphors can serve a broader proto-explanatory function. And this may help explain why the mind metaphors have been mistaken for a theory or proto-theory. As Susan Haack notes, metaphors are often the precursors of genuine theory:

. . . in the process of developing a specific, detailed, precise theory a vague idea may be a very useful stage along the way. A figurative comparison is well-fitted to serve in this capacity because it is open-ended and unspecific, but at the same time invites a certain process of specification and filling-in of details. . . . At any rate, a metaphor's combination of lack of specificity, of directedness, and of novelty is indeed what makes it useful in the early, fumbling-around phases of inquiry.[14]

Haack is talking about metaphor as a way station on the road to knowledge. We begin with analogies, models, and metaphors; then, as we get to know a topic better, we replace these with detailed literal descriptions, and perhaps (depending on the nature of the subject matter) quantifications and/or mathematical formulas.

Arguably, progress on both lay and philosophical theories of thinking has stalled at Haack's fumbling-around stage. In chapters 8 and 9, I have suggested that the biggest fumble might be our too-credulous rehearsal of the "impersonal process" metaphors. This has led to a mere figment of the metaphors and/or a rhetorical prop for them, "mind," being mistaken for their subject matter. A theory of thinking is required, not a theory of mind. Perhaps it is "mind" that has stalled progress. Perhaps also, people's assumption that a scientific explanation is required has exacerbated the situation. Or perhaps it is the sheer cultural inertia of the metaphors and their domination of our view of thinking. Anyway, Haack's observations seem not to apply so well to the mind metaphors and our other stock metaphors for thinking. Rather than preliminary sketches of explanations, they look more like long-term substitutes for them.

Almost certainly, our ignorance of thinking is increased by the metaphors themselves. Once the metaphors attracted by a topic reach a certain critical mass, a kind of heuristic fatigue sets in whereby the metaphors begin to dominate and constrain our perception of the topic, obscuring more than they illuminate. Our metaphors for thinking, and the mind metaphors in particular, have acquired this kind of hypnotic influence. Their effect is akin to that of subliminal advertising or propaganda. Apart from the sheer number of the metaphors, the factors contributing to their influence seem to be as follows.

First, their use is more or less subliminal: the expressions are so familiar, we use them so frequently, that we are hardly aware of using them at all, let alone aware that they are metaphors and not to be taken at face value. Second, the repetition that comes with frequent use of certain metaphors tends to give the messages the metaphors carry a cultural acceptability that we come to rely on psychologically and mistake for literal credibility. Third, the variations on a theme that some of the mind metaphors exhibit—with the posited non-physical entity inside the head portrayed in several different ways—add to the impression that the metaphors are true, and true *of* something (the mind). Finally, the importance of the subject matter is a factor. Despite our ignorance of it, thinking is very important in our daily lives, both practically and as an expression of our togetherness.

The above factors tend to cement our initial ignorance by making it difficult for us to imagine thinking in ways other than the fanciful ways the metaphors prescribe. Long-term reliance on fantasy may diminish the ability to perceive reality. At any rate, our level of dependence on the colloquial thinking metaphors leads us to accept them as literally true—at least, it keeps us from realizing that they might not be literally true. This is not necessarily a disadvantage for the ordinary person. In everyday situations, it is only certain features of thinking that are relevant at all often, and the mind metaphors and the others pick most of these out nicely. For everyday purposes, we may not need to know what general kind of action or activity thinking is.

As I speculated above, it is also possible that the metaphors are useful in the way in which myths were useful in pre-scientific cultures. The idea of an impersonal inner agency controlling the other person's actions may usefully disguise the conflict—which often arises in interpersonal dealings—between empathizing with another person and viewing him objectively. So it might be useful in rationalizing impersonal treatment of others.

In any event, by obliging us to imagine thinking as an inner process, the metaphors distance and/or veil an important aspect of our lives. Seeing past the metaphors—seeing thinking as learned and as founded in concerted activity, and appreciating the ramifications of this—might have some beneficial effects. For the philosopher, a realistic overview of thinking would be a boon and the disadvantages of unaware addiction to figures of speech are more obvious. Unless the colloquial metaphors for thinking and their associated nominalizations and synecdoches are seen for what they are and set aside, then the desired philosophical overview will remain elusive. This is what Wittgenstein and Strawson are saying in the passages I quote at the end of chapter 8.

Mistaking Empathizing for Imagined Perceiving

Most actions involve easily observable and empathizable movements. We seldom fail to recognize them as actions. The situation is somewhat different with acts of thinking. As I say, we are predisposed by figurative expressions to imagine that thinking is unobservable—thus we tend to disqualify behaviors such as speech, inaudible mutterings, facial expressions, and ostentatious pauses from counting as constituent parts of the thinking. The image of thinking going on inside the person persuades us to view these behaviors as effects of thinking, rather than its constituents. In the case of thinking, we do not (we believe) see anything we could recognize as voluntary action. Yet we know that thinking is going on. So, we conclude that thinking cannot be an action, but must be an inner process.

Our being convinced that thinking goes on inside the person's head and is thus unobservable means that the format we assume for our references to people's thinking is that of absent-referent referring. The internality metaphors predispose us to regard thinking on the model of something hidden (and in this sense absent), such as a mouse scratching inside a wall. Even when the thinking is going on right in front of us, we assume, because we believe we can never actually observe thinking, that we are obliged to merely imagine observing it. A problem then arises: How do we visualize the other's thinking? It is easy enough to visualize a mouse in a wall. But what does a thought process look like? How does one covertly token the perceiving of this particular absent referent?

Often the thought being talked about is referred to via metaphor, and some content for visualizing is prescribed by the metaphor: *It crossed her mind that. . . . I formed the belief that. . . . He tried to think through the situation.* In other cases, there is no metaphor nearby. There is just *P thought again of Carolina,* or *I suddenly remembered the anchovies,* or *He was furious.* What imagined absent-referent-perceiving, what covertly tokened perceptual behavior, can the hearer contribute in these cases?

It is safe to say that we never visualize brain events in this connection. Even the most rigorously physicalist philosopher does not respond to *P thought of going to Carolina* by visualizing constellations of interneuron firings coursing through P's brain. The fact is that, in response to *P thought of going to Carolina,* none of us, including physicalists, would attempt to visualize goings-on of any kind inside P's head.

What we would all actually do instead is try to empathize with P. That is, we would attempt to do what P is doing. We would attempt to covertly token going to Carolina. Inevitably, when P's thinking is being talked about, it is an empathic response that we come up with. Empathy is our primary heuristic recourse when we witness or hear about actions. But only actions. If what is being talked about is an impersonal process going on inside P, then an attempt at (covertly tokened) objective scrutiny will be appropriate.

Probably, the main function of the colloquial thinking vocabulary is not to assist hearers to imagine objective intracranial realities, or indeed any objective realities, but rather to assist hearers to empathize with the person whose thinking is being talked about. If this is so, the colloquial thinking vocabulary is a set of expressions devised to assist in inducing empathy in the "covert tokening" area of our shared repertoire. The expressions in it help us empathize—or actually imitate—the thinking of others. We may respond to the mind talk and the metaphors with some cursory covert tokening of objective scrutiny (of putative intracranial goings-on). We do process the metaphors, albeit perfunctorily. But our primary response is empathy for the thinking, the covert tokening, that the person being talked about is doing. We reassure ourselves that we know what action is being talked about by "doing" it too.

That it is logically necessary to empathize in order to identify others' actions, including their acts of thinking, is shown by the empathy argument I present in the next chapter. Actions are specified by reference to the things in the world that the action has to do with. To identify any act of thinking, or any "mental phenomenon," one must know what it is "about." If P's thinking is about going to Carolina, then, for the speaker to describe P's thinking to you, she must mention going to Carolina. When she does, and you respond by thinking of going to Carolina, then you are doing what P is doing.

That is not all. The speaker is also empathizing with P, and by referring you to what P is thinking she is communicating her own empathizing-with-P to you. You end up empathizing with both her and P. All three of you are covertly tokening going to Carolina. In fact, we all are.

It is perhaps the main source of confusion in the philosophy of mind that philosophers mistake the empathic responses elicited by colloquial mentalist talk for successful attempts on the hearer's part to imagine perceiving mental phenomena. We have a description of someone thinking of going somewhere, or remembering something, or feeling angry. And the hearer makes an imaginative response to that description. But the kind of imaginative response that is appropriate for this kind of description is not the same as the kind of imaginative response that is appropriate when we are hearing about, or hearing, the intramural mouse.

The imagining we actually do in response to the apparent referrals to internal mental phenomena is not imagining of objective observings. It is much more like the kind of empathic imagining with which one would respond to a hortation to do something, or to a picture of someone doing something, or to a demonstration of an action. The imagining we do in response to *P has the belief that snow is white* is empathic. It is a matter of our covertly and "on P's behalf" rehearsing that proposition about snow. However, when the philosopher goes on about intracranial entities and processes, we all too easily misinterpret this empathizing of ours as a kind of imagined perceiving. That is, we misconstrue it as covertly tokened, in lieu of actual, perceivings of something sitting there in P's head—some "mental representation," perhaps, or a special brain state.

11 Our Knowledge of Actions

The belief that science is in principle capable of explaining everything and that scientific knowledge is the most fundamental and reliable kind is often called *scientism*. One corollary of scientism is the assumption that human beings are essentially biologically evolved organisms, their behavior determined by in-principle identifiable, scientifically explicable and predictable physical (especially physiological) causes. This assumption underpins cognitive science. I call it *action physicalism*.

The preferred explanatory strategy in cognitive science is as follows: Confronted by a given instance or type of human behavior, the scientist seeks to identify a neurophysiological mechanism in the brain—a mechanism that has been installed there by evolutionary influences over many generations—that is triggered by specific environmental circumstances and that directly causes the behavior in question. The behavior might be anything from the ability to recognize faces or estimate distance to increased competitive behavior among females in the presence of males. The explanatory strategy is basically the same as that employed for any animal. In the human case, most behavior is thought to be determined by an advanced cognitive system, an assembly of information-processing mechanisms installed by evolution in our brains. These mechanisms enable us to respond rationally to our environment.

In the introduction I argued that people's learned actions and natural (in particular, biological) processes are two very different categories, and I gave reasons for believing that thinking is a learned action and not a natural process. The chapters since then have continued the argument that thinking is a learned action. I have attempted to show, among other things, what kind of action thinking is and how it is learned. However, even if it is true that thinking is a learned action, if action physicalism is true, it would still be true that thinking—not just despite being an action but *because* it is an action—is ultimately a biological process. In this case, cognitive science's assumption that thinking is the functioning of the cognitive system in the brain could be fully justified. So, it is up to me—if my efforts to establish the actionality of thinking are not to be undone at the end, with thinking sliding back down into the biological in action's arms—to provide good reasons why action physicalism should be discarded. In the following sections I present two. They are, respectively, the *empathy* argument and the argument about *action metaphors in science*.

The Empathy Argument

One of the reasons action physicalism seems plausible at first is that our witnessings of people's actions, such as P tying his shoelace, seem very similar to our witnessings of natural events and processes—a tree bending in wind or water turning to steam in a pot. Whether watching the tree bend or P tie his shoelace, it seems, we simply "stand back and observe." What we are observing is objectively "there." It is occurring in the world in an apparently similar way in both cases. Certain rhetorical ploys, including act nominalization and metaphor, abet this impression. They encourage our tendency to put people's actions on the pile of "things happening in the world." I discuss the linguistic influences later. In this section I argue that, despite first impressions, there are essential differences between the way we perceive people's actions and the way we perceive natural processes and events.

Roughly speaking, action physicalists claim that actions are physiological events. For this claim to be verifiable, it would have to be possible to temporally and spatially correlate observations of actions with observations of physiological events. I argue that we are unable to correlate people's actions with physiological events, because the two subject matters require different heuristic methods for their individuation and observation. Actions require empathy. To perceive and/or specify an action, its external accessories must be perceived and/or specified. To do this, the observer must imitate or empathize perceivings and referrings that the agent of the observed action is performing. Scientific observation requires objective observation methods, measurements, and experiments. These are incompatible with an imitative or empathic heuristic. Because the respective heuristic procedures are incompatible, actions can never be observed side by side with physiological events. That is, the two can never be "correlated."

Empathy as a Heuristic Vehicle

In order to perceive actions, we must empathize. In order to see what someone else is doing, we must put ourselves in the other's position—that is, we must imagine doing what the other is doing. We use our own covert tokening of the action as a "heuristic vehicle," an investigative strategy according to which we perceive and identify the action the other is performing.

In addition to viewing perceiving as itself an action (see chapter 6), I am assuming here what might be called a "pragmatic" or an "operational" story about the context in which perceiving is done. I assume that we perceive things only in the course of, and as part of, the performance of wider actions. We encounter things in the world not in a vacuum but in the course of practical, recreational, or investigative activity, and the view we get of any particular thing—how we encounter it and what about it we attend to—is determined by the nature of the activity we are currently engaged in. We view things in terms of the activity and/or as accessories to it. If we are chopping firewood, we will see the wood in one way. If we want to whittle something from the wood, or throw a piece of it for a dog to retrieve, or find out how old it is by counting the rings, we will see it in other ways. We will use different perception recipes. One inspects thing T from a checklist determined by the nature of activity X. One looks for and ticks off just those features of T that bear on X-ing.

The need for an activity context from which to perceive things carries over into the absent-referent referring done in descriptions and explanations. The speaker or writer must sketch in some activity for us to imagine engaging in—as the heuristic vehicle from which we can imagine encountering and perceiving the things being talked about.

When the thing T we are being asked to perceive or imagine perceiving is an action, the situation is the same. We still need some action to serve as a heuristic vehicle. In one sense, however, the situation is simpler when it is an action that we are witnessing or imagining. There is one obvious candidate for heuristic vehicle, and it is already at hand. The heuristic vehicle—the actual or covertly tokened action "via" or "in the course of which" we do or imagine doing the relevant perceivings—can be the action in front of us, the observed action itself. We observe P doing X while tokening doing X ourselves. We observe X "from the point of view of" someone doing X.

Although we observe the action from a distance, and make no move to actually participate, we are nevertheless construing that action from the standpoint of the performer. We learn this trick—this empathy at a distance—by adapting the format of the innumerable concertings we engaged in as children in which seeing the other do something does go with our doing it too. Initially, our *actual* performance of the action is the heuristic frame on which our perceptions of the other's doings hang. Subsequently, once we are able to unilaterally withdraw from concerted activity into the detached and immobile spectator role, we learn to correlate the perceived doings of the other not with our actual doings but with our imagined or "covertly tokened" doings. It is the phases and termini in our covertly tokened doings that orchestrate our perceptions of the other's actual doings.

Naturally, there are different interests one might have in a given action— hence different checklists and corresponding ways of scrutinizing that action. One might be intent on cooperating with the action, evaluating it, stopping it, encouraging it, learning how to do it, reporting it for a newspaper, or responding cleverly to it. However, an observer must first identify what he is seeing. When what one is observing is an action, the way to do this is to covertly token doing what one is witnessing and look from there.

The Practical Necessity of Empathy

Many reasons have been cited as to why it is necessary that our perception of actions be underpinned by empathy or *verstehen*.[1] It has been argued by Strawson that the empathic or "participant" attitude toward others is essential for practical reasons, in that all our interpersonal dealings—in effect, all society and the concert and cooperation it involves—depend on our adopting it.[2] And society is essential for our survival. So we empathize to survive. The theologian Martin Buber, in his book *I and Thou*, has speculated a fundamental moral obligation to adopt the empathic attitude—and to eschew a range of objective attitudes toward others.

Dennett has argued that it is necessary for reasons of heuristic convenience for us to adopt "the intentional stance" toward others.[3] The intentional stance is a close relative of what I am calling empathy. According to Dennett, if we assume that the other is a rational agent and put ourselves in his shoes, we can predict his behavior more efficiently and reliably than we could on the assumption that he is a biological mechanism or a complex nexus of physico-chemical phenomena. This argument is similar to that of simulation theory,[4] a version of theory theory that claims that empathy—as opposed to logical and inductive inferences from observed behavior—is our preferred means of determining what mental states prevail in the minds of others. Here again, empathy is thought to be justified on the grounds of heuristic necessity.

In addition, an argument for the practical inevitability of empathy could perhaps be developed around my definition of empathy as inhibited concerting. It could be argued that the power of our natural urge to do things in concert with others means that we have a tendency to imitate (with a view to acting in concert with) every action we see; however, because of practicalities, we are normally obliged to inhibit or abort this incipient response. The result is that, instead of imitating, we merely covertly commence and abort the concerting of the action. That is, we covertly token it, or "empathize."

A Logical Requirement for Empathy

It can also be argued that, for observing actions, an empathic attitude is logically necessary. Actions are by definition interventions in an environment. Any action involves manipulation of ambient things and is aimed at achieving some change in the prevailing situation. As I put it before, actions necessarily have accessories—things in the world that are essential to their performance and which they by definition have to do with. We are logically obliged to specify actions in terms of these accessories. We plot actions by reference to their external coordinates. I cannot specify the act of feeding the hens without mentioning the hens. And the more detailed my specification is, the more accessories get mentioned.

Many actions, such as some gestures, involve movements that seem to have no accessories, no patients. They seem to be "intransitive" movements, not interactions with an environment. They look unanchored in their respective contexts. However, it could be argued (though I will not attempt it here) that reference to external things is essential in defining even these apparently unattached movements. Granted this, there is no possibility of "methodological solipsism" as far as observation of actions is concerned. Actions have intentionality. Every action possesses at least one (and let us for argument's sake assume just one) "core accessory"—an external thing that must be mentioned in a specification of that action.

One feature of the core accessory is that the agent logically must be aware of it (though in some cases he can make do with imagining perceiving it) in order to perform the action in question. Attention to that accessory (the hens) is a sine qua non of performing the action (feeding the hens). Furthermore, in order for any observer to perceive an action, the observer must perceive (though in some cases he can make do with imagining) at least the action's core accessory.

Thus, if T is the core accessory of action X, then, in order to observe P performing action X, any observer O must attend to at least thing T. Since attending to T is an essential part of the performance of action X, P is also attending to T. This means that, at least with respect to attending to T, the observer and the agent are doing the same thing. They are both performing the same X-related "T" perceptual behavior. The observer is imitating the agent in this respect. Furthermore, at least this degree of imitation is necessary if O is to observe P doing X.

In a scenario that involves O actually observing P doing X, O's duplication of P's perceptual behavior need not be fully realized and may be in large part merely tokened. When O is hearing about X rather than witnessing it, the relevant perceptual behavior will usually be entirely tokened (and usually covertly). Exceptions would include cases where T (Cock Robin lying dead) is actually being inspected while the (heinous) act is being overtly and/or covertly tokened. However, the same applies: either actual or imagined perceiving of the core accessory is essential, not only to performing action X, but also to perceiving or imagining perceiving action X.

The Correlation Thesis

Action physicalism takes diverse forms. Actions may be claimed to be identical with physiological (plus other) events, or to be caused by physiological (plus other) events, or to be partly composed of physiological events, or to be a function of physiological mechanisms. Alternatively, actions are said to stand in some other intimate relation to physiological events. These other relations are usually expressed in metaphor. Actions are, for example, "supervenient on," "mediated by," or "based on" physiological mechanisms or events. Or physiological events or mechanisms "are the substrate for," "are responsible for," "are employed in," "participate in," or "underpin" relevant actions. However, all forms of action physicalism require at least that a given action and a given physiological event (or a disjunct of physiological events) can in principle be correlated. No matter what, precisely, is the relation between them, you must still be able to put, on the one side, an action and, on the other side, a physiological event (or a disjunct of them). The concept of correlation logically includes the condition that the items correlated (in this case, actions and physiological events) may be placed side by side and viewed simultaneously.

Correlation is the essence of action physicalism. Without repeated observations of P performing action X simultaneously with observations of P's physiological states, there is no way of determining which physiological events of the multitude going on in P are relevant to P's performance of X.[5] Action physicalism is a meaningful thesis only if it is possible to identify physiological events (or disjuncts of them) that occur always and only when X is being performed. Temporal correlation is required for this.

However, if it is true that actions require their observer to empathize, the necessary correlation of actions and physiological events can never be achieved. The observation of physiological events presupposes an objective, scientific stance that is incompatible with empathy. Thus, actions and physiological events cannot be correlated. They cannot both be encompassed within the one view, because the heuristic stances they respectively require are incompatible.

Why Scientists Are Not Allowed to Empathize

The distinctive thing about science as an activity is the care and rigor with which it defines and manages its heuristic vehicles. The experimental and other investigative procedures, and the measuring and recording techniques by which scientists observe the things they are interested in, are by design "objective." Scientific observations must at every stage be in principle publicly observable, explicitly definable, and repeatable by anyone, and must include no human intervention that might affect the repeatability of the results. Not just any investigative technique will do. Science is defined by its specialized yet highly versatile, efficient, and productive heuristic procedures as much as by its subject matter.

The reason why empathizing the subject matter is out of bounds for scientists (in the course of their work), and hence the reason why actions are out of bounds as subject matters, is as follows: To empathize action X is to employ the covert tokening of action X as one's heuristic vehicle for observing P's performance of X—which includes P's perceivings of core accessory

T. Empathizing precludes the employment as heuristic vehicle of any distinctively scientific procedure. That is, whatever action X is, the actual or token performance of X necessary (as a heuristic vehicle) for the observing of X is bound to preclude the practice of any of the restricted set of "scientific" procedures. The scientist can empathize actions with the rest of us, but cannot remain a practicing scientist while doing so.

With reservations for heuristic use of anthropomorphic metaphors (see next section), the observer of an impersonal natural process does not empathize it. The heuristic vehicle for one's observations of a natural process cannot be that process itself. The heuristic vehicle must be some independent and objective investigative approach to the phenomenon—for example, observing it from several angles, measuring and timing it under controlled conditions with customary scales, or viewing it through standard heuristic instruments. When such investigative procedures are formal, disciplined, reliably transferable, and repeatable, they become scientific procedures. The closest parallel science can offer to "one person observing another person do something" is a scenario in which trainee scientist P observes scientist Q demonstrating a certain scientific procedure X. P is observing Q doing X, certainly, but this is not objective, scientific observation. Only Q is doing science.

Summary

The substance of the above argument is that physiological events require to be viewed from a scientific context—they require scientific procedures as their "heuristic vehicle"—whereas actions require to be viewed with empathy, with the observed action also doing duty as the observer's heuristic vehicle. A scientist may view another person's action qua physiological event; however, the moment he does so, what is being observed ceases to be an action. Similarly, viewing someone's action qua action precludes seeing it as a physiological event. There is no possibility of correlating the "two."

Action Metaphors in Science

My second argument against action physicalism is that scientific explanation—as opposed to mere observation and documentation—of physiological events requires the use of action metaphors, and this makes physiological descriptions incapable of explaining things that literally are actions.

The task of biological science is to both document and explain biological phenomena. As in any science, the documenting task is a matter of establishing—by means of objective observation and experiment, and statistical analysis—reliable laws, or constant conjunctions, of this form: If (biological) state of affairs A obtains, then state of affairs B will follow. Of course, the "if A then B" format is a simplification. In principle, any suitable mathematical formula can be employed to state the law to which the biological phenomena in question are observed to conform. One aim of scientific documentation is parsimony—to describe the largest possible range of phenomena with the simplest possible formula.

The borderline between documentation and explanation is in theory sharp enough. To document is to say (preferably in the simplest possible way) what is so. And to explain is to say (again preferably in the simplest possible way) why what is so must be so. That is, as well as accurately and objectively recording natural phenomena, scientists look for their *causes*. Pre-scientific thinkers did not hesitate to attribute human-like powers to inanimate objects and processes, to speak of natural phenomena "doing things," "exerting influences," and so on. Scientists have abandoned such explicit anthropomorphism, but they still rely heavily—at least when it comes to explaining biological phenomena—on the words *function, perform, system, operate, task, organized, structure, device, mechanism, organ, organism, agent, means, role, purpose, law, forces, behavior, action, activity, process, interaction, effect, contribute, provide, enable, cope, adjust, adapt, survive, trigger, produce, engender,* and *cause*. These words are endemic in both professional and popular biological writing.

Although I do not argue it here, in their various biological contexts all these terms are anthropomorphic metaphors. They are borrowed from our everyday vocabulary of personal action, and they construe biological phenomena as if they were the work of some agent or agency. The model of agency assumed is that of personal agency—simply, someone doing something. The source of the metaphors in concepts of personal action is obvious in most cases. Anything that is literally a system, a device, or a mechanism, for example, must have been designed and constructed, and must be operated, by a person or multiple persons. Perhaps the least obvious action metaphor is *cause*. However, Reid,[6] Macmurray,[7] Collingwood,[8] Gasking,[9] and Strawson[10] all argue—convincingly in my opinion—that the scientist's notion of cause is essentially a metaphor depicting natural phenomena as actions as of a person. There is no reason why we should not treat ourselves to a sample of what these philosophers say—and, for good measure, add a J. L. Austin passage:

It is very probable, that the very conception or idea of active power, and of efficient causes, is derived from our voluntary exertions in producing effects; and that, if we were not conscious of such exertions, we should have no conception at all of a cause, or of active power, and consequently no conviction of the necessity of a cause of every change which we observe in nature. (Reid 1977, p. 278)

. . . the idea of an event having a cause is an attempt to think an event on the analogy of an act, while at the same time denying that it can be referred to an agent. The cause is that which is responsible for the production of the event. It is also something which is not an agent, and therefore cannot be responsible for anything, or produce anything. Thus the cause is at once an agent and not an agent. (Macmurray 1938, p. 82)

The natural scientist is trying to construct a science of nature in terms of analogies drawn from the conscious life of man. It is only through such analogies that nature becomes intelligible to man; a science of nature which renounced their use would accordingly be no science at all. When Darwin in *The Origin of Species* announces "the highly important fact that an organ constructed for one purpose may be converted into one for a widely different purpose" (Ch. VI), his use of frankly teleological language need bring no blush to the cheek of his disciples. Thus described, the facts of animal anatomy become intelligible. Described without appeal to the human activities of constructing and adapting, means and ends, they would be unintelligible. (Collingwood 1940, p. 335)

In general, then, the search for causal theories is a search for modes of action and reaction which are not observable at the ordinary level (or not observable at all, but postulated or hypothesized) and which we find intelligible because we model them on, or think of them on analogy with, those various modes of action and reaction which experience presents to gross observation or which we are conscious of engaging in, or suffering, ourselves. (Strawson 1986, p. 125)

"Causing," I suppose, was a notion taken from man's own experience of doing simple actions, and by primitive man every event was construed in terms of this model: every event has a cause, that is, every event is an action done by somebody—if not by a man, then by a quasi-man, a spirit. When, later, events which are *not* actions are realized to be such, we still say that they must be "caused," and the word snares us: we are struggling to ascribe to it a new, unanthropomorphic meaning, yet constantly, in searching for its analysis, we unearth and incorporate the lineaments of the ancient model. (Austin 1961, pp. 150–151)

The claim here is that we do not take a natural phenomenon to be explained, we do not feel we understand it, unless we can empathize it as an action we might ourselves perform. And if this impression of empathy is to be achieved, action metaphors must be mixed in with the bare documented facts. As I say, action metaphors are endemic in biological writing. Not only do they seem to be essential for explaining biological phenomena to the public; they are apparently very useful—in the case of neurophysiology, at least—in the reports in which scientists document their findings in academic journals. Presumably, the metaphors are not indispensable in this latter context. Presumably, they do not influence either what data are gathered or the objectivity of the means by which the data are gathered. These academic reports could in theory always be couched in purely statistical terms, and perhaps it is only for interpreting the data in everyday language that the metaphors are necessary. However, it is possible that the metaphors of system, function, mechanism, etc. also serve as heuristic and mnemonic aids to scientists, helping them to organize raw data into familiar and easily surveyable patterns.

If it is true that action metaphors are necessary to give us an impression of grasp, and that they are useful in scientists' reports and in their thoughts, this would in no way challenge the propriety or objectivity of the techniques by which data are gathered and parsimonious statistical reports are formulated. You can always pull the metaphors and get back to the teleologically neutral constant conjunctions research has established. The "teleologically neutral" here may equate to "inexplicable" or "meaningless," but if the statistical analysis is accurate and efficient we can still use it for prediction. If people need to empathize in order to "understand" natural phenomena, and if strategically placed action metaphors are necessary for this, then so be it. The metaphor-garnished explanations the scientist presents to the public are not frauds if their factual basis is sound. The talk of laws, of intricate mechanisms designed by evolution, of animals doing things to ensure their survival, and so on, is all fine. For biology's usual purposes, no harm is done, either, if people take as "scientific facts" not only the findings and regularities that scientists report but also the superimposed explanations—in terms of forces, mechanisms, and so on.

The employment of action metaphors to construe the raw data must be inappropriate, however, when the phenomenon presented for biological explanation is something that literally is an action. For the cognitive scientist to explicitly appeal, in explanation of someone's action, to a quasi-agent—some internal mechanism or system, some neurophysiological module programmed in by evolution—is to imply that talk of inner agents can be taken literally. It is to imply that the existence and operation of the internal mechanism (or whatever) is a scientifically established fact. However, if what I have said is true, the mechanistic "explanation" is merely a metaphorical gloss on the facts. Mechanistic and other action metaphors are not scientifically established facts. They are merely ad hoc fancies that provide a way of understanding the raw data that happens to be convenient for mnemonic, heuristic, and expository purposes. The scientist cannot explain the real action of a real person by redescribing it as the fancied "action" of a metaphor-generated fiction.

If we do take the action metaphors (the talk of inner agencies, systems and mechanisms) literally, we come up against a regress. We now have to explain the ulterior actions of the inner agent, or of the designer, the installer, and the operator of the mechanism or system. And if we use mechanism or system talk to explain these, the regress continues. At no stage can we spell out the actional explanation in purely objective, non-actional terms. If we do, our explanation reduces to a statement of the brute physiological facts. It then ceases to be an explanation and reverts to being an observational report of inherently "meaningless" phenomena.

Action metaphors are not going to help explain what actions are. We would already have to know what actions are to understand the metaphors in the explanation. Action metaphors may help us explain the workings of the earthworm's gut, the hunting strategies employed by polar bears in summer, and the structure of the human hypothalamus, but they are never going to help us explain people's actions. If nowhere else, we should hold action metaphors in abeyance here. And if we do hold these metaphors in abeyance, this reduces the options for "physiological explanation" of a given action X to providing a list—as long as it would be meaningless—of the physiological events that occur when and only when action X is performed. At best, we would have this list, which would not explain anything, to put beside our specification of X.

Our specification of X would be couched in terms of our everyday designed-to-induce-empathy vocabulary for actions. Or, depending on what X is, some specialized language or an actual demonstration might be needed to specify X. If X is, say, "whistling the Hoagy Carmichael song *Skylark*," the action specification will be a musical score (or, better, a whistled demonstration). And this brings us up against the methodological and logical difficulties described in the empathy argument. How does one put the list of physiological events *beside* the informal action specification—the informal description or the score or the whistling? How does one establish a connection between the two?

The Rhetoric of Action Physicalism

If I am right, action physicalism benightedly attempts to conflate two incompatible heuristic strategies and hence two incommensurable subject matters. If action physicalism is as wrong as this, why do so many believe it? How could anyone believe that science, which has been developed to explain natural phenomena, could have anything to say about things people do?

On the surface, action physicalism does not seem implausible at all. It seems quite reasonable to assume that one's body—which is, surely, essentially involved in the actions one performs—is a biological system, the structure and functioning of which has been determined by physical (especially evolutionary) causes. My suggestion in this section is that one reason—perhaps the main reason—why action physicalism seems so plausible is that we are misled here, as elsewhere, by figures of speech. I suggest that the impression of a seamless transition between talk about actions and talk about physiological processes is the work of three figures of speech in particular.

The Actions-as-Use-of-Body-Parts Metaphor

The first kind of figurative expression contributing to the apparent plausibility of action physicalism is well entrenched in everyday speech. This is the metaphor whereby we speak of "using" parts of the body in the course of performing actions, as if the relevant body parts were tools or instruments. Sometimes, to speak in this way is merely periphrastic and jocose, as when one is exhorted to use one's eyes (or ears, or head, or brain). This is still metaphor, however. One's eyes are not literally—as a telescope or an infrared sight is literally—something one uses to see "with" or "through." *Use your eyes* is not really an injunction to make use of equipment; it is only an injunction to look. In the normal case, simple looking requires no accessory hardware.

At other times, a use-of-body-part metaphor is employed where there is a question of alternative ways of performing an action—say, a baby's pushing himself across the floor with his knees, or one's using one's feet instead of one's hands to steer a car, or beating on a door with one's head instead of one's fists. In these cases, to speak of "using" the relevant body part is pointful and informative. It highlights the addition, to a normally mundane action, of a degree of ingenuity and innovation characteristic of tool use. On my calculation, *using the bottle* (in reference to feeding an infant) is literal, since a tool or instrument really is being used, but *using the breast* is metaphorical. The mother breastfeeds but does not use anything to do so.

The use-of-body-part metaphor is also used in regard to a physical ability lost or regained. One may "lose the use" of one's fingers because of the cold and then, having warmed them, be able to "use them" again. Here the "use" metaphor highlights the necessary bodily preconditions of the manipulative actions in question. The metaphorical character of the idiom is clear here too. The body parts one may "lose the use of" are not literally tools, instruments, or use objects of any kind.

The Biologist's Mechanism Metaphor

The second ingredient in the rhetoric of action physicalism is one of the action metaphors commonly employed in the biological sciences, as described in the previous section. It is the metaphor of body parts as mechanisms (devices, systems). As it is used in biological explanations, this metaphor serves to highlight an important feature of normal intra-bodily processes and events: they occur in interdependent, regular, systematic ways reminiscent of the functioning of components in complex machines. An easy extension of the mechanism metaphor is also invaluable in providing a simple and vivid way to characterize the effects of biological evolution. A body part (heart, liver, brain, eye, etc.) is described as having been designed and/or installed by evolution to serve a particular purpose, to fulfill a necessary bodily function, and to thus help ensure the organism's survival. Because of their aptness and utility, both the original metaphor and its extension have acquired—particularly in explanations of biological phenomena for the layperson—currency and credibility that distract us from their figurative status.

The Tool-as-Agent Synecdoche

Third, there is a certain way of talking about tools, instruments, and mechanisms (and devices, machines, systems, and other man-made equipment) generally. We talk of the tool or whatever as doing a job, performing a task, playing a role, or serving a function. That is, we speak of the tool as an *agent* and we talk about what it *does*. This is not so much a metaphor as a synecdoche.

As I have mentioned, synecdoche is kind of shorthand, an ellipsis whereby the name of a part of something is used for referring to the whole. In the present "tool doing a job" case, as in the "words refer to things" case, the synecdoche involves taking what is merely one contributing factor in an activity or a process and attributing the effect of the whole activity or process to just that one factor. This is often a convenient way to speak about use-objects. We often have to describe an activity that involves the use of a certain tool. Rather than go to the trouble of specifying how the tool is deployed and operated—and describing other relevant aspects of the context in which it is used, and relevant ancillary activities—we can simply, but figuratively, attribute the efficacy of the whole complex of activities to the tool. So, we forget about the people wielding the tool and the ancillary personnel, including those who designed, made, and supplied the tool. We speak as if the tool does the work itself—as if the computer works out and issues the invoices, the train transports us across the country, or the waste-management system cleans up the environment. Strictly, literally, and long-windedly speaking, the *people* who designed, made, and/or are using the computer, the train, and the waste-management system collectively bring about those results.

How We Judge Size at a Distance

In combination, the action-as-use-of-body-part metaphor, the body-part-as-mechanism-designed-by-evolution metaphor, and the tool-as-agent synecdoche can effect a verbal sleight that creates an illusion of seamlessness between actions and physiological events and gives action physicalism its appearance of plausibility. To appreciate the respective roles of the three figures in fostering the illusion, imagine a brain scientist explaining on television how we judge the sizes of distant objects.

We are told first that in estimating the size of a distant object we use not only our eyes but also our brain. We accept this as the reasonable and very probably true statement—albeit couched in terms of the familiar action-as-use-of-body-part metaphor—that, in order to estimate size at a distance, we not only have to look, we have to think too. However, the metaphor has also insinuated the notion of body parts' having "technical" relevance to the action.

The scientist then goes on to describe a neurophysiological mechanism, designed and installed by evolution, by which eye and brain interact to interpret the visual information and compute an estimate of the object's size. This introduction of the mechanism metaphor gives us a easy and efficient way to construe the specialized physiological data. However, it serves also to revive and corroborate the notion of body part as use object that is implied by the initial action-as-use-of-body-part metaphor. What we "use" when we see things at a distance has now been further specified for us, by the expert scientist, as not just our eyes and our brain but also the intricate mechanism that coordinates them. This complex tool for estimating size at a distance has been supplied to us by the natural process of evolution.

The effect of this corroboration and further specification is to make us rethink the original use-of-body-part metaphor and make us take it more seriously. We sense that "using one's eyes and brain" cannot be just a manner of speaking. There really is something there, developed and supplied by evolution, specifically for us to use for the size-estimating job. The initial suggestion of body parts' active role in performing the action is now firmed up and made explicit.

It is worth noting that the two metaphors employed so far were devised for very different referring jobs in very different contexts. The everyday action-as-use-of-body-parts metaphor is designed for talking about actions, particularly actions involving a modicum of ingenuity. Our scientist is using it to talk about the everyday skill of estimating size at a distance. On the other hand, the mechanism metaphor is used by biologists to help them describe certain features of physiological processes. Our scientist is employing the mechanism metaphor to help describe certain coordinated eye and brain events.

With the introduction of the mechanism metaphor, our television scientist is no longer talking (figuratively, in terms of the use of body-parts) about the *action* of estimating size at a distance. He has moved on to talking about anatomy and physiology. He is now describing structures and processes inside the body—structures and processes of which the person doing the estimating has no knowledge or control and which he certainly cannot "use." There has been a radical change of subject, from an action that people perform (estimating size) to certain physiological processes in the eyes and the brain. It is only because of the (apparent) affinity between the two metaphors—"using" and "mechanism"—that we do not notice the change. Even though the two metaphors were devised for different jobs in different contexts, one reconciles and combines them in the back of one's mind. This back-of-the-mind entertaining of what is effectively a mixed metaphor is what sustains—and simultaneously elides or conceals—the transition from action talk to physiology talk.

The "argument" that has been transacted is as follows: The use metaphor and the mechanism metaphor are familiar, apt, and useful in their respective home contexts, and therefore they can be taken as valid or "true" in those contexts. The present contexts are using-one's-eyes-to-see-distant-objects for the use metaphor and physiological-processes-involving-the-eye-and-the-brain for the mechanism metaphor. These present contexts seem relevantly similar to the metaphors' usual contexts, therefore we accept both metaphors as true in their present contexts too. Because the two metaphors seem to combine easily and fruitfully, and to corroborate each other, we also accept that they are true taken together. We conclude that, in judging size at a distance, we make use of a mechanism inside our bodies—a mechanism designed for the job and installed in us by evolution.

However, the question cannot help but arise (if only at the back of the mind again) just how we "use" the internal eye-brain mechanism. Prima facie, the locating and putting to use of one's own internal body parts is not going to be easy. A third rhetorical device—the tool-as-agent synecdoche—is now brought to bear to dissolve the problem of how we use the internal mechanism. The scientist/presenter brings the (personal) action of estimating size back into focus. He informs us that (the action of) estimating size is *done by* the internal mechanism. It is not, after all, as if the person needs to actively "use" the mechanism. The mechanism functions automatically. The size-estimating just appears to be done by the person. Science has revealed that, actually, the internal mechanism is doing it for us. The physiology is where the action is.

In my view, the physicalist account of thinking seems plausible only because we follow a similar rhetorical route. We come to believe thinking is done by the brain because we respond naively to a certain sequence of figures of speech. First, the action-as-use-of-body-part metaphor persuades us that thinking is "using one's mind/brain." Second, the utility and the scientific respectability of the body-part-as-mechanism-designed-by-evolution metaphor persuade us that there literally are systems and mechanisms inside our bodies—and that the brain is one of them. Third, the convenient synecdoche whereby tools and mechanisms can do things, fulfill functions, and serve purposes on their own allows us to believe that the effective agents of our actions are in reality the internal physiological mechanisms that science is bringing to light. Accordingly, we are led to believe that the effective agent of our thinking is not ourselves but a system of neuro-computational mechanisms in our brains—the mechanisms cognitive neuroscience has been tasked with identifying.

Cultural Determinants of Actions

As I say, the standard assumption in cognitive science and psychology is that people's actions are largely and/or ultimately determined by biologically evolved internal mechanisms. The assumption is that these mechanisms, in the brain and elsewhere, "underpin," "are responsible for," "are the causal basis of," and generally provide the impetus for, the things we do. Sometimes, especially in material for a popular audience, the talk of mechanisms is supplemented by talk of instincts, urges, genes, genetic predispositions, and innate modules. An innate competitive instinct is often mentioned. There are said to be genes for greed. There is a language instinct.

If valid, my empathy and action-metaphors-in-science arguments rule out any biological influence on our actions. At least they say that, if there are biological influences, we can't know them. This might seem extreme, or just wrong, but we can bear with it for a while. Apart from biology, the only likely-looking candidate for "ultimate cause of human behavior" must be culture. Thus, we can briefly consider the possibility that our behavior is governed, not by biological influences, but by cultural influences, and cultural influences exclusively. At least culture is not going to get disqualified by the empathy and action-metaphors-in-science arguments. The study of culture is not an objective science, and it employs the same empathic heuristic we use to understand everyday actions (albeit in a more disciplined way).

Largely by dint of the meta-behaviors I describe in this book—imitating, concerting, communicating, cooperating, and thinking—human beings have been able to pool their behavioral resources, including their perceptual resources. "Culture" in the anthropologist's broad sense is, roughly, our behavior (or meme) pool itself, our shared doings—the repertoire of behaviors disseminated by concert and communication. Culture is what is kept ticking over in incipient form by the constant minuscule recollective, redintegrative, and anticipatory commencings and abortings, the thinking, of individuals. It is that covert chorus going on, as we say, in our minds.

Taking a lead from chapters 3–7, we can roughly itemize the cultural influences on our actions as follows: Long-term, *educative concerting* and its variants determine what we are able and motivated to do. Generally, we do what we have been prepared for doing by our numerous informal and formal teachers. In the shorter term, cues such as others' hortations or other *overt tokenings*, or the sight of others engaged in activity (e.g., practical or recreational concerting), will normally elicit an appropriate cooperative response from us. The conjunction of two other kinds of cultural influence, the application of two culturally acquired skills, is able to prompt solitary action. Short-term or long-term *thinking* (in the form of anticipatory covert tokening of some action X), when combined with *perception* of relevant things in the environment, often brings about performance of X. That both thought and perception are cultural products and not biologically given I have already argued.

The cultural determinism I am contemplating would see our lives spent in a cultural cocoon, insulated from any biological influence by the extent to which every detail of our behavior is directed by cultural means for cultural purposes. Effectively all our post-natal behavior is created or bent—by the four long-term and short-term influences above—to accommodate and foster existing shared practices. If we are going to speak of an *über*-agency "determining," "governing," "underpinning," or "providing the causal basis of" our actions, it had better be culture rather than biology.

We can test this view against likely objections. First, it could be objected that, despite the empathy and action-metaphor arguments, our actions are, if not determined, at least "enabled" by the physiological hardware in our bodies. For example, there are sense organs to initiate behavior, complex neural firing programs to orchestrate it, and glands and muscles to physically realize it. Here, surely, is an unarguable biological contribution to behavior. Well, yes. Our bodies are involved in our actions. However, it can be denied that this involvement is in any sense biological.

Suppose we could identify the specific physical indices of somatic enablement for a given action—the attunement of sensory receptors, the development of muscles, and the installation of a viable neural firing program specific to the action. These specific enablers would simply not exist without prior cultural intervention. In many ways this is the crucial point. Somatic enabling—or just enabling—for specific actions is what educative concerting and related educative techniques bring about and are meant to bring about. Teaching brings about changes in the body (and, presumably, particularly in the brain) that enable pupils to perform actions they couldn't perform before. These changes include the creation of anatomical structures—such as effective new synapses and other elements of a firing program, and muscle mass—that would not otherwise have existed. If you teach a person how to drive a car, you change that person physically. A skilled tennis player is anatomically different from a novice. A speaking child is anatomically different from an infant.

When we reflect that the anatomical or physiological enablers of action, if that is what they are, are the results of deliberate cultural intervention (education), and that what they enable is itself a cultural product (a learned action), we may be less inclined to speak of biological influences. Neither learning how to perform particular actions nor performing them is biology. If the input and the output are both cultural, the body is not so much a biological organism as culture's instrument.

Varying the above objection slightly, one could claim that culture needs a "healthy standard human" to operate on in order to elicit the required behavior from individuals. This essential behavioral parameter is supplied (or not) by biology. Biology produces and maintains culture's "instrument," the individual human being. Well, we might grant that biology supplies the neonate—although planned pregnancy, artificial fertilization, and hospital birth are beginning to cast doubt on even this. However, to keep the infant, then the child, and then the adult flourishing requires massive and sustained cultural input, including feeding, nourishing, loving, training, and employing. Though the survival of *Homo sapiens'* far distant ancestors must have been the outcome of purely biological vicissitudes, the survival of individual *Homo sapiens* never has been. The healthy standard *Homo sapiens* is a cultural achievement.

A third objection locates biological input at the inception of culture-generating activity itself. Plausibly, our initial ability to pool behavior is a result of biological evolution—and we can usefully, if figuratively, talk about inbuilt physiological mechanisms here. For example, one mechanism might enable neonatal imitation. Another might be the huge uncommitted cerebral cortex available for behavior-dedication by educative concerting. *Homo sapiens* has genetically evolved to be culturally available, culturally biddable. To ensure that culture gets under way and is sustainable, innate mechanisms such as the above are required. Here, it might be claimed, is a clear enabling influence exerted by biology on human, culture-based action.

It is true that culture would never have taken root if *Homo sapiens* were not born to imitate and did not have that roomy brain. However, this objection ignores the fact that behavioral strategy and anatomical evolution are incremental and interdependent. The evolution of the relevant mechanisms is as much due to the survival advantages of culture-based behavior as culture-based behavior is due to the evolution of the mechanisms. This is an important point. In a sense, here too culture is determining biology.

The third objection also misses the point. It does not adduce any biological influence on our actions, because actions don't enter the repertoire until well after birth. As I described it in chapter 3, the advent of concerting follows birth by several weeks and comes after considerable and persistent cultural inducement. Solo actions follow much later still. Thus, having the relevant biological mechanisms installed does not enable or otherwise affect personal action; it enables only the forerunner of personal action: concerting. And it enables concerting only in the sense of being one necessary condition among many.

In culture's earliest days, when *Australopithecus* or whoever was first trying it on and when much "behavior" was still biologically determined, a hypothetical observer could perhaps have spoken realistically of competing cultural and biological influences on behavior. Perhaps the early pre-humans had both of these caregivers ensuring their survival. Now however, biology leaves newborn *Homo sapiens* on culture's doorstep and goes away. The infant might come from nature, but the adult person comes from culture, and culture comes from concerting. Nature's work is finished when the infant first smiles.

Verbs and Actions and Things

. . . action is that which is expressed by verbs. The distinction between substantives and verbs is the most fundamental distinction in the field of language. The substantive is primarily the linguistic form which denotes an object. This at least suggests that the distinction between *object* and *action* is a fundamental distinction in reality. . . . And any analysis of action which treats it as if it were an object, must ignore or at least misrepresent the nature of action.

—John Macmurray, "What is action?"[11]

If actions are not scientifically observable things (nor events nor processes) in the world, what are they? What is the point of showing that thinking is neither a supernatural nor a natural process, but an action, and showing what kind of action it is, if we do not know what actions are in the first place? It looks as if I have replaced the traditional Mind/Body problem with an Action/Body problem that is just as intractable.

After all, what is the relation between actions and the body? Much of the philosophical literature on actions is taken up with discussion of the possibility that "bodily movements" might be a useful intermediary between actions and physiological events. Actions seem to consist at least in part of bodily movements. And surely bodily movements are physiologically explicable. But what are these bodily movements, these movements "of" the body? Are they movements the body makes? Or is the body moved by something? Well, no. Nor can we say that actions are performed "by" the body or by parts of it, or that the person "uses" his body to perform actions. And what is "performing"? If we look at how we come to know actions, and look at the general characteristics of our responses to action words, verbs, we may get closer to appreciating what kind of thing an action is—that is, if it is a kind of "thing" at all.

In the introduction I quoted a passage from Wittgenstein—"doing is something that one can give someone an *exhibition* of"[12]—that might serve as the starting point for a definition of action. We can take it Wittgenstein is saying that the notion of demonstrating is basic to the concept of action—that actions are, by definition, demonstrable. However, there are procedures other than demonstrating that are characteristically appropriate to actions: concerted performing, solo performing; demonstrating to solicit imitation and/or concerted performance; overt tokening; covert tokening; witnessing and empathizing; hortating; verbally instructing how; explaining the efficacy of; cooperating in the performance of; adapting the method of; responding in kind to; and so on. And we may recognize, verbally identify, and evaluate actions. These meta-actional abilities are our ways of knowing actions, the heuristic vehicles via which we experience them. If the account in chapters 3–7 of this book is right, the font of actional knowledge, the prototype from which the above ways of knowing actions all derive, is educative concerting. Wittgenstein's "demonstrating" is just one early descendent of concerting.

Various Uses of Action Verbs

In their earliest form, action verbs are simply vocal accompaniments distinctive of (concerted performances and demonstrations of) particular actions. They are *markers* serving to concentrate attention on actions and aspects of them. The next usefulness they acquire is as means of overtly tokening those same actions, to incite the hearer to join in concerted performances of them or, later, to incite the hearer to solo performances of them. This is their *hortative* or imperative use. Later, action verbs may also be employed *reportively*, in descriptions of what specified and unspecified agents did, will do, or are doing elsewhere. There is also a *referential* usage, wherein either of the two kinds of act nominalization is employed to refer to either a particular instance of X-ing, or to X-ing in general, qua phenomenon. Thus, as well as reporting that we swam right across the river on Saturday, I can talk about "the swim" we had on Saturday, or how good "swimming" is for keeping you fit.

Presumably, the developmentally later reportive and referential uses are modifications of the developmentally earlier marker and imperative uses. Thus we might speculate that the primary function of action verbs is not to name or refer to actions, but to mark and/or incite them. Action verbs are, first, attention-and-excitement-adding markers of actions. Second, they are imperatives to action. It is only third or fourth that they are, or they approximate, referring expressions.

Presumably also, as the child learns more verbal action markers and hears a greater variety of them directed toward himself as incitements to action, he will often have to pause before embarking on a response, in order to ready the response by covertly tokening it—to remind himself of the action in question, to reassure himself that this action is in his repertoire. The covert tokening of specific actions will thus become the hearer's habitual preliminary response to action verbs heard as imperatives. Whether an actual performance follows the hearer's covert tokening of it depends on other factors.

The child subsequently gets accustomed to reportive use of verbs. Presumably, the preliminary covert tokening still occurs, and the child at first assumes an imperative use of the verb and anticipates actually doing X. Suppose, however, that the verbal cues distinctive of imperative use are absent and are replaced by others. Suppose there are grammatical cues signaling reporting or referring instead. Perhaps there is reference to a third party as agent of the reported action and the imperative interpretation is thus precluded. The verb may say initially to the hearer *do X*, but then the X-ing is further specified as "P did X," and our hearer, whose name happens to be Q, cannot do "P doing X"—especially if it is to be done in the past. Thus, in response to reportive use of the verb *X*, the hearer will prevent his preliminary covert tokening of action X from developing into an actual performance of X. The hortation has been "spiked." Q's hands are tied, and the initial covert tokening can inflate only into something like "covertly tokened witnessing-with-empathy of P doing X." That is, on realizing that the verb is not being used imperatively, Q adjusts his initial self-educative imagining-doing-X in a likely alternative direction—say, imagining-looking-at-P-doing-X—rather than in the familiar I-do-X-now direction.

Other reportive and referential uses of verbs may prescribe similar inhibitings of and departures from the actual doing that imperative use prescribes. Act nominalizations—e.g., *having a swim* and *swimming is boring*—make a noun of the verb and so establish an instance of X-ing or X-ing in general as a topic, a thing. Perhaps the referential overlay here, with its prescription of an observer viewing from a distance, is what stymies incipient actual X-ing. Here again we have a kind of pre-aborted imperative, a "look but don't do" message leading the hearer to adjust his preliminary covert tokening toward an empathic-but-passive-spectator stance.

I am suggesting that, no matter how the action verb is being employed by the speaker, the hearer always makes a similar initial orienting response. And that response consists of a self-educative covert tokening of the action in question, reassuring the hearer that he knows the action the speaker is talking about. Subsequently, depending on what other verbal and circumstantial cues accrue, this initial tokening will develop in different ways. To provide a label for the verb's capacity to elicit the initial covert tokening response on the hearer's part, we can speak of verbs' *evoking* actions. To "evoke" is thus to get the hearer to imagine performing the action.

Evoking Actions vs. Referring to Things

What is the difference between what I call the "evoking" of actions and referring to actions? First, we should note that referring to things is one *kind* of action-evoking. Referring is the evoking of activity of a special kind—namely, perceptual behavior. In its paradigm concerted form, perceptual behavior involves two or more people looking at or otherwise investigating some object or other variety of thing that is separate from them. (At least, an object is perceivable separately from the person(s) perceiving it in a way that an action is not perceivable separately from the person performing it.) Apart from a small number of action verbs—*look, perceive, observe, scrutinize, attend*, etc.—the speech used to evoke this kind and format of activity consists of nouns and other referring expressions. Thus, in response to a referring expression, the hearer's initial (reassurative, self-educative) response is to covertly token some sort of joint scrutiny of an object (or other thing).

Our initial tendency is probably to assimilate verbs to nouns and to say that verbs refer to, or are the names of, actions. If the above is reasonable, however, it makes more sense to construe nouns as verbs of a special kind.

The specialized referring role of nouns and other referring expressions is signaled by their distinctive grammar. In referring (here I am talking primarily about absent-referent referring), the specific perceptual behavior is not *explicitly* evoked verbally. The speaker does not say, in the imperative, *do perceptual behavior appropriate to a cat*. Rather, he performs an abbreviated version of this hortation and just says *cat*. We do a huge amount of referring in everyday life, and this saves a lot of repetition. The *"do perceptual behavior appropriate to . . ."* part of the perceptual hortation can be taken for granted and remain tacit. We need verbalize only the salient "what specific kind of perceptual behavior" part. When, as children, we learn to recognize and learn the names of innumerable things, we learn to forgo marking and/or inciting the repetitious part—the procedural "concerted perceptual investigation" part, which happens every time—and we learn to concentrate only on marking and/or inciting the specific perceptual part. It is this abbreviated and efficient kind of action-evoking, unique to our evokings of perceptual behavior, that is signaled by the distinctive grammatical forms and roles of nouns and other referring expressions.

Referring to Actions?

Is it possible to *refer to* an *action*? Can actions play the referent role that objects and other things customarily fill? Can act nominalization, in converting a verb into a noun (or honorary noun), take us from merely evoking an action to referring to it? Actions don't sit there like things in the world. Like any motion, an action is gone as soon as it is complete. We see actions only bit by bit, never entire. As Reid says, "no kind of succession can be an object, either of the senses, or of consciousness; because the operations of both are confined to the present point of time, and there can be no succession in a point of time; and on that account the motion of a body, which is a successive change of place, could not be observed by the senses alone. . . ."[13]

Whether one chooses to classify reportive use of action verbs as reference to actions depends on whether one is prepared to admit empathy—the observer actually "doing" the referent in covertly tokened form—as an observational technique. Obviously, empathy can never be a valid observational technique in science. Equally obviously, we rely on empathy, and yet we still accept actions as "things," in everyday life. The ball is in the philosopher's court. Is empathy an acceptable variant of the "detached and objective joint scrutiny" that characterizes referring to things? The "joint" is satisfiable. The football crowd roars as one. However, the "detached and objective" is problematic. The empathizer is not exactly holding the referent at arms' length in the classic objective style if he is imagining actually *doing* the referent.

At any rate, if empathy is acceptable as an observation technique, then acts of swimming are things in the world alongside rivers and wet bathing togs. If, on the other hand, action verbs are held to be basically imperatives (or action-markers), and their occasional referential dress held to be purely formal, then there are no more things called "swims" in the world than there are things called *get your feet off the table*. And in this case we should conclude that getting one's feet off the table is not a thing in the world. Rather, it is something we do.

The situation is much the same with act nominalizations that purport to refer not to particular swims or swimmings but to swimming in general. In this case, the spectator scenario the hearer is to envisage is indeterminate as to agent, time, or place. However, the hearer's imagining *doing* the putative referent must still be an essential part of the "joint scrutiny" that is guaranteed to be possible (and is covertly tokened accordingly) if it is genuine absent-referent *referring* that is going on.

Is Knowledge of Actions Epistemologically Primary?

Our certainty about action is of a higher order than our knowledge of events.
—John Macmurray, "What is action?"[14]

Whatever the splendors of the exact sciences there was a sense in which we could know more about our own and other men's experiences—in which we acted as participants, indeed authors, and not as mere observers—than we could ever know about non-human nature which we could only observe from outside.
—Isaiah Berlin, *Vico and Herder*[15]

I have said that our ways of knowing actions include teaching and/or learning an action or activity by example, demonstrating or miming an action, abbreviating an action into a gesture, spectating an action and empathizing, listening to the verbal specification of an action and empathizing, verbally specifying an action, encouraging or inciting an action, solo rehearsal or practice of an action, arguing the efficiency or morality of an action, and so on. These are our heuristic strategies for actions. They all involve, to a greater or lesser degree, participation in or "trying out" of the actions in question.

Action physicalism implies that an objective, scientific knowledge of actions would be in some sense more basic and reliable than our everyday knowledge of actions. Action physicalists assume that, in contrast to the depth and discipline and the steadfast objectivity of science's heuristic methods, our everyday empathy-based ways of knowing actions are superficial and undisciplined, subject to personal bias, etc. Against this assumption, the eighteenth-century Italian philosopher Vico advanced the *verum factum* principle, according to which our knowledge of the things we make or do ourselves is more fundamental and more certain than any knowledge we can obtain of natural phenomena.[16] Vico was the avatar of the *verstehen* tradition in social science and history. The advocates of this approach believe that people's actions and other cultural products can be understood only via empathy—the exercise of which is incompatible with the practice of science. It will be clear from my empathy argument that Vico has my vote on this issue.

Whether our knowledge of actions is necessarily more informal, less disciplined, shallower, less certain, or less reliable than objective knowledge of things is debatable. Sometimes we want to get clear about an action or activity in a theoretical way. Rather than just learning roughly what X is for, or what it is like to do X, or sharing P's experience of X-ing, or learning how to manage X-ing in everyday contexts, we want to engage in a more formal, disciplined study of it. We want a broad view of the practicalities of X-ing— its rationale, techniques, logistics, personnel requirements, etc. We want this broad view for purposes, perhaps, of improving the activity's efficiency, or introducing it as a practice, or eliminating it, or making legal decisions about it. Or our interest in the activity is academic—within anthropology, psychology, linguistics, or philosophy, for example.

There is no question of our abandoning, for purposes of studying an action formally, the distinctive empathic heuristic methods that actions require. If we don't empathize, we simply don't see the action. The new task is just to empathize in a more disciplined, sustained, detailed, and comprehensive way—and to so closely hedge about one's imaginative participation in the activity with (usually verbal) overt tokenings that anyone following will make the same observations and reports you do. Concerting our perceptions and descriptions of actions and activities is no less difficult, in principle or practice, than concerting perceptions and descriptions of physical objects and natural processes. As teachers and lawyers know, even though you might not get to wear a white coat, teaching and describing actions is just as demanding of perceptual and verbal abilities, imagination and intellectual discipline as describing objects. And the knowledge communicated is not necessarily less certain or less valuable.

Vico may be right that actional knowledge is more "basic" than objective knowledge. I argued in chapters 3–6 that actional knowledge is more basic, at least in the sense of its being developmentally prior to knowledge of things in the world. Does developmental priority equate to epistemological priority? One thing we can say after chapter 6 is that objective knowledge can plausibly be construed as one *kind* of actional knowledge. Despite what epistemologists have for the last two millennia said about the provenance of objective knowledge, it seems that objective knowing—perceiving in concert, referring, recording, experimenting, verifying, measuring, describing, etc., culminating in the practice of science—is a skill-based activity that a person has to learn by example, by empathy and practice. In my account, objective knowledge—and every other kind of knowledge, and consciousness itself—has its developmental roots in the concerting of activity, especially perceptual activity.

The fact that we must employ action metaphors in order to understand natural processes—and this seems true in biology and in other sciences—is another reason to surmise that actional knowledge may be epistemologically prior to objective knowledge.

Appendix: A Sample of Mind Metaphors

Attending

it concentrates (focuses) the mind wonderfully

have (set, put, focus, fix, keep) one's mind on (the job in hand, higher things)

I turned my mind to other things

(something to) occupy (engage, exercise) the (my) mind

my mind was occupied with other things

mind-riveting

pay no mind to

have (keep) uppermost in (my) mind

have (keep) in the front of my mind

give my mind (over) to

my mind turned to thoughts of

too many things (a lot, lots) going on in my mind

my mind was too active (for sleep)

thoughts crowded (into) my mind

out of sight, out of mind

empty my mind of (all thoughts of . . .)

I put (shut) it out of my mind

it crossed (entered, came into, passed through) my mind

prominent in my mind

impressed on (fixed in) my mind that

my mind wandered

absent-minded

my mind was elsewhere (far away)

it took my mind off my troubles

I've got a lot on my mind

a weight (load) off my mind

he withdrew (retreated) into his own mind

my mind was distracted by

my mind was racing

running in (through) my mind

mind-set

it couldn't be further from my mind

the last thing on my mind

Understanding

get clear in my mind

get my mind around it

penetrate my mind

my mind went (is a) blank

the suspicion (certainty) grew in his mind that

couldn't get clear in my mind

his mind was confused

her mind couldn't grasp that

a mental block

Intending and Opining

set his mind on (a red one)

to have one's mind set on

in my own mind (I wasn't so sure)

be in two minds

be of one mind

of similar (the same) mind

like minds (like-minded)

great minds think alike

have it in one's mind to

to know one's own mind

make up your mind

change one's mind

what do you have in mind?

what's on your mind?

a mind of my (its) own

be of a mind (minded) to

have a (good, half a) mind to

my mind said yes but my body said no (and vice versa)

speak my mind

give him a piece of my mind

to my mind

keep an open mind

close (shut) my mind to the possibility

poisoned his mind against them

get it off my mind

Being of a Certain Disposition

frame (cast, turn, state) of mind

peace of mind

set (put) one's mind at rest (ease)

calm (ease) your mind

an enquiring mind

strength of mind

reconciled to it in my mind

his mind was composed

has a brilliant (twisted, warped, dirty, suspicious, sick) mind

the criminal mind

that's how his mind works

high- (bloody-, dirty-, broad-, narrow-, open-, closed-, clear-, small-, dull-, simple-, single-, fair-, public-, civic-, petty-, feeble-, strong-) minded

qualities of mind

mental qualities

a win-at-all-costs mentality

travel broadens the mind

mental outlook (defective, deficiency, patient, illness, disease, disorder, health, breakdown, collapse, exhaustion, problem, condition, tenacity, toughness, fortitude, ability, burden, capacity, equilibrium, state, attitude, stability, condition, retardation, suffering, torment, pain, cruelty, abuse, torture, powers, activity)

Remembering

burden his mind with

if I cast my mind back to when

have (bear, keep) in mind

what springs (comes) to mind is

it brings (calls) to mind

try and call to mind

be reminded of

it puts me in mind of

(kept, stored) at (in) the back of my mind

something (at) in the back of my mind kept saying

still fresh in my mind

it went clean out of my mind

I (all the other things I had to think about) put it right out of my mind

it slipped my mind

make a mental note (promise, etc.)

be mindful of

it stuck (lodged) in my mind

my mind kept repeating (returning to)

I kept returning to it in my mind

replaying the episode in my mind

over and over in my mind

(her words) echoed in my mind

couldn't get it out of my mind

one-track mind

I had just one thing in mind

it preyed (weighed) on my mind

Imagining and Fancying

(all) in my (the) mind

I got (took) it into my mind (head) that

my mind seized on the idea that

see (picture) in my mind

see in my mind's eye

see (have) a mental image (picture)

conjure up (evoke) a mental image (picture) of

an image (picture) rose (formed) in my mind

it rose up before (in) my mind

mind filled with notions of

Communicating

mind games

you must be a mind reader

his mind was an open book

she read my mind

I saw into his mind

she was playing with his mind

mental telepathy

meeting of minds

Cogitating

set my mind to work

apply (devote) his (whole) mind to

if you put your mind to it

what was going through (going on in) his mind?

going over it in my mind

tossing up in my mind whether

turning it over in my mind

it kept turning over (revolving) in my mind

I weighed things up (compared the two, went over it again) in my mind

you could see his mind ticking over

you could see it ticking over in his mind

(the mysterious) workings of her mind

the inner recesses of her mind

doing mental arithmetic

my mind was working overtime

mastermind

Inability or Ability to Think

my mind was in a turmoil (tizzy)

my mind was playing tricks on me

it affected his mind

be (go) out of my mind (with)(anxiety, grief, etc.)

are you out of your mind?

lose my mind

not in his right mind

of sound (unsound) mind

his mind is gone

his mind's grasp (hold) on reality

her mind is (still) good (sharp, active, clear)

my mind was clouded by (thoughts of, grief)

his mind was unbalanced

mentally unbalanced

his mind was unhinged (destroyed) by

my mind couldn't cope

he has the mind of a child

he has a mental age of

she went (was a bit) mental

my mind snapped/cracked (under the strain)

in your tiny mind

a mind like a steel trap

it boggles the mind

the mind boggles

it blew my mind

mindless

eager young minds

improve your mind

mind-expanding (-altering, -blowing, -boggling, -numbing, -bending)

presence of mind

mind control

mind-power

she has a good mind

Anticipating

his mind ran on ahead

looking forward in my mind to

mentally prepared

she prepared her mind

his mind was prepared

mental rehearsal

rehearsed it in my mind

Current Uses of *Mind* as a Verb

mind the baby, mind out! mind out for (the baby, the step, etc.)

mind the step (how you go, what you say, your back (eye, Ps and Qs, manners), etc.)

if you don't mind

do you mind?

I don't mind

never mind

mind your own business

mind (that) you (don't forget to) water the plants

remind

mind you

Obsolete Meanings of *Mind* as a Verb (*Oxford English Dictionary*)

[Sometimes in constructions: *to mind of, to mind on, to mind upon, to mind toward*, etc.]

to remind, admonish, exhort (someone)

to remember, recollect, bring to mind, think of (something past or absent)

to bear in mind, be aware of, have in one's memory, take care to remember

to mention, record, pray for, remember in a will

to heed, perceive, notice, have one's attention caught by, attend to

to intend, contemplate, aim at, plan, provide for

to wish, desire, be inclined to

to care for, like, value, wish for

to direct or apply oneself to, concentrate on, practice diligently

Obsolete Uses of *Mind* as a Noun, with Meanings (*OED*)

fall or run to P's mind (occur to P's recollection)

be (go, pass) out of mind (be forgotten)

to set out of mind (to forget, ignore)

put P in mind of (remind or suggest to P that)

of good mind (of happy memory)

have mind of (*on, upon, how, that*) or *take mind to* (*upon*)—here "mind" is the action or state of thinking about something, or the thought of something

out of mind (more than one can calculate)

against the mind of P (against P's judgment or wishes)

fulfill one's mind, bring one's mind to pass, have (*obtain*) *one's mind* (achieve one's aim, satisfy one's desire)

for one's mind's sake (to gratify one's whim)

be of diverse (*many*) *minds* (vacillate)

be in (*of*) *mind to,* or *be of great mind* (*of good mind, in a good mind*) *to* (do X) (be disposed to, or intend to do X)

bring P in mind (persuade P)

have a mind to or *bear good mind to* (be favorably disposed toward, have a liking for, wish to possess)

P is whole of mind (*in good mind*) (P is legally sane)

Note: Some of these obsolete uses of the noun seem more like act nominalizations than like my "metaphorical accessory nominalization." It is a question of whether, in expressions like *to have mind of*, or *to be of mind to*, or *out of mind*, the surrounding words (*to have, to be of, out of*) are metaphorical or not. In some of the obsolete cases it is arguable whether they are. It may also be arguable whether some current usages, like *to be of a good mind to* and *to have a mind to*, which are very similar to some of the obsolete ones above, are really metaphorical. However, what is clear is that the above noun uses of *mind* are not just formal, in the way ordinary act nominalizations are. The "mind" being referred to in each case is more than a pure "doing"—that is, more just an episode or state of minding (intending, desiring, thinking of, etc.). The referent has pretensions to thinghood. And I can only think that these pretensions are fostered by the accompanying words—*having, being in, good,* and so on. The *OED* gives as meaning III, 18, for the noun *mind* "The cognitive or intellectual powers, as distinguished from the will and emotions." Among the quotations given in illustration of this meaning are the following, both embodying a fine equivocation of verb and noun senses. The first is from Disraeli: "Blue eyes, lit up by a smile of such mind and meaning." The second is from Ouida: ". . . there can be no mind in an imitation." Is minding (in the old sense) being referred to here, or a thing called mind?

In the passage I use as an epigraph in chapter 9, the *OED* lexicographer comments that "unfortunately the word mind has been almost universally employed to signify both that which thinks and the phenomena of thinking." Clearly he believes there is (or was) a viable act nominalization of the verb *mind*—referring to particular acts of minding/thinking or to minding/thinking in general (i.e., to "the phenomena of thinking")—in addition to the usual metaphorical accessory nominalizations. However, the *OED* quotes from Reid to exemplify the philosophical use of *mind*, and Reid insists that this philosophical use, at least, does not refer to acts of minding/thinking (i.e., it has no act-nominalization use): "We do not give the name of mind to thought, reason, or desire; but to that being which thinks, which reasons, which desires." (Reid 1785, I, ii, 42)

The Entry for *Mind* in the *Oxford Dictionary of English Etymology*

mind maind memory (surviving in phr. *in m., to m., time out of m.*); thought, purpose, intention; mental faculty. XII. Early ME. *mind(e)*, with dial. vars. *münd(e)*, *mend(e)*, later *meende*; aphetic of *imünd*, etc. :—OE. *gemynd*, corr. to OHG. *gimunt*, Goth. *gamunds* memory :—Germ. *gamundix, f. **ga-* Y- + **mun-*, weak grade of the series **men-* **man-* **mun-* :—IE. **men-* **mon-* **mn-* revolve in the mind, think. Other Germ. derivs. are: OFris. *minne*, OS. *minnea*, OHG. *minna* (G. *minne*) love; ON. *minni*, Goth. *gaminþi* memory (:—*gamenþjam); OE. *manian* remind, exhort, advise, *ge-munan* (present *geman*) remember, OS. *far-munan* deny, despise, Goth. *munan* (present *man*) think, believe, *muns* thought, OE. *myne* (:—*muniz) memory, desire, love. Hence **mind** vb. REMIND; remember, give heed to XIV; (dial.) perceive, notice XV; contemplate XVI; be careful about XVIII. ¶ The IE. base was very prolific; many derivs. are given in the articles AUTOMATON, COMMENT, DEMENTIA, MANIA, MATHESIS, MEMENTO, MEMORY, MENTAL, MENTION, MENTOR, MNEMONIC, MONITION, REMEMBER, REMINISCENT

Notes and Citations

Introduction

1. See Gardner 1985.

2. Crick and Koch 2002, p. 94.

3. Wittgenstein 1980, #655.

4. Ryle 1971b, p. 299.

Chapter 1

1. See Flanagan 1995, p. 81.

2. Ryle 1949.

3. Ibid., pp. 134–135.

4. See Zikmund 1972; Scheerer 1984; Jeannerod 1994; Melser 2000.

5. Hume 1960, pp. 1, 86, 96.

6. See Decety 2002a.

7. Watson 1919.

8. Skinner 1957, chapter 19.

9. Drake 1933, p. 329.

10. Jacobson 1931.

11. See Davidson and Schwartz 1977.

12. Decety et al. 1991.

13. Rizzolatti and Arbib 1998.

14. See also Decety and Chaminade 2005; Decety et al. 2002; Decety 2002b; Paccalin and Jeannerod 2000.

15. Washburn 1910.

16. Watson 1919.

17. de Laguna 1963.

18. Pavlov 1927.

19. Hull 1931.

20. Guthrie 1935, p. 206.

21. Hebb 1958, 1968, 1980.

22. Monod 1972; Jeannerod 1995; Currie 1995; Decety 2002a.

23. Neisser 1976, 1985.

24. Annett 1996.

25. Washburn 1910, p. 58.

26. Skinner 1957, p. 438. For Skinner's version of the "weakness" hypothesis, see pp. 434–438.

27. Hofstadter 1979, p. 364.

28. Jeannerod 1995, p. 88.

29. Frijda 1986, pp. 392–393.

30. Ibid., p. 405.

31. Neisser 1976, p. 145.

32. Research on "mental practice" in sport is comprehensively reviewed in Jones and Stuth 1997.

33. Neisser 1985, p. 104.

34. de Laguna 1963, p. 175. See also p. 178.

35. See Jeannerod 1995, pp. 91–96; 1994, p. 191.

36. However, see Jeannerod 1994.

37. Skinner 1957, p. 438.

38. Sarbin 1972.

39. Dennett 1991, p. 197.

40. Ryle's adverbial theory is expounded in *The Concept of Mind* (1949, pp. 40–51, 135–149), in volume 2 of *Collected Papers* (1971b, pp. 465–496), and in *On Thinking* (1979, pp. 17–49, 65–93). See also Sibley 1970; Bestor 1979.

41. Ryle 1971b, p. 471.

42. Ryle 1949, p. 48.

43. Ryle 1979, p. 24.

44. See Ryle 1949, pp. 144–146; Ryle 1971b, p. 481; Ryle 1979, p. 18ff.; Bestor 1979.

45. See Ryle 1949, p. 136ff.

46. Ibid., p. 48.

47. See ibid., pp. 138–139, 143.

48. Ryle 1979, p. 23.

49. See Ryle 1971b, p. 258.

50. Ryle 1949, p. 313.

51. Ryle 1979, pp. 74–75.

52. Ibid., p. 77.

53. Ibid., p. 24.

54. Ryle 1971b, p. 473.

55. Ryle 1949, p. 34.

56. Ryle 1971b, p. 259.

57. Ryle 1949, p. 34.

58. Ryle 1979, p. 77.

59. See Hampshire 1970, note to p. 35.

60. See Ryle 1949, pp. 36–37.

Chapter 2

1. Ryle 1949, especially pp. 261–270.

2. Ibid., pp. 269–270 (my italics).

3. Ibid., p. 270.

4. Ryle 1979, pp. 105–119.

5. Ibid., p. 105.

6. Ibid., p. 108.

7. Ibid., p. 114.

8. Ibid., p. 107.

9. Ibid., p. 108.

10. Ibid., p. 114.

11. Ibid., p. 110.

12. Ryle 1971b, p. 477.

13. Ryle 1979, p. 118.

14. Ibid., p. 105.

15. Ryle 1949, p. 265.

16. Ibid., p. 270.

17. See Walton 1990, p. 23.

18. Ryle 1949, p. 270.

19. Ibid., p. 97.

20. Leontyev 1978, p. 60.

21. Vygotsky 1978, p. 88.

22. Vygotsky 1962, p. 104; 1986, p. 188.

23. Vygotsky 1962, pp. 34–35; 1986, pp. 71–72.

24. Luria 1981, p. 89.

25. Vygotsky 1978, pp. 56–57.

26. Ibid., p. 27.

27. Vygotsky 1962, p. 18; 1986, pp. 32–33.

28. Leontyev 1978, p. 60.

29. Hampshire's account is contained in two papers, "Feeling and Expression" and "Disposition and Memory," both written in 1960 and reprinted in *Freedom of Mind* (1971). The first paper is also published, along with five pages omitted from the 1971 edition, as *Feeling and Expression* (1961).

30. Hampshire 1965, pp. 34–35.

31. Hampshire 1971, p. 163.

32. Ibid., p. 144ff.

33. Ibid., p. 164ff.

34. Ibid., pp. 145, 151, 155.

35. Ibid., p. 148.

36. Ibid., pp. 145–146.

37. Ibid., pp. 153–154.

38. See Wittgenstein 1963, #244 and #257.

39. Hampshire 1971, p. 154.

40. Ibid., p. 164.

41. Personal communication to the author.

42. Hampshire 2000a, pp. 11–12.

43. Ibid., p. 7.

44. Ibid., p. 11.

45. Ibid., p. 12.

46. Ibid.

47. Personal communication to the author.

48. Ryle 1949, p. 27.

49. de Laguna 1963.

50. Ibid., pp. 352–353.

51. Mead 1962.

52. Ibid., p. 47.

53. Ibid., p. 50.

54. Leontyev 1978, p. 60.

55. Leontyev, quoted in Lektorsky 1984, p. 145.

56. Sarbin 1972.

57. Ibid., p. 342.

58. Ibid., p. 344.

59. See Ryle 1949, pp. 258–272.

60. Sarbin 1972, p. 341.

61. Ibid., pp. 341–342.

62. Lawrence and Valsiner 1993, pp. 151–152.

Chapter 3

1. Taylor 1973, p. 16.

2. Donald 1991, p. 189.

3. Lock 1980.

4. See Savage-Rumbaugh, Shanker, and Taylor 1998.

5. See Stern 1985, p. 107.

6. See, for example, Gillett 1999.

7. Trevarthen 1987, p. 364.

8. See Slater 2004.

9. Rizzolatti and Arbib 1998, p. 190.

10. Meltzoff 1996, p. 363.

11. Ibid., p. 358.

12. Bruner 1975, p. 8.

13. See Bremner 1994, p. 241.

14. See Sheldrake 1999 and earlier works.

15. See Stern 1985, pp. 37, 100–102.

16. Trevarthen 1979, p. 347.

17. Meltzoff and Gopnik 1993, p. 355.

18. Meltzoff 1996, p. 364.

19. Stern 1985, p. 107.

20. Baldwin 1905.

21. Stern 1985, p. 102.

22. Ibid., p. 107.

23. Trevarthen 1992, p. 113.

24. Kaye 1982, pp. 180–181.

25. Lessing 1995, p. 49.

26. Macmurray 1961, p. 60.

27. Donald 1991, pp. 176–177.

28. Iacoboni 2005.

29. Meltzoff 1996, pp. 356–357.

30. Stern 1985, pp. 139–140.

31. Meares 1992, pp. 29–30.

32. Ibid., p. 124.

33. Ibid., p. 27.

34. Ibid., p. 123.

35. Papousek and Papousek 1977, p. 82.

36. Kaye 1979, p. 199.

37. Trevarthen 1987, p. 364.

38. Carpenter et al. 1998, p. 26.

39. Bruner 1975, p. 7.

40. Savage-Rumbaugh et al. 1993, p. 27.

41. Bruner 1975, p. 13 (his upper case).

42. Trevarthen 1979, p. 336.

43. Wallman 1992, p. 51.

44. Savage-Rumbaugh et al. 1993, p. 32.

45. Stern 1985, pp. 140–141.

Chapter 4

1. Trevarthen 1979, p. 334.

2. Ibid., p. 335.

3. Bruner 1975, p. 13.

4. Lorenz 1977, p. 215.

5. Lock 1978 (pp. 5–6 and elsewhere) provides fascinating detail about the origin of the classic child's gesture of arm-raising as an invitation to be picked up. See also Savage-Rumbaugh et al. 1993.

6. Savage-Rumbaugh, Shanker, and Taylor 1998, pp. 122–123.

7. Vygotsky 1978, pp. 110–111.

8. Macmurray 1961, p. 60.

9. See, for example, de Laguna 1963; Hewes 1996; Lock 1997, 2004; Corballis 1999.

10. Hampshire 1971, pp. 145–146.

11. Ibid., p. 169.

12. Ibid., p. 154.

13. Savage-Rumbaugh et al. 1993, pp. 29–30.

14. Ryle 1949, p. 270.

15. Ibid., p. 27.

16. Burke 1969, p. 242.

17. See Neisser 1976, p. 145.

18. de Laguna 1963, p. 175.

19. Pavlov 1927.

20. Harris 1994, p. 257.

21. Savage-Rumbaugh, Shanker, and Taylor 1998, p. 59.

22. Walton 1990, p. 21.

23. Ibid., p. 23.

24. Hampshire 1971, p. 168.

25. Ibid., p. 160.

26. Ibid., p. 165.

Chapter 5

1. Cooley 1964, p. 38.

2. Stern 1985, p. 114.

3. Mead 1962, p. 141, note 3.

4. Luria 1981, p. 89.

5. Jaynes 1976, p. 79.

6. Again see Lock 1978, pp. 5–6. See also Savage-Rumbaugh, Shanker, and Taylor 1998 and the accounts of chimpanzee cooperation in de Waal 1982, pp. 200–204.

7. See Ryle 1979, pp. 65–78.

8. Ibid., p. 75.

9. Stern 1985, p. 118.

10. Cooley 1964, p. 90. See also ibid., pp. 89–90, 95.

Chapter 6

1. Davidson 1997, p. 27.

2. Ryle 1949, pp. 149–153.

3. Churchland and Sejnowski 1992, p. 143.

4. Thomas (1999) provides a useful adumbration of, and an extensive bibliography for, what he calls "perceptual activity theory." See also Ryle 1949, pp. 218–219, 228–234; Neisser 1976; Trevarthen 1984; O'Regan and Noë 2001.

5. Mead 1938, p. 3.

6. Schiffman 1996, pp. 100–108.

7. See Noton and Stark 1971a,b.

8. Schiffman 1996, p. 107.

9. Ibid.

10. Sacks 1995, note to p. 111.

11. Macmurray 1961, p. 53.

12. Bruner 1975, p. 9.

13. Collis 1977.

14. Bruner 1975, p. 13.

15. Stern 1985, p. 129.

16. Butterworth 1998, p. 157.

17. Butterworth 2004.

18. Bruner 1975, p. 9.

19. Papousek and Papousek 1977, p. 82.

20. Collingwood 1938, p. 227.

21. Collis 1977.

22. Bruner 1975, p. 16.

23. Savage-Rumbaugh et al. 1993, pp. 32–33.

24. Davidson 1984, p. 251.

25. Quinton 1965, p. 526.

26. Sartre 1968, p. 209.

27. Werner and Kaplan 1963, pp. 42–43.

28. Vygotsky 1978, p. 56.

29. Stern 1985, p. 130.

30. Carpenter et al. 1998, p. 20.

31. See, for example, ibid. pp. 17–22.

32. Sartre 1966, pp. 22–77.

33. Fowler 1983, p. 611.

34. Sartre 1966.

35. Butterworth 1994, p. 117.

Chapter 7

1. Piaget 1974, p. 59.

2. Hampshire 2000a, p. 9.

3. de Laguna 1963, pp. xi–xii.

4. Savage-Rumbaugh, Shanker, and Taylor 1998, p. 191.

5. de Laguna 1963, pp. 352–353.

6. Ryle 1971b, p. 258.

7. See Rorty 1984, pp. 547–548.

8. Watson 1919, p. 324.

Chapter 8

1. Stich 1996, p. 126.

2. Churchland 1981, p. 70.

3. Ibid., p. 68.

4. Dennett 1993, p. 124.

5. Meltzoff and Gopnik 1993, p. 335.

6. Churchland 1981, p. 70.

7. Astington 1995, p. 185.

8. Dennett 1993, p. 125.

9. Meltzoff and Gopnik 1993, p. 340.

10. Ibid.

11. Astington 1995, p. 185.

12. The phrase is Fodor's; see Davies and Stone 1995, p. 11.

13. Churchland 1981, p. 68.

14. Dennett 1993, pp. 124–125.

15. Fodor 1987, pp. 131–133, presumably following Humphrey 1983, p. 53ff.

16. Fodor 1987, p. 132.

17. Churchland 1986, p. 302.

18. Meltzoff and Gopnik 1993, p. 340.

19. Gregory 1987, p. 158.

20. Wisdom 1964, p. 248.

21. Richards 1936.

22. Black 1962.

23. Lakoff and Johnson 1980.

24. Davidson 1984, p. 252.

25. Rorty 1991, p. 167.

26. Henle 1958, p. 183.

27. Ibid., p. 187.

28. Sharpe 1995, p. 555.

29. Fowler 1983, p. 359.

30. Orwell 1957, p. 151.

31. Lakoff and Johnson 1980.

32. Cooper 1986.

33. Lakoff and Johnson 1980, p. 85.

34. Lakoff 1993, pp. 244–245.

35. Cooper 1986, p. 135.

36. Strawson 1974, p. 131.

37. Wittgenstein 1963, #109.

38. Ibid., #115.

39. Ibid., #422–#425.

40. Hacker 1990, p. 541.

Chapter 9

1. Berkeley 1953, p. 89.

2. Berkeley 1949, p. 250.

3. Berkeley 1950, p. 306.

4. Berkeley 1948, p. 24.

5. Cooper 1986, pp. 140–141.

6. Hampshire 1970, p. 21. See also Jaynes 1976, p. 55; Sweetser 1990, pp. 28, 41–45.

7. Aristotle, *Rhetoric* 1404B.

8. As far as I know, I am only the second person to attempt this—after Thomas Reid (1969, pp. 389–421).

9. Sarbin 1972, p. 338.

10. *Oxford English Dictionary*, mind: 17.

11. The entry for *mind* in the *Oxford Dictionary of English Etymology* is reproduced in the appendix of this book.

12. See Reid 1969, pp. 15, 389–391, 420–421; Collingwood 1938, p. 254; Taylor 1966, pp. 155–157. See also Sarbin 1972, pp. 337–338.

13. Taylor 1966, p. 248.

14. Hornsby 1997, p. 157.

15. Ibid.

Chapter 10

1. Skinner 1957, pp. 436–437.

2. Hampshire 1971, p. 163.

3. Dennett 1991, p. 197.

4. Ryle 1949, p. 34.

5. Taylor 1966, p. 248.

6. Berkeley 1949, p. 250.

7. Searle 1983, p. 4.

8. Fodor 1975.

9. Lévi-Strauss 1963, p. 229.

10. Reddy 1993.

11. Harris 1998, pp. 20–22, 32–33.

12. Saussure 1922, p. 27.

13. Toolan 1998, p. 70.

14. Haack 1994, pp. 15–16.

Chapter 11

1. See Pettit 1987 for an excellent brief summary of the *verstehen* tradition in philosophy.

2. Strawson 1968.

3. Dennett 1973, 1987, 1996.

4. See, for example, Goldman 1996 and Gordon 1996.

5. Again see Rorty 1984, pp. 547–548.

6. Reid 1977, pp. 17, 278, 282–284.

7. Macmurray 1938, p. 82.

8. Collingwood 1940, p. 335.

9. Gasking 1955.

10. Strawson 1986, pp. 122–125.

11. Macmurray 1938, p. 71.

12. Wittgenstein 1980a, #655.

13. Reid 1969, p. 349.

14. Macmurray 1938, p. 81.

15. Berlin 1977, p. 12.

16. See Pompa 1975.

Bibliography

Annett, J. 1995. "Motor imagery: Perception or action?" In M. Behrmann et al., eds., *The Neuropsychology of Mental Imagery*. Pergamon.

Annett, J. 1996. "On knowing how to do things: A theory of motor imagery." *Cognitive Brain Research* 3: 65–69.

Astington, J. 1995. "What is theoretical about the child's theory of mind?: A Vygotskian perspective." In P. Carruthers and P. Smith, eds., *Theories of Theories of Mind*. Cambridge University Press.

Austin, J. L. 1961. *Philosophical Papers*. Oxford University Press.

Baldwin, J. M. 1905. *Dictionary of Philosophy and Psychology*. Macmillan.

Berkeley, G. 1948. "Philosophical commentaries." In A. Luce and T. Jessop, eds., *The Works of George Berkeley, Bishop of Cloyne*, volume 1. Nelson. First published in 1708.

Berkeley, G. 1949. "Three dialogues between Hylas and Philonous." In A. Luce and T. Jessop, eds., *The Works of George Berkeley, Bishop of Cloyne*, volume 2. Nelson. First published in 1734.

Berkeley, G. 1950. "Alciphron." In A. Luce and T. Jessop, eds., *The Works of George Berkeley, Bishop of Cloyne*, volume 3. Nelson. First published in 1732.

Berkeley, G. 1953. "Siris." In A. Luce and T. Jessop, eds., *The Works of George Berkeley, Bishop of Cloyne*, volume 5. Nelson. First published in 1744.

Berlin, I. 1977. *Vico and Herder: Two Studies in the History of Ideas*. Vintage.

Bestor, T. W. 1979. "Gilbert Ryle and the adverbial theory of mind." *The Personalist* 60, no. 3: 233–242.

Black, M. 1962. *Models and Metaphors*. Cornell University Press.

Bremner, J. G. 1994. *Infancy*, second edition. Blackwell.

Bruner, J. 1975. "The ontogenesis of speech acts." *Journal of Child Language* 2: 1–19.

Burke, K. 1969. *A Grammar of Motives*. University of Califormia Press.

Butterworth, G. 1994. "Theory of mind and the facts of embodiment." In C. Lewis and P. Mitchell, eds., *Early Understanding of Mind*. Erlbaum.

Butterworth, G. 1998. "Origins of joint attention in infancy." In M. Carpenter et al., eds., *Social Cognition, Joint Attention and Communicative Competence from 9 to 15 Months of Age*. University of Chicago Press.

Butterworth, G. 2004. "Joint visual attention in infancy." In G. Butterworth and A. Fogel, eds., *Blackwell Handbook of Infant Development*. Blackwell.

Carpenter, M., et al., eds. 1998. *Social Cognition, Joint Attention and Communicative Competence from 9 to 15 Months of Age*. University of Chicago Press.

Churchland, P. M. 1981. "Eliminative materialism and the propositional attitudes." *Journal of Philosophy* 78: 67–90.

Churchland, P. S. 1986. *Neurophilosophy: Towards a Unified Science of the Mind/Brain*. MIT Press.

Churchland, P. S., and Sejnowski, T. J. 1992. *The Computational Brain*. MIT Press.

Collingwood, R. G. 1938. *The Principles of Art*. Oxford University Press.

Collingwood, R. G. 1940. *An Essay on Metaphysics* (*Philosophical Papers*, volume II). Oxford University Press.

Collis, G. M. 1977. "Visual co-orientation and maternal speech." In H. R. Schaffer, ed., *Studies in Mother-Infant Interaction*. Academic Press.

Cooley, C. H. 1964. *Human Nature and the Social Order*. Schocken. First published in 1902.

Cooper, D. E. 1986. *Metaphor*. Blackwell.

Corballis, M. C. 1999, "The gestural origins of language." *American Scientist* 87, no. 2: 138–145.

Crick, F., and Koch, C. 2002. "Why neuroscience may be able to explain consciousness." *Scientific American* 12, no. 1: 94–95.

Currie, G. 1995. "Visual imagery as the simulation of vision." *Mind and Language* 10: 25–44.

Davidson, D. 1984. "What metaphors mean." In *Inquiries into Truth and Interpretation*. Clarendon.

Davidson, D. 1997. "Seeing through language." *Royal Institute of Philosophy Supplement*: 42: 15–28.

Davidson, R. J., and Schwartz, G. E. 1977. "Brain mechanisms subserving self-generated imagery: Electrophysiological specificity and patterning." *Psychophysiology* 14: 598–601.

Davies, M., and Stone, T., eds. 1995. *Folk Psychology: The Theory of Mind Debate.* Blackwell.

Decety, J. 2002a. "Neurophysiological evidence for simulation of action." In J. Dokic and J. Proust, eds., *Simulation and Knowledge of Action.* Benjamins.

Decety, J. 2002b. "Naturaliser l'empathie." *L'Encéphale* 28: 9–20.

Decety, J., et al. 1991. "Vegetative response during imagined movement is proportional to mental effort." *Behavioural Brain Research* 42: 1–5.

Decety, J., et al. 1993. "Central activation of autonomic effectors during mental simulation of motor actions in man." *Journal of Physiology* 461: 549–563.

Decety, J., et al. 2002. "A PET exploration of the neural mechanisms involved in reciprocal imitation." *NeuroImage* 15: 265–272.

Decety, J., and Chaminade, T. 2005. "The neurophysiology of imitation and intersubjectivity." In S. Hurley and N. Chater, eds., *Perspectives on Imitation.* MIT Press.

de Laguna, G. A. 1963. *Speech: Its Function and Development.* Indiana University Press. First published in 1927.

Dennett, D. C. 1973, "Mechanism and responsibility." In T. Honderich, ed., *Essays on Freedom of Action*, Routledge and Kegan Paul.

Dennett, D. C. 1987. *The Intentional Stance.* MIT Press.

Dennett, D. C. 1991. *Consciousness Explained.* Penguin/Allan Lane.

Dennett, D. C. 1993. "Three kinds of Intentional Psychology." In S. Christensen and D. Turner, eds., *Folk Psychology and the Philosophy of Mind.* Erlbaum.

Dennett, D. C. 1996. *Kinds of Minds.* Weidenfeld & Nicolson.

de Waal, F. 1982. *Chimpanzee Politics.* Unwin Counterpoint.

Donald, M. 1991. *Origins of the Modern Mind: Three Stages in the Evolution of Culture and Cognition.* Harvard University Press.

Drake, D. 1933. *Invitation to Philosophy.* Houghton Mifflin.

Flanagan, O. 1995. "Behaviourism." In T. Honderich, ed., *The Oxford Companion to Philosophy*, Oxford University Press.

Fodor, J. A. 1975. *The Language of Thought.* Crowell.

Fodor, J. A. 1987. *Psychosemantics: The Problem of Meaning in the Philosophy of Mind.* MIT Press.

Fodor, J. A. 1992. "A theory of the child's theory of mind." *Cognition* 44: 283–296.

Fowler, H. W. 1983. *A Dictionary of Modern English Usage*, second edition. Oxford University Press.

Frijda, N. H. 1986. *The Emotions*. Cambridge University Press.

Gardner, H. 1985. *The Mind's New Science*. Basic Books.

Gasking, D. 1955. "Causation and recipes." *Mind* 64: 479–487.

Gillett, G. 1999. "Dennett, Foucault, and the selection of memes." *Inquiry* 42: 3–24.

Goldman, A. I. 1996. "Simulation and interpersonal utility." In L. May et al., eds., *Mind and Morals*. MIT Press.

Gordon, R. M. 1996. "Radical simulationism." In P. Carruthers and P. K. Smith, eds., *Theories of Theories of Mind*. Cambridge University Press.

Gregory, R. L., ed. 1987. *The Oxford Companion to the Mind*. Oxford University Press.

Guthrie, E. R. 1935. *The Psychology of Learning*. Harper.

Haack, S. 1994. "Dry truth and real knowledge." In J. Hintikka, ed., *Aspects of Metaphor*. Kluwer.

Hacker, P. M. S. 1990. *Wittgenstein: Meaning and Mind*. Blackwell.

Hampshire, S. 1961. *Feeling and Expression*. University of London/H. K. Lewis.

Hampshire, S. 1965. *Freedom of the Individual*. Chatto and Windus/University of Otago Press.

Hampshire, S. 1970. "Critical review of *The Concept of Mind*." In O. Wood and G. Pitcher, eds., *Ryle*. Doubleday/Macmillan.

Hampshire, S. 1971. *Freedom of Mind*. Princeton University Press.

Hampshire, S. 2000a. *Justice Is Conflict*. Princeton University Press.

Harris, P. L. 1994. "Understanding pretence." In C. Lewis and P. Mitchell, eds., *Children's Early Understanding of Mind*. Erlbaum.

Harris, R. 1998. *Introduction to Integrational Linguistics*. Pergamon.

Hebb, D. O. 1958. *A Textbook of Psychology*. Saunders.

Hebb, D. O. 1968. "Concerning imagery." *Psychological Review* 75: 466–77.

Hebb, D. O. 1980. *Essay on Mind*. Erlbaum.

Henle, P. 1958. "Metaphor." In P. Henle, ed., *Language, Thought and Culture*. University of Michigan Press.

Hewes, G. W. 1996. "A history of the study of language origins and the gestural primacy hypothesis." In A. Lock and C. Peters, eds., *Handbook of Human Symbolic Evolution*. Clarendon.

Hochberg, J. 1987. "Gestalt theory." In R. Gregory, ed., *The Oxford Companion to the Mind*. Oxford University Press.

Hofstadter, D. R. 1979. *Gödel, Escher, Bach: An Eternal Golden Braid*. Harvester.

Hornsby, J. 1997. *Simple Mindedness: In Defence of Naïve Naturalism in the Philosophy of Mind*. Harvard University Press.

Hull, C. 1931. "Goal attraction and directing ideas conceived as habit phenomena." *Psychological Review* 38: 487–506.

Hume, D. 1960. *A Treatise of Human Nature*. Oxford University Press. First published in 1739.

Humphrey, N. 1983. *Consciousness Regained: Chapters in the Development of Mind*. Oxford University Press.

Iacoboni, M. 2005. "Understanding others: Imitation, language, empathy." In S. Hurley and N. Chater, eds., *Perspectives on Imitation*. MIT Press.

Jacobson, E. 1930. "Electrical measurements of neuromuscular states during mental activities. I. Imagination of movement involving skeletal muscle." *American Journal of Physiology* 92: 567–608. II. "Imagination and recollection of various muscular acts." Ibid. 94: 22–34. III. "Visual imagination and recollection." Ibid. 95: 694–702. IV. "Evidence of contraction of specific muscles during imagination." Ibid. 95: 703–712.

Jacobson, E. 1931. V. "Variation of specific muscles contracting during imagination." *American Journal of Physiology* 96: 115–121. VI. "A note on mental activities concerning an amputated limb." Ibid. 96: 122–125. VII. "Imagination, recollection and abstract thinking involving the speech musculature." Ibid. 97: 200–209.

Jacobson, E. 1932. "Electrophysiology of mental activities." *American Journal of Psychology* 44: 677–694.

Jaynes, J. 1976. *The Origin of Consciousness in the Breakdown of the Bicameral Mind*. Houghton Mifflin.

Jeannerod, M. 1994. "The representing brain: Neural correlates of motor intention and imagery." *Behavioral and Brain Sciences* 17: 187–245.

Jeannerod, M. 1995. "Mental imagery in the motor context." In M. Behrmann et al., eds., *The Neuropsychology of Mental Imagery*. Pergamon.

Jones, L., and Stuth, G. 1997. "The uses of mental imagery in athletics: An overview." *Applied and Preventive Psychology* 6: 101–115.

Kaye, K. 1979. "Thickening thin data: The maternal role in developing communication and language." In M. Bullowa, ed., *Before Speech*. Cambridge University Press.

Kaye, K. 1982. *The Mental and Social Life of Babies*. University of Chicago Press.

Lakoff, G. 1993: "Contemporary theory of metaphor." In A. Ortony, ed., *Metaphor and Thought*, second edition. Cambridge University Press.

Lakoff, G., and Johnson, M. 1980. *Metaphors We Live By*. University of Chicago Press.

Lawrence, J. A., and Valsiner, J. 1993. "Conceptual Roots of Internalisation: From Transmission to Transformation." *Human Development* 36: 150–167.

Lektorsky, V. A. 1984. *Subject Object Cognition*. Progress.

Lessing, D. 1995. *The Memoirs of a Survivor*. Flamingo/HarperCollins.

Lévi-Strauss, C. 1963. *Structural Anthropology*. Basic Books.

Lock, A., ed. 1978. *Action, Gesture and Symbol*. Academic Press.

Lock, A. 1980. *The Guided Re-invention of Language*. Academic Press.

Lock, A. 1997. "The role of gesture in the establishment of symbolic abilities: continuities and discontinuities in early language development." *Evolution of Communication* 1: 159–192.

Lock, A. 2004. "Preverbal communication." In G. Butterworth and A. Fogel, eds., *Blackwell Handbook of Infant Development*. Blackwell.

Lorenz, K. 1977. *Behind the Mirror*. Methuen.

Luria, A. R. 1981. *Language and Cognition*. Wiley.

Leontyev, A. N. 1978. *Activity, Consciousness and Personality*. Prentice-Hall.

Macmurray, J. 1938. "What is action?" *Aristotelian Society Proceedings*, supplementary volume 17: 69–85.

Macmurray, J. 1961. *Persons in Relation*. Faber and Faber.

Mead, G. H. 1938. *The Philosophy of the Act*. University of Chicago Press.

Mead, G. H. 1962. *Mind, Self and Society*. University of Chicago Press. First published in 1934.

Meares, R. 1992. *The Metaphor of Play*. Hill of Content.

Melser, D. J. 2000. Incipient Action. Ph.D. thesis, Massey University, Palmerston North, New Zealand.

Meltzoff, A. N. 1996. "The human infant as imitative generalist." In C. Heyes and B. Galef, eds., *Social Learning in Animals*. Academic Press.

Meltzoff, A. N., and Gopnik, A. 1993. "The role of imitation in understanding persons and developing a theory of mind." In S. Baron-Cohen et al., eds., *Understanding Other Minds*. Oxford University Press.

Meltzoff, A. N., and Moore, M. H. 1983. "Newborn infants imitate adult facial gestures." *Child Development* 54: 702–709.

Monod, J. 1972. *Chance and Necessity*. Collins.

Neisser, U. 1976. *Cognition and Reality*. Freeman.

Neisser, U. 1985. "The role of invariant structures in the control of movement." In M. Frese and J. Sabini, eds., *Goal Directed Behavior*. Erlbaum.

Noton, D., and Stark, L. 1971a. "Scanpaths in saccadic eye movements while viewing and recognising patterns." *Vision Research* 11: 929–942.

Noton, D., and Stark, L. 1971b. "Eye movements and visual perception." In *Perception*. Freeman.

O'Regan, J. K., and Noë, A. 2001. "A sensorimotor account of vision and visual consciousness." *Behavioral and Brain Sciences* 24: 5.

Orwell, G. 1957. *Selected Essays*. Penguin.

Paccalin, C., and Jeannerod, M. 2000. Changes in Breathing during Observation of Effortful Actions. Working paper 2000-02, Institut des Sciences Cognitives, Bron, France.

Papousek, H., and Papousek, M. 1977. "Mothering and the cognitive head-start: Psychobiological consideration." In H. Schaffer, ed., *Studies in Mother-Infant Interaction*. Academic Press.

Pavlov, I. P. 1927. *Conditioned Reflexes*. Oxford University Press.

Pettit, P. 1987, "Verstehen." In R. Gregory, ed., *The Oxford Companion to the Mind*, Oxford University Press.

Piaget, J. 1974. *The Language and Thought of the Child*. New American Library.

Pompa, L. 1975. *Vico*. Cambridge University Press.

Quinton, A. M. 1965. "The problem of perception." In R. Schwartz, ed., *Perceiving, Sensing, and Knowing*. Anchor.

Reddy, M. J. 1993. "The conduit metaphor." In Ortony, A. ed., *Metaphor and Thought*, second edition. Cambridge University Press.

Reid, T. 1969. *Essays on the Intellectual Powers of Man*. MIT Press. First published in 1785.

Reid, T. 1977. *Essays on the Active Powers of Man*. Garland. First published in 1788.

Richards, I. A. 1936. *The Philosophy of Rhetoric*. Oxford University Press.

Rizzolatti, G., and Arbib, M. 1998. "Language within our grasp." *Trends in Neuroscience* 21, no. 5: 190–191.

Rorty, A. O. 1984. "Formal traces in Cartesian functional explanation." *Canadian Journal of Philosophy* 14, no. 4: 545–560.

Rorty, R. 1991. "Unfamiliar noises: Hesse and Davidson on metaphor." In *Objectivity, Relativism and Truth. Philosophical Papers*, volume 1. Cambridge University Press.

Ryle, G. 1949. *The Concept of Mind*. Hutchinson.

Ryle, G. 1960. *Dilemmas*. Cambridge University Press.

Ryle, G. 1971a. *Collected Papers*, volume 1. Hutchinson.

Ryle, G. 1971b. *Collected Papers*, volume II. Hutchinson.

Ryle, G. 1979. *On Thinking*. Blackwell.

Sacks, O. 1995. *An Anthropologist on Mars*. Knopf.

Sarbin, T. R. 1972. "Imagining as muted role-taking: A historical-linguistic analysis." In P. Sheehan, ed., *The Function and Nature of Imagery*. Academic Press.

Sartre, J.-P. 1966. *The Psychology of Imagination*. Citadel.

Sartre, J.-P. 1968. *Being and Nothingness*. Citadel.

Saussure, F. de. 1922. *Cours de Linguistique Générale*, second edition. Payot.

Savage-Rumbaugh, E. S., et al. 1993. *Language Comprehension in Ape and Child*. Monographs of the Society for Research in Child Development no. 233, Georgia State University.

Savage-Rumbaugh, S., Shanker, S. G., and Taylor, T. J. 1998. *Apes, Language and the Human Mind*. Oxford University Press.

Scheerer, E. 1984. "Motor theories of cognitive structure: A historical review." In W. Prinz and A. Sanders, eds., *Cognition and Motor Processes*. Springer-Verlag.

Schiffman, H. R. 1996. *Sensation and Perception: An Integrated Approach*. Wiley.

Sharpe, R. A. 1995. "Metaphor." In T. Honderich, ed., *The Oxford Companion to Philosophy*. Oxford University Press.

Sheldrake, R. 1999. *Dogs That Know When Their Owners Are Coming Home and Other Unexplained Powers of Animals*. Hutchinson.

Sibley, F. N. 1970. "Ryle and Thinking." In O. Wood and G. Pitcher, eds., *Ryle*. Macmillan.

Skinner, B. F. 1957. *Verbal Behavior*. Methuen.

Slater, A. 2004. "Visual perception." In G. Butterworth and A. Fogel, eds., *Blackwell Handbook of Infant Development*. Blackwell.

Stern, D. N. 1985. *The Interpersonal World of the Infant*. Basic Books.

Stich, S. P. 1996. *Deconstructing the Mind*. Oxford University Press.

Strawson, P. F. 1968. "Freedom and resentment." In P. Strawson, ed., *Studies in the Philosophy of Thought and Action*. Oxford University Press.

Strawson, P. F. 1974. *Freedom and Resentment*. Methuen.

Strawson, P. F. 1986. "Causation and Explanation." In B. Vermazen and M. Hintikka, eds., *Essays on Davidson—Actions and Events*. Oxford University Press.

Sweetser, E. 1990. *From Etymology to Pragmatics: Metaphorical and Cultural Aspects of Semantic Structure*. Cambridge University Press.

Taylor, R. 1966. *Action and Purpose*. Prentice-Hall.

Taylor, R. 1973. *With Heart and Mind*. St. Martin's Press.

Thomas, N. J. T. 1999. "Are theories of imagery theories of imagination? An *active perception* approach to conscious mental content." *Cognitive Science* 23: 207–245.

Toolan, M. 1998. "A few words on telementation." In R. Harris and G. Wolf, eds., *Integrational Linguisitics*. Elsevier.

Trevarthen, C. 1977. "Descriptive analyses of infant communicative behaviour." In H. Schaffer, ed., *Studies in Mother-Infant Interaction*. Academic Press.

Trevarthen, C. 1979. "Communication and cooperation in early infancy: A description of primary intersubjectivity." In M. Bullowa, ed., *Before Speech*. Cambridge University Press.

Trevarthen, C. 1984. "Biodynamic structures, cognitive correlates of motive sets and the development of motives in infants." In W. Prinz and W. Sanders, eds., *Cognition and Motor Processes*. Springer-Verlag.

Trevarthen, C. 1987. "Infancy, mind in." In R. Gregory, ed., *The Oxford Companion to the Mind*. Oxford University Press.

Trevarthen, C. 1992. "An infant's motives for speaking and thinking in the culture." In A. Wold, ed., *Language and Mind*. Oxford University Press.

Vygotsky, L. S. 1962. *Thought and Language*. MIT Press.

Vygotsky, L. S. 1978. *Mind in Society: The Development of Higher Psychological Processes*. MIT Press.

Vygotsky, L. S. 1986. *Thought and Language*, revised edition. MIT Press.

Vygotsky, L. S. 1994. *The Vygotsky Reader*. Blackwell.

Wallman, J. 1992. *Aping Language*. Cambridge University Press.

Walton, K. L. 1990. *Mimesis as Make-Believe*. Harvard University Press.

Washburn, M. F. 1910. *Movement and Mental Imagery*. University of Chicago Press.

Washburn, M. F. 1914. "The function of incipient motor processes." *Psychological Review* 21: 376–390.

Watson, J. B. 1919. *Psychology from the Standpoint of a Behaviourist*. Lippincott.

Werner, H., and Kaplan, B. 1963. *Symbol Formation*. Wiley.

Wisdom, J. 1964. *Philosophy and Psychoanalysis*. Blackwell.

Wisdom, J. 1965. *Paradox and Discovery*. Blackwell.

Wittgenstein, L. 1963. *Philosophical Investigations*. Blackwell.

Wittgenstein, L. 1980. *Remarks on the Philosophy of Psychology*, volume 1. Blackwell.

Zikmund, V. 1972. "Physiological correlates of visual imagery." In P. Sheehan, ed., *The Function and Nature of Imagery*. Academic Press.

Index